THE HOUSE IS NOT A HOME

THE HOUSE IS NOT A HOME

Erik Nielsen *(signature)*

Macmillan of Canada
A Division of Canada Publishing Corporation
Toronto, Ontario, Canada

Canadian Cataloguing in Publication Data
Nielsen, Erik, date.
The house is not a home

Includes index.
ISBN 0-7715-9426-7

1. Nielsen, Erik, 1924–   . 2. Canada—Politics and government—1957–1963.* 3. Canada—Politics and government—1963-   .*
4. Canada. Parliament. House of Commons—Biography.
5. Legislators—Canada—Biography. 6. Politicians—Canada—Biography.
I. Title.

FC601.N54A3   1989   328.71′092′4   C89-094326-5
F1034.3.N54A3 1989

Printed and bound in Canada by
T. H. Best Printing Company Limited

Macmillan of Canada
A Division of Canada Publishing Corporation
Toronto, Ontario, Canada

Contents

Wicks' Outcast

Acknowledgments

The first name on the list of eligible voters in Dawson City for the general election of 1957 was Alec Adams, a placer miner, and at Elsa, a mining community also in Yukon, the last name on the list was Ralph Zachareli. Both men are now deceased, and both were among my earliest supporters. These men are representative of the hundreds of men and women in Yukon whose support, hard work, and encouragement first propelled me into a political career and then, with the help of many others from all parts of Canada, kept me at it—sometimes against my better judgment. Though I was never asked by them for explanations for any of my actions, I now provide them here in the hope that they might have a better understanding of the personal problems and motives that I felt compelled to take into account in arriving at some of the critical decisions which I had to make from time to time. I do so with a profound sense of gratitude for their generous support and loyalty to me over the years. I often felt unworthy of their faith in me and frustrated by self-imposed barriers to providing them with explanations. I hope that this book makes up for these deficiencies and restores any loss of personal regard that they might have felt for me.

More than twenty-five years ago, Walter Stewart travelled to Yukon to acquire first-hand data about my private, business, and political life for an article. He stayed for several days, visiting my friends and business acquaintances with me, accompanying me on a visit to my constituents living in the Whitehorse Indian Village, where he saw the appalling living conditions of the people there, and mainstreeting with me and my constituents. I was impressed by the lengths to which Walter would go to gather background material, and by the accuracy of his writing. As a result, I continued to follow his career and to enjoy his books and articles. Early on I formed the opinion that Walter was unique among the journalists

I knew or read in that he had a finely honed sense of journalistic (and other) ethical standards.

When I decided that it was important to construct an account of my experiences, particularly of the political years, I knew at once that I would require the help of a professional writer. One does not become a writer simply by writing or by having the desire to write (although some people do not share this belief). It was only natural that I would think of Walter Stewart, even though I had not seen him in more than twenty-five years and did not even know where to find him. Eventually a literary agent brought us together.

Walter Stewart is the architect of this book. Without his writing skills, the book would not have happened. I consider myself very fortunate indeed to have had the experience of working with him and I acknowledge my deep gratitude to him for his invaluable collaboration. I hope that it will not be the last writing venture that we share together.

Finally, both Walter and I are grateful to Suzanne Frenette for the many evenings and weekends which she devoted to the preparation of the final draft of the manuscript.

Cartoon copyright Ben Wicks, distributed by Southam Syndicate.

Prologue

In air navigation, in flying from the point of departure to a destination, there is a point along the route that marks the last opportunity to turn around and return safely to base, given the quantity of fuel remaining on board. That point is known as the point of no return, or PNR; if it is passed, there can be no safe return to the point of departure, and the flight must continue to its destination. I reached the PNR of my political career when I decided to run for re-election in 1972. Until then, I had made continual but unsuccessful efforts to leave the political scene; afterwards, for various reasons, I was locked into successive decisions to continue to seek re-election. It is a common situation in politics, and anyone seeking public office should determine the length of time he or she intends to commit to public service and, having made that decision, abide by it.

When I made my commitment in 1972, I assumed that I would be able to choose my own destination. It was not to be. My eventual departure from politics occurred in circumstances that were certainly not of my choosing, nor indeed of my making. Any flight ought to end in a safe landing at a destination chosen by the pilot. My departure from the political scene, however, can by no means be described as the successful completion of a flight. That I walked away from the landing is nothing short of miraculous.

I did not realize how close I was to a forced landing until one day when I was having a telephone conversation with Sinclair Stevens, at that time the minister of Regional and Industrial Expansion in the Progressive Conservative government of Prime Minister Brian Mulroney. For two weeks I, as deputy prime minister, had been the focus of considerable heat in the House of Commons, wrestling with what had become the Sinc Stevens Affair. My conversation with him dealt with the establishment of an inquiry to determine whether

Stevens had, in fact, complied with the conflict-of-interest code governing the behaviour of cabinet ministers. At one point he complained to me, "You mustn't forget that my political future is at stake here."

To which I replied, "You have company, Sinc, because my own political future has been very much tied to yours from the outset of this business, and it is just as much at stake as your own."

I did not say to him that at that moment I would not have given a plugged nickel for the political future of either of us. Had I expressed that blunt opinion on the telephone, I very much doubt that he would have agreed to tendering his resignation later that week—a resignation that led, not long afterwards, to my own departure.

The course that we should have followed, naturally, would have been to recognize at once that a conflict existed and to apply the only possible remedy in the circumstances, namely, to request the immediate resignation of the minister. A little preventive maintenance five months earlier would have avoided the difficulties entirely. Instead, we carried on until we crashed. My "good [air]ship politic" was a total write-off and I sustained injuries that prevented me from making any further useful contribution in the government or in the House of Commons.

Nonetheless, during the course of more than thirty years of active political life—twenty-eight and a half of them on active service in the House of Commons—I ought to have remembered that the political flight is never a simple trip from A to B; along the way, there are always many stopovers. My own flightpath crossed the lives of many in politics and in the private sector. I was often embroiled in party or national affairs and in political events, some of which have already been recorded; others I am certain will find their way into historical annals some day.

In the course of those stops along the route, my life was enriched enormously. I take a considerable measure of satisfaction in the belief that I somehow affected—always favorably, I hope—the lives of those involved insofar as these events touched the well-being of our country, and that I had a hand in building a better Canada, especially in my own particular part of Canada, Yukon, and influencing the destinies of the Canadians who live there.

The purpose of this book is to describe fully for the first time the part I played in some of the significant events of our time. The telling of my story has been, for me, a sometimes painful experience; many of the things I have to say about myself, as well as others, are far from flattering. It is not my purpose here to pen another volume of chatty reminiscences, but to set down, as honestly as I can, exactly what happened. I have been described as "Velcro Lips"—the man who clams up and takes his secrets to the grave. I do not intend to do that, so I will explain for the first time, for example, the motives and events that reshaped Canadian political life in the Rivard Affair and the Munsinger scandal, and what actually happened in the so-called Eavesdropping Affair. I will describe what life was really like in the caucuses of John Diefenbaker, Robert Stanfield, Joe Clark, and Brian Mulroney, and what was behind my much-criticized behaviour in the Sinc Stevens Affair. From a modest position on the back benches of the governing party, I was thrust by circumstances into the centre of politics, first as an opposition MP, later as opposition house leader, then Leader of the Opposition, and finally a series of cabinet posts, including that of deputy prime minister. I have remained silent on a number of questions concerning which there have been various distorted accounts— most of them authored by representatives of the media.

There were times, I confess, during the writing of this story, when I wondered about what I was doing. Some parts of my story reawakened pain and resentment and made me relive some of my own anguish. I am a very private person, and such a telling does not come easily to me. Nevertheless, if Canadians are to understand today's events, they must have before them a true record of what went before. Much of what has been written about myself, my activities, my party, and my colleagues has been, not to put too fine a point on it, utter balderdash. If Canadians are to have an accurate and adequate record of the span of time that embraces the Diefenbaker era, the Trudeau regime and the Mulroney period (history will substitute its own noun for the last), this story ought to form part of it, and it must be a revealing and blunt account, whatever the resentment and pain it causes. Time and space have constrained me—there is much, much more that could be said— but a desire to spare anyone's feelings, including my own, has not.

My political life had many happy moments, many exciting and constructive times, as well as some rough spots; most are here. There have been many turning points, when every decision constituted a new challenge. I hope that, by the time this story is told, the reader will agree with my assessment of the challenges and decisions—or, at least, will better understand why these decisions were made.

At the end of this volume, I will try to draw the lessons that flow from my experiences. It's a little late for me to benefit from them, but they might provide some guidance to others.

A style note for southern readers: like most Yukoners, I say "Yukon," not "the Yukon." After all, we do not say "the Alberta" or "the Ontario," do we?

Chapter One
Growing Pains

The day the child realizes that all adults are
imperfect, he becomes an adolescent; the day he
forgives them, he becomes an adult; the day he
forgives himself, he becomes wise.
                                        Alden Nowlan, 1971

The cliché holds that the child is father of the man, and it may explain some of the things that later happened to me; mine was a childhood full of accidents, some of them painful, some just silly. It was also, at least by modern standards, a tough childhood—tough in the physical sense—and yet I consider it a happy childhood, in which the bonds of discipline and of love were both present. It was an outdoor childhood, spent in the North, a childhood of adventure, competition, and fun, and of pain and hard work, a childhood admirably suited to equip me for the struggles I would later endure.

My father, Ingvard Evesen Nielsen, was born in Esbjerg, a little fishing village on the west coast of the Danish peninsula, where his father was a shoemaker. He had two brothers and two sisters. The family was not poor, but they were not well-to-do, either. Dad went to work very early, first as a milk delivery boy, then as an acrobat in a circus (he pursued acrobatics until well into his sixties and drilled the skills into his children, with mixed results). In 1914, when he was fourteen, the entire family emigrated to Canada, just before the outbreak of World War I.

Their ship landed them in Montreal, where Dad managed to find work as a "blocker" in a boiler factory. He was the guy on the inside who provided a hard surface for the riveter on the outside to work against with his gun. Noisy work.

Although they had come to Canada intending to stay, like so many before them, they succumbed to the more attractive opportunities in the United States. All except my father went on to the

U.S. in search of a better life. One brother married a French Canadian in Montreal and took her to Detroit, where he became a production foreman in one of the automobile plants. The other brother
went to Chicago and did quite well in the interior decorating business. Both had families, so I have countless cousins. One of Dad's
sisters, my Aunt Via, wound up in Los Angeles, where she married
Jean Hersholt, the Danish actor, who bequeathed me my middle
name, Hersholt. He played Dr. Dafoe in the film about the Dionne
quintuplets, *Five of a Kind*, and had the doctor's role in the original
Dracula with Bela Lugosi. (I'm glad none of my political opponents
were aware of that! Can't you just see the headlines: "The Dracula
Connection"?) Cousins resulted from that union, too, one of whom,
Osa Massen, was an actress who married Jean Hersholt Jr. (Alan).
Aunt Via's family gave the Nielsens a bit of a foothold in Los
Angeles: my father went there to live after he retired, and he died
there at the age of seventy-five, and my brother Leslie is quite a
famous denizen of Hollywood. The other sister, my Aunt Erna, is
now living in the southern U.S.

All that was a long way in the future as my sixteen-year-old
father crouched inside a boiler at Canadian Car and Foundry in
Montreal, contemplating a future in which the only thing he could
be sure of was that he would eventually become deaf. When he
learned that the Royal North-West Mounted Police were accepting
young boys as recruits, he leapt at the chance, because the RNWMP
was, to him, a very glamorous outfit. They sent him to Regina,
where his exclusive duties were to maintain the highest standards
of hygiene in the horse barns. Undoubtedly that was where he
learned to shovel so well.

During the First World War, the RNWMP formed a regiment
to go overseas as a unit, and Dad managed to sign up in the artillery
still looking after horses. He served overseas, and then returned to
Regina.

In the meantime, my mother, Mabel Elizabeth Davies, who was
born of Welsh parents in Fulham, a suburb of London, had also
wound up in Regina, working for the telephone company. They
met—probably by my father flirting on the phone—and secretly
became engaged.

My father was a constable in the RNWMP, which seemed pretty
grand to him, but he was still subject to the most rigid discipline.
Among other things, in those days no member of the force could

marry before he had served at least five years, and then only with the force's permission. Dad defied the rules, and my parents were married, secretly, in Regina. Dad was posted to Brandon, Manitoba, shortly thereafter, and it was not long before it became clear that the secret marriage could be kept secret no longer. My mother was pregnant with my brother Gordon, who was born on June 30, 1922. Dad was recalled to Regina—back to the stables, I imagine. He was not dismissed from the service, as he might have been, but he was in the doghouse—or the stables, take your pick. He was given only the most routine assignments for several years.

Meanwhile, I was born on February 24, 1924, and my brother Leslie on February 11, 1926. I have been back to look for the houses in which we lived in Regina, the first on Dewdney Street, almost directly opposite the RCMP barracks, and the second at 1454 Grace, just around the corner. The Dewdney Street property has been rebuilt, and the address on Grace Street no longer exists; it is a strange feeling to find that your roots have been, well, uprooted.

I was born on a Sunday. Friday's *Morning Leader Post* contained the news that King Tut's tomb had been opened in Egypt; that Leon Trotsky, commissioner for war for the Soviet Union, had written a strong article praising the Red Army on its sixth anniversary ("Its force," he wrote—and who knows, somebody may have believed him—"is only directed against oppressors and exploiters"), and that down at the Capitol Theatre, Edna Wallace Hopper ("She's 62, but you'll swear not") was giving a talk on how she retained her youth. Wares Limited on Scarth Street was advertising men's pants for three dollars, but they wanted twenty-five dollars for a suit with two pairs of pants. My father could never have afforded that.

Dad's first substantial posting came in the spring of 1927, when I was three. It was to Fort Norman, in the Northwest Territories. We travelled there on the paddlewheeler *Distributor*, down the Mackenzie River from Fort McMurray, although I do not remember the trip.

My memories begin in Fort Norman, and they are mostly pleasant ones. I have a clear recollection of my mother mixing bread in a huge galvanized washtub, and of the aroma of baking bread. There were no shops in Fort Norman; everything was shipped there and to other Mackenzie River destinations in the spring and summer, when the river was open. The supplies we received therefore had to last us through the winter, until the river broke up.

Dad was alone for a good portion of his tour there, though he was later joined by a fellow constable named George Kirk, who eventually wound up in Yukon as a corporal in charge of the Old Crow detachment. My father did his one-man patrols on a river boat during the summer, and in the winter with the aid of dog-teams. There were twenty-one dogs in all, in three teams, kennelled at the back of the RCMP detachment house, which was close to the river bank.

The local population consisted mostly of Dogrib Indians, and Dad's kind of police work was pretty routine. He was good at his job, and the people throughout his vast area of responsibility liked him. We were the only non-native family in that community for the two years of my father's tour there. During this time, my father, who still had only a rudimentary command of English, enlisted my mother's tutelage and an American correspondence course to improve his English so that he could use proper syntax and grammar in his police reports. He never lost his accent, though, and when he became annoyed at any one of his boys, he would chew us out in Danish, or in accented English: "I tol' you a *tusind* times not to do that." (*Tusind* is Danish for thousand.)

I learned the names of the parts of the body in Danish, but my grasp of the language never progressed much past that; once Dad had learned English well, he had little opportunity to speak his native tongue.

One of my clearest memories of Fort Norman is of pounding on empty steel barrels at the back of the house. This usually made the dogs howl, but in the summer it attracted curious bear cubs. One day, one of them wandered towards the sound, and my brothers and I took it into the house and gave it milk. When my mother found us, she was horrified. No doubt she had visions of Mrs. Bear coming to look for her cub. She put it outside and it wandered off; had the mother bear been in the vicinity, we would have been in trouble from her as well as from Mother.

Another vivid memory concerns a contest I carried on with my elder brother, Gordon, hammering nails into a stump to see who could sink his nail out of sight first. One day when we were doing this, he suddenly started hammering on the nail that I was supposed to be driving, so I put out my left hand to stop him. Gordon's hammer came down full force on my finger, smashing the last joint, which hung by a thin strip of skin. My mother rushed out, grasped the end of my finger, forced it tightly back onto the stump, then tightly bandaged the whole together. It worked! To this day, I have no bone in that joint, but I do have the end of the finger.

Mother, besides being a housewife and nurse, made all of our clothing as well. The RCMP clothing issue included a pea jacket, and one day mother was cutting one of these down to make three coats for her three boys. I was gathering up all the bits of thread and cloth that had fallen to the floor and was putting them into a coffee tin from which the smooth top rim had been removed, exposing a very sharp edge. George Kirk, the RCMP constable who worked with Dad, was sprawled in a chair nearby. I tripped over his outstretched legs, fell on the sharp-edged rim of the tin, and cut my upper lip and chin to the bone. To patch me up was going to require some skilled suturing, but there was no doctor available— he, like the supplies, came only once a year in the spring. My mother went to find the Oblate priest to come and assist my father while he did the suturing. Mother returned with the priest, then left the house, since she could not bear to listen to my screams. Dad put in half a dozen stitches with ordinary needle and thread while Kirk and Father Benami held me on the kitchen table. There was no anaesthetic.

Between accidents, my life was quiet, and I suppose that if it had not been for my brother Gordon, who was nearly seven and ready for school, we would have stayed at Fort Norman for some time. It was late enough for him to start formal classes, and there were no such things in Fort Norman.

Before we left, we had one final adventure. My father had given Gordon a beautiful big coal-black sled dog, which we immediately named Nigger. (People were not so sensitive to such names in those days.) The local people made a small sled for Gordon, a miniature of Dad's patrol sled, and Gordon had a great time mushing his dog all over the frozen river and tundra.

Gordon and I decided to run away from home. I cannot remember why we came to this decision, but Gordon put me in the sled and we left, in the dead of winter, across the frozen Mackenzie River, which at Fort Norman was well over half a mile wide. The ice was very rough, with numerous pressure ridges looming more than three or four times the height of a four-year-old boy. The going was pretty tough for the dog, pulling that sled with me in it, up the ridges, down into the hollows, and up again. About halfway across the river, Gordon stopped the sled and said, "Look, you can't ride any more; you get out and go home." It was now quite late in the northern afternoon where winter days are very short.

Gordon kicked me out and carried on, and I started back in the rapidly gathering dusk. I had not gone very far before I was pretty miserable. I was not exactly a seasoned explorer. Back at home, my parents were getting frantic, when they realized that we were gone with the sled in a rapidly advancing Arctic night. Dad organized a search party with the native people. They found me on the river minutes before total darkness descended. To this day I can remember how cold I was, and I can remember looking up at the ice ridges towering over me.

I had not made much headway after leaving Gordon. As soon as the Indian people found me, I told them which way Gordon had gone. They followed his tracks and found him, not long after, in the dark and cold, trying to extract the dog's front paw from a wolf trap he had stumbled into. Gordon was not strong enough to push down the springs of the trap to release the dog's paw but he was not going to desert him.

In 1930 my family moved out of the North, and my father was posted briefly to Edmonton, where we lived for a few months in a little bungalow on 95th Street, near Jasper Avenue. I started at Alex Taylor School. I was still accident-prone and suffered a rash of mishaps in that period. While jumping during play from a wooden apple box to the floor, I fell and broke my left arm at the elbow. It never did set properly, and as a result I have about a fifteen-degree limitation in its movement. (Much later, I was dreadfully concerned that this limitation would keep me out of the Air Force, but it did not interfere with flying at all.) The other serious accident happened while I was chasing a ball in the front yard, and the ball landed in the middle of Mother's sweet peas, which were supported with wooden stakes. I tripped and fell, driving one of the sticks deeply into my right eye socket. Fortunately, the wooden splinter entered on the outer side, but it was driven in a good inch or two. This required a hospital operation, during which my eyeball had to be removed so the wooden splinters could be taken out. The doctor did a marvellous job, and I have never suffered any ill effects.

I also discovered at this time that when one sticks a wet tongue onto a frozen metal shovel, the tongue tends to become very painfully attached to the shovel. My early years were tough, but I learned a number of useful things.

My brother Gordon had another adventure during this Edmonton sojourn. There was a road under construction—Grierson Avenue, which is there to this day—running down an incline to the south bank of the Saskatchewan River from 96th Street to the Low Level Bridge. The earthmoving equipment was at work, and Gordon was on hand to watch the excitement, when an earth slide caught and totally covered his playmate. No one saw this except Gordon, who ran around yelling and screaming, trying to get help. Finally, one of the construction workers listened to him, and the boy was rescued. The *Edmonton Journal* duly recorded his heroism, complete with picture and a reference to his earlier adventure on the frozen Mackenzie River.

At one point during our stay in Edmonton, my mother was very ill and confined to her bed, and I had my first experience playing with matches. I had a merry blaze going in the clothes closet, and my mother had to get out of her sickbed to put it out as I watched. I was properly admonished, but apparently it did not take. During that same illness of my mother, I found my father's service revolver, a .45 calibre pistol. It was not loaded—I probably would have tried to load it myself if I had found the bullets. In my efforts to pull the hammer back, I clutched the gun tightly against myself. The spring of the hammer was strong and my hands and strength were those of a five and a half year old. While I was hugging the revolver to my stomach, the hammer slipped from my thumbs and the firing pin caught a fold of the flesh of my stomach. I now had a .45 dangling from my stomach. Naturally I screamed blue murder, and my mother had to come and free me, and again an admonition was administered.

Leslie didn't seem to get into such scrapes; all the problems seemed to happen to Gordon and me. We managed to get into these scrapes even though we were brought up under the stern discipline of my father. The threat of his leather belt or RCMP riding crop certainly did not prevent us from being ever more venturesome. When I was ten, I crawled through one of the hollow bridge girders that support Edmonton's High Level Bridge. The girder is about a foot-and-a-half square, and if I had slipped, that would have been the end, since the High Level Bridge is several hundred feet above the river. It was a hair-raising adventure, and not one I felt the need to tell my parents about. I also walked across the top of the spans on the Fifth Street Bridge, and obviously survived that as well.

I roamed a lot, and one of the places I used to visit was a wood-working shop close by the Low Level Bridge. There they made parts for airplanes, and I was fascinated to see bits of wood and fabric turned into the parts of a flying machine. This fascination would stay with me throughout my life.

My father was flush with money when he left the North, since there had been no place to spend his wages in Fort Norman. His savings proved to be enough for him to buy a new Buick Durant. After getting around with a river boat and a dogsled for more than two years, that automobile was the apple of his eye. No boy could ever forget such a car: the new smell of it, the thrill of going on family picnics in it, the fun of sitting behind the wheel pretending to drive it when it was standing still. I marvelled at the complexity of the two or three instruments on the dashboard and the lovely finish inside and outside, and at the overall workmanship of this state-of-the-art Buick. For a third-class constable, the lowest rank in the RCMP, to own a Buick Durant was a miracle. And as with most young fellows, Dad wanted to see how fast it could go. He found out, much to his regret.

After our few months in Edmonton, Dad was posted to Rochfort Bridge, near Whitecourt. He was out driving one Sunday, off duty (to the extent that an RCMP officer on detachment can be off duty). Although most of the roads were dirt, they were hard-packed enough to accommodate a fair burst of speed. Dad was going at a pretty good clip when he suddenly came upon a huge dray, pulled by a team of horses and piled about eight feet high with hay. When you took in the height of the wagon itself, the whole thing was more than ten feet high. This one was crossing the road, blocking out everything. Dad pulled out to pass it at a high speed—and had a head-on collision with an oncoming car. The driver's wife, who was in the front seat of the other vehicle, was seriously injured. Because the victims were successful in showing that the accident occurred during the course of my father's employment and that he was driving negligently, the resulting legal proceedings involved a judgment against the government. To the RCMP, that was as bad as getting married before you had completed five years of service, so now Dad had two black marks against him, which were to limit his future progress in the RCMP.

He knew he was going nowhere in the force. Whether he chose to get out or was asked to leave, I am not certain, but it was at this point—in 1930 or 1931—that he joined the Alberta Provincial Police. In 1935 the provincial force was merged with the RCMP, so he found himself back with the Mounted again. He was posted to Thorhild, in today's Pembina riding, a small town of about 250 people, sixty miles northeast of Edmonton.

These were the days when the salary of a constable in the RCMP was about $100 a month, and on that my parents had to maintain a family of three growing children. It became a little easier when my father was transferred to Thorhild, where prices were slightly lower, but there was never much money for extras. We got a nickel every once in a while to go to the movies; but when some of the higher-class movies came to town, at a cost of a dime, we were priced out of the market.

The years we spent in Thorhild, when I was between eleven and fifteen, were the most happy and carefree of my life. As well, they were formative years for me, growing up at a time when the most important fundamental values were self-reliance, self-initiative, competition, physical fitness, and tolerance for others and for different values, all of which contributed significantly to my survival as an adult.

It was my mother's task to make things work at home, and she did, never complaining, always cheerful and affectionate. She died of cancer in 1958, just after I was first elected to Parliament. I often reflect on the hardships that she suffered, and yet, to me at least, she always seemed to enjoy herself, so perhaps the simple, hardworking life she led had its compensations.

Whatever else can be said of my father, he was a top-notch policeman and a rigid disciplinarian, but he had a sense of fairness, and always, behind it, a sense of control. He never lost his cool, even when he was raging inside. When he had to chastise us, no matter how annoyed he might be, the punishment would be calculated. If he wanted to hit hard, he hit hard, but always with his temper under control. He expected the same control of others.

There was nothing unusual at that time in a father administering corporal punishment to his children, but it was unusual to get it with an RCMP riding crop, which is what Dad used if he thought the occasion warranted it. At any rate, I cannot see that it ever did us any harm.

At Thorhild, after Dad was placed in charge of the detachment, one of his subordinates drew a cartoon of him that showed him as a typical Scandinavian, with the unmistakable Roman nose, thin lips, square jaw, and ice-blue eyes. Dad was blond, and that caricatured face looked like something out of a Norse legend; not quite glowering, but on the verge of it, looking down a great length of Roman nose. It was captioned "Rasputin of Thorhild."

One of our school principals at Thorhild was a man named Jack Zubick. He was a physical fitness fanatic. Every day he had us out in the schoolyard for fifteen minutes in the morning and fifteen minutes in the afternoon doing pushups, leg strides—what today is called aerobics. Nowadays he would probably be fired for the rigorous routines he put his students through, but we thrived on it. One day, I committed some sin—I cannot now remember what it was, probably something in the order of snipping off the hair of the girl in the seat in front of me—and Jack Zubick gave me the strap. In those days, the strap was permitted, but only directly on the hands. Zubick was careless, and the leather belt landed part way up my wrists, bruising them quite badly. When I went home, I did not say anything—whining was the unforgivable sin in our household—but while at the supper table my father noticed the swelling and bruising and asked me about it. Lying was a capital offence in our house, so I told him that I had been strapped and why.

"Who did it?"

"Jack Zubick."

Dad later left the house. The next day in school I noticed that the principal had a shiner. It transpired that Dad had gone to his house, knocked on his door, and hit him in the eye. Again, today that would have led to great repercussions, but nothing came of it then. Zubick, who was a younger man than my father, later joined the RCMP and rose to commissioned rank, while Dad remained a constable. Obviously, he had not been scarred by the ordeal, but he did learn something of how my father operated.

We lived in Thorhild the best part of five years, although the normal tour of duty is only three. This extended posting came about in a curious way. My father was very tough on some of the townsfolk. His position was that the law was the law; he did not make it, but he was going to see that it was enforced. One group, led by the man who ran the local pool hall, initiated a petition to the officer commanding K Division in Edmonton—Dad's boss—complaining about his strictness and asking for his removal. The real cause of complaint was that Dad would not allow the pool hall and beverage room to operate beyond the legal hours.

This petition prompted an inspection from headquarters. Inspector Montezambert turned up for that. (While he was there, I remember clearly his asking me what I was going to be when I grew up. "A lawyer," I promptly told him.) He was a fine, silver-haired man, and very shrewd. He quickly learned that the locals loved it when my father disarmed a berserk drunk armed with a meat cleaver (as he had once), but when he stopped the locals from drinking in the butcher shop, they thought he was going too far.

When the inspection was over—the inspector obviously gave Dad a favourable report, since his tour was extended—Dad dropped around to the pool hall and hinted obliquely that he would not be around forever. Without ever saying so, he managed to convey the impression that he was on the verge of leaving. Word got around town very quickly, and some of the locals—grateful that they were getting rid of him—organized a surprise party for him. Dozens of townspeople descended on our house and presented Dad with a lovely brown leather briefcase as a going-away present. There was even a little speech by the pool hall proprietor, touching on how much the town had appreciated having my father on the job against crime.

We kids were able to take all this in by listening at the head of the stairs, peering through the banister rails. Dad acknowledged the gift and the speech by telling the crowd that he enjoyed being among the citizens of the community every bit as much as they enjoyed having him. Then he stayed on for another two years.

Our two-storey house had a steel holding-cell where people could be kept in custody and where drunks were put to dry out. We came to meet some of the town's more colourful characters there. One of these was a man I remember now only as Big John, a giant of a man, well over six feet tall and broad in proportion. He was a farmer and, as far as I know, a good one, but his weakness was beer, and he was an abusive and violent drunk. (It was Big John, with a meat cleaver, who had been disarmed by Dad in the butcher shop.) One evening, when Big John had been clapped into durance vile for disorderly behaviour, he started stomping his boots on the cell floor; it sounded like the beating of a big drum. Dad told him to be quiet, but he paid no attention, so Dad handcuffed him with his arms through the bars at a level where he could neither stand up straight nor sit down. He was left thus until he was sober enough to be released, whereupon he promptly fell asleep.

In the Dirty Thirties, I used to go with my father on some of his patrols. One of these was to a farm where a report had come in that the farmer had taken his life. That was my first view of death—an immigrant farmer from Germany, hanging from a rafter in his barn. Dad had to cut him down and take the body to town.

Another farm visit worked out more happily. A farmer had caught his leg in a hay bailer and had broken it in several places. My father straightened the leg, put it in splints, and sped the injured man sixty miles to the hospital in Edmonton. Thanks to Dad's competent and immediate first aid, the leg was saved. No one complained then about Dad's fast driving, nor did they when he rushed to hospital a woman who had tried to commit suicide by swallowing lye; nor when he was speeding down the main street at sixty miles an hour to apprehend the perpetrators of a robbery at the general store.

In those days, a Mountie was much more than just a law enforcement officer. No one had any money, and my father had a continuous stream of people at the front door every day applying for relief. Dad and his subordinates were the administrators who filled in the forms and dispensed the limited funds available to help a stricken populace.

Many of the locals took to making moonshine, an activity frowned upon by the law but which provided an income, since the product was always in demand. So, in addition to relief, my father administered a revolving fund to pay informers who told him who had a still on the back forty. The going rate for this information was twenty-five dollars, a very attractive sum at that time.

Whenever Dad drove into Edmonton, I or my brothers would

ask to go with him. It was a nice break from life in a town of 250 souls. I can remember driving along with him when he would stop the car and stick that wonderful schnozzle of his out the window and pick up the unmistakable odour of working mash. He would follow it like a hound on the scent. Once, hot on the scent, he went into a farm, and a little old farm wife told him that yes, she had a little of the stuff, but only to bathe her poor aching feet. She suffered something terrible from rheumatism, she said. When Dad made her show him where the supply was, she lifted the kitchen floorboards, and there were enough gallons of foot balm to ease the rheumatic pains of the Red Army Chorus. The still was nearby.

Once, Dad and another constable had to transport a prisoner to Edmonton; when they arrived in the city, my father briefly left the prisoner in the custody of the other officer, and that worthy decided to pop into the King Edward Hotel to buy some cigarettes, leaving the prisoner free to walk away. As senior officer, Dad had to bear the responsibility, even though it clearly was not his fault. Now there were three black marks against him. Despite his success as a policeman, my father was never promoted during his thirty-year career, and retired as a first-class constable.

Thorhild was a happy place for me, and it was there at the age of fourteen that I wrote my first—and only—play. I wrote it on the typewriter in my father's office for a province-wide school festival. It was a medical drama, and I played the role of the doctor and directed the production. I even won an award for acting. At the same festival, my brother Leslie won the award for oratory with a recital of the Gettysburg Address and "Abou Ben Adhem." Clearly we had not settled on our career paths at that point.

It was a simple time, a time when farmers would drive in from the countryside with a wagonload of fresh meat and produce, and sell it around the town pump. Each summer Dad would find a different farm where we boys would go to work, so that we would be exposed to the benefits of honest toil and would learn tolerance for others. I learned tolerance in the broadest sense of that word: the sense that a non-English-speaking Ukrainian works every bit as hard and deserves every bit as much respect as the English-speaking son of a middle-class family, that a German is no better or worse than a Finn or a Pole. Everyone I knew worked hard to survive; they were all equal in that.

I wound up once on a farm with a Ukrainian family who spoke no English whatever. I learned to ask for *borabolia* (potato), and *capusta* (cabbage), and I learned to say *ya holodnye* (I am hungry)— which I usually was. I was growing up by then, and they had a very nice daughter, so my education included more than merely the language of the dining room. I also learned much Ukrainian scatology from her brothers. I fetched in the cows and milked them, I slopped the hogs and pitched hay, I watched the mating and birthing of animals, watched the butchery, separated the cream from the milk, worked hard, and learned much. We were up before dawn and to bed by eight or nine o'clock at night. Young people are the poorer today who have not been exposed to such experiences.

Another summer I spent on a Finnish farm, where I learned what it is to take a proper sauna. I also learned to weave, in a room occupied only by a large loom. Naturally, I learned some of the language as well, and years later I was able to startle the minister of mines, Judy Erola, who is of Finnish extraction, by demonstrating that I knew the Finnish for "son of a bitch." She seemed impressed.

On the farm I learned to ride, to give a horse its head and rush like the wind over fields and along country roads and trails. For a boy of twelve, it was a fine thrill. Bringing in the cows while riding a horse was to me at that young age the most rewarding part of farming. The least rewarding was going after those accursed cows on foot, in the rain, in the dark, in the middle of a swamp. Being entrusted at the age of twelve to drive a team of horses and wagon eight miles to town without anyone accompanying me was a sobering responsibility and a thrilling adventure.

In town I learned about the law with my father. I went on circuit with him to some of the outlying villages where he acted as the prosecutor in minor cases. A judge heard more serious cases in Thorhild, with a regular Crown lawyer, but for theft, drunkenness, and other summary conviction offences, Dad did the work. Even at that age, as I watched the defence attorneys at work, I recognized that some lawyers were good and some terrible; some were sober and some were drinkers; some dressed well and some did not. But what fascinated me was the process of the law, the meting out of justice—or, on occasion, what appeared to be injustice.

I also taught myself something of flying, which, with the law, was to become a lifelong passion. I do not recall exactly when the joy of flying first came to me. I suppose it had something to do with my environment; in such spaces, you had to conquer the air if you really wanted to see the land. That yearning was somehow built into me, and has never left.

I built model airplanes of balsa and tissue paper, powered by rubber bands, miniatures of the ones I had seen built in that workshop down by the Low Level Bridge, down to the last grommet.

The models I was sure would fly I launched by hand. When I was not so sure, I would climb up to the roof of our house and give them a better chance from there. There were, needless to say, many crashes, but I went on building, and at one time had forty or fifty model airplanes in my collection. So I learned, without knowing any of the theory, what in fact made an airplane fly. I knew about the thickness of wing cords and the length of wings, and about torque and centres of gravity. I never flew in an airplane until I joined the Air Force, but my brother Gordon took a demonstration flight with a barnstorming pilot who visited Thorhild in an old Jenny, which thrilled me vicariously. The ride cost the enormous sum of one dollar.

I also learned to drive a car. Dad would sit us in his lap in the police patrol car and allow us to steer. When we were a bit bigger and could reach the pedals, we would sit between his legs and drive, and he would be right there to kick a foot off the gas pedal if he thought we were going too fast. Sometimes, during work trips to a farm on which the farmer owned a Model T Ford, I would be permitted to drive that around the pasture, manipulating the three clutch pedals on the floor and the hand brake on the left side of the driver's seat.

I developed as well a love of books. From the very first, I was a voracious reader. I obtained then and still obtain enormous pleasure, not merely in the knowledge books impart, but in the stimulation of the imagination that comes with them. I was later to haunt libraries and book stores everywhere I went and I still remember my overwhelming sense of inadequacy when I realized that I would never in my lifetime be able to read all of the books that were published. If anything, my passion for reading has increased with the passage of time.

Perhaps—and I would not be the first to fall victim to this besetting sin—I am looking at my childhood through rose-coloured glasses, but I do not believe so. It was truly a happy time, in a much simpler world.

Sports were tremendously important, and we played them all: hockey, baseball, football, and others. The Thorhild community centred on the hockey rink, as do so many small prairie towns in a cold climate. There were dances in the community hall, and a movie once a week, brought on circuit by an entrepreneur with a 16-mm projector.

The radio brought us the outside world. Every family had a battery-powered radio—battery-powered because not every family in town had electricity. We did, because of Dad's job, but we had the same battery-radio as everyone else. It became a tradition for the family to gather around the radio on Sunday evening to listen to Fibber McGee and Molly, The Shadow, Jack Benny, Inner Sanctum, Lux Radio Theatre, and many other shows.

I learned as well something of money and commerce in those early years. I had a paper route and delivered the *Edmonton Journal* and the *Edmonton Bulletin*. Some of my customers lived on farms a considerable distance from town and when I was not able to borrow a bicycle to deliver their papers, I walked. I was soon itching to move on and become a conglomerate. I began hoarding my nickels and dimes. I had an old Brownie camera, and I learned to develop my own pictures, so I thought I would go into the film processing business. That was when I discovered that if hard well water was used in the developing mixture, it ruined the film; soft water was required. Once I had that mastered, I did all right, but the market, after my first efforts, was a little leery.

When I was fifteen, I received my last thrashing. We three boys were playing outside while my parents were playing bridge with some neighbours. A real dandy of a squabble broke out, and Leslie ran over to the neighbours to enlist aid. He was sent back with strict orders that we were to settle down and behave. The fight went on, and Leslie went back. A few minutes later, there was Dad, with the riding crop. In those conditions, we were all nailed, without much attempt to sort out who had started what, so, in my turn, I was laid over my father's knee and the riding crop was put to work. I wriggled sideways just as a blow was descending, and the crop hit Dad's knee with such force that it put him right out of action for a few minutes. He realized what a punishing thing the crop was, and it was put away forever.

Soon after that, we moved back to Edmonton, in September 1939, a few days after the declaration of World War II. At first we lived in a house by the Dawson Bridge, in the north end of the city, and we walked about three miles every day to Victoria High School. Then we moved farther up the hill, just below 95th Street and not far from RCMP K Division headquarters, where Dad worked. This was just as well, as we could no longer afford a car. His salary was now $120 a month, not much for life in the city.

Finally, we moved to the corner of 95th Street and 102 A Avenue, two and a half blocks from Dad's work. He was promptly transferred to the Criminal Investigation Branch, which took him away from home for long stretches at a time. First, there was a course in Regina, where he trained with a special anti-safecracking team. At the tail end of the Depression, when crime was still rampant, one of the favourite routines for robbers was to travel the rail lines, and break into the safes in the rail depots. Dad was part of a police group set up to put a stop to that. When he returned home, he brought with him a neat little fingerprint kit, which included vials of various-coloured powders. One day when there was no one home, I decided to try my hand at fingerprinting on the mirrorlike finish of our brand-new walnut dining-room table. I pressed my fingers on the gleaming tabletop and with a wet brush applied quite a large quantity of yellowish powder to the prints. Had I used a dry brush, the experiment would have been a complete success. As it was, I ruined the tabletop, which had to be refinished.

I joined the Edmonton School Boys Band, where I played the drums. In point of fact, I could not play the drums, but I had taken piano lessons in Thorhild and could read music, which was all that was required. It was a good band, with about seventy-five members, under the direction of T.V. Newlove. We played at all the football games, gave concerts, and played some classical music besides the usual John Philip Sousa marching repertoire. The lead B-flat bass player, Lee Hepner, later became the first director of the Edmonton Symphony Orchestra.

I also became a regular visitor to the Edmonton Municipal Airport on Kingsway Avenue, where I would stand by the hour watching the airplanes take off and land. I would soon be flying myself, although I had no inkling of that at the time. I built my first gas-powered model airplane at this time, a WACO biplane with a five-foot wingspan, and flew it successfully.

During my first summer in Edmonton, I walked into the Northwest Industries plant at the municipal airport and asked for a job, saying that I would do anything around airplanes. They decided to give me a try. They were doing contract work on Fairey Battle aircraft, and I worked on flying controls, electrics, splicing steel cable—all sorts of jobs connected with building an airplane.

The next summer, I worked for an electrical contractor, and I dropped out of high school—although I continued to study by correspondence course—to be an apprenticed electrician. I was sixteen years old and the pay was five dollars a month. The contractor's agreement, which my father had to sign, was that I would pay for my teaching with my services. I accepted that; I did not drive a hard bargain in those days.

I liked the work and learned the fundamentals of house wiring. I also learned that when you are repairing pipe organs, you do not crawl along the lead pipes that carry the air to the organ. I flattened them, ruining a good part of the instrument. That cost my employer a pretty penny to repair.

I was also put on the job of wiring the new Hudson's Bay Store, which still stands on Jasper Avenue between 102nd and 103rd streets. The job required putting a ten-foot length of five-inch conduit on my shoulder and carrying it up a stepladder to the ceiling, twenty feet up; measuring and marking it; bringing it down the ladder; clamping it in the vise; cutting it, double-checking it, and then threading it so it could be coupled to the next length.

I was several months at that exhausting work; I do not suppose I had encountered any harder work in my life. Going up and down the ladder so often, I developed infected ingrown toenails, and that put me off work. I had to go to a chiropodist and have them cut out—it was excruciatingly painful. I could not walk; it was quite a while before I could even ride my bike. While I was recuperating, I decided that there had to be an easier way to make a living. My conclusion was that I had better return to school full time, which I did.

That Christmas, I narrowly escaped what might have been another sound thrashing from my father. I was nearly eighteen, and I went out on Christmas Eve with a number of my close friends. As it happened, all of them were Jewish. One, an older boy named Joe Loomer (who later joined the Department of Finance and now lives in Ottawa), had purchased a bottle of Queen Anne Scotch.

I have been drunk three times in my life; this was the first. There were periods of that evening that I could not recall later, and that was a frightening new experience for me. What was even more worrying was the thought of what my father would do to me if I turned up drunk on Christmas Eve. Joe took me to his home and the next morning we had a real kosher breakfast, which almost made me throw up again. When I finally arrived home at about nine o'clock Christmas morning, very much hung over, Dad gave me a stern look and said, "If I thought you had been out drinking last night, I would lambaste you something terrible."

Silence.

That was the kind of disciplinarian he was.

Very soon after this, Dad was away again. The RCMP had decided to take advantage of his ability for languages (besides Danish and English, he spoke French, German, Norwegian, and some Italian). They posted him to the Criminal Investigation Branch in Halifax, where he spent most of the rest of the war undercover on the docks. His cover was to work as a stevedore, while his real work was to flush out spies and saboteurs.

Combined with the innate fascination I'd always had for flying, the urge to do something worthwhile in the war, as my father was doing, took me down to the Air Force recruiting office on Jasper Avenue. The enlistment officer there, surveying my youthful appearance, declined to take my word for it that I was the eighteen I claimed to be. He told me I would have to bring my mother in to swear to it.

Mother was unwilling to swear a falsehood, but I was only three or four months away from the required age, and that time was to be spent on bringing my math and other necessary subjects up to the Air Force standard. That was a compelling argument, as were the tears in my eyes when I begged her to lie for me. She caved in. I will never forget her holding the Bible in the recruiting office, with her fingers crossed underneath the holy book. My father's typical blunt reaction, when he learned I had joined the Air Force, was, in so many words, "Who are you trying to kid? You don't have what it takes."

That remark harks back to our days in Thorhild, when part of his regimen of training the young Nielsen boys was to teach us some of the tumbling he had learned as a youngster—handsprings, headstands, flips, and all the rest of it. The three Nielsen brothers were known for their tumbling skills at school. I remember one of the stunts involved doing a backward flip with a boost from Dad's cupped hands, and I was always sure I was going to break my back. Gordon and Leslie had no such qualms.

Gordon eventually reached a height of six foot three, and Leslie, a body-building fanatic, reached six two. Dad took to referring to me as "the runt of the litter." I was as good on the horse, the rings, and the springboard as they were, but that was when the performance was voluntary. When we were required to perform, I complained, and Dad formed the conclusion that I was lacking the "right stuff," and hence would not do well in the armed forces.

When I returned from active service in 1945 and reminded him of what he had said, he looked at me down the entire length of his magnificent nose and replied, "Well, I was wrong, wasn't I?"

But that was a war, and several medals, later.

Chapter Two

The War Years

We didn't cross the Channel to fight for England,
but felt rather that we were going forth to fight,
along with England, for Canada.
                              Abbé J.-Armand Sabourin, 1942

When in 1942 I moved from the shelter of family life and youthful teenage existence into the highly disciplined environment of the Air Force, the change was a substantial shock. The discipline at home may have been above average for a normal family, but the discipline in the forces was absolute: instant obedience to orders was required on the pain of instant punishment.

My first recollection is of numbers—thousands of young men drawn together at the manning depot in Edmonton, where they were housed in horse stables converted to bunkhouses, and other outbuildings of the Edmonton Exhibition grounds. From the moment we were issued our kit, I did not see much of civilian clothes until after the war, when I returned to Canada.

Each morning, we were awakened at five, while it was still quite dark. We fought for a place in the long queues of men waiting to perform their ablutions and then rushed back to the sleeping area. There was no time to waste; everything had to be done—including cleaning the bed space, making the bed, and all the myriad duties that had to be achieved to escape punishment—before breakfast parade, sharp at six.

I can still hear the sergeant banging together two garbage can lids in the bunkhouse to awaken us, with the shout, "Wakey, wakey, wakey; leggo your cocks and grab your socks and get up and piss, 'cause the world's on fire!" The first time I heard it I did not know what was happening. I had just turned eighteen and was about to learn that what I had judged to be oppressive discipline at home would soon look like a snap.

21

Life seem to consist mainly of marching and drill and physical training, all day long, seven days a week. I was exhausted by the end of the day, though by the end of six weeks, I was as fit as anyone there. We did our physical training—pushups and acrobatics—in the Edmonton Arena. Then outside for the marching, on the huge macadammed spaces of the Ex grounds. Everywhere you looked, men were marching, turning, wheeling, with and without rifles.

The bunkhouses were H-shaped huts with approximately 100 men in each side of the H in row upon row of double-bunk beds. The middle of the H housed the washrooms, with their rows of sinks and toilets. There was no privacy anywhere. From the first cold February dawn when you arrived, your neighbour had no secrets from you, not even his goose bumps. We were expected to discipline and organize ourselves to keep every inch of that building immaculate. If a hospital corner on a blanket was inadvertently left hanging rather than tucked in, it was good for seven days' CB (which meant confined to barracks). We were all aiming for air crew postings, but the discipline had to do with being in the military, not being in the air. We complained about it, thrived on it, and, as time would prove, survived on it.

After ten weeks of basic training and one month of tarmac duty (working around the hangars) at No. 3 Service Flying Training School in Calgary, the next posting for air crew intake was No. 4 ITS—Initial Training School. ITS was housed in the University of Alberta buildings in Edmonton, which had been taken over by the Air Force. There, in addition to the daily drill and physical training, we had lengthy and demanding classes in trigonometry, navigation, armaments, the theory of flight, airmanship, meteorology—virtually every matter having to do with flight, airplanes, and their armaments. Again, the hours were long; we started at six in the morning and finished, exhausted, about twelve hours later. After dinner, we had to clean up our kit and uniforms, do our washing, and complete academic assignments for the next day.

Quite apart from academic studies, drill, and physical training, the Air Force offered us another treat—medicals. The medical on entrance to the service was quite rigorous. It went hand-in-hand with IQ tests. (IQ tests were applied to sort out air crew categories such as air gunner, bomb aimer, pilot, wireless operator, navigator, and so on. I had applied to be a wireless operator/air gunner because

I had enjoyed tinkering with radios as a teenager.) At ITS, the medical was ten times as rigorous as the recruiting medical; this was the school for those who were expected to be allotted duties in the air. Many recruits were recategorized at the ITS level because they could not do the academics or could not pass the physical.

The doctors who administered the medical in ITS did more than confirm that you were sound of mind and body, that your coordination was perfect, that your eyesight was perfect, and that your other senses and reactions were of a high order. They also drew conclusions about your mental attitude. For instance, one test had you blow into a tube with a glass mouthpiece, surmounted by a crossbar to prevent you from using your tongue to hold the pressure up. You were required to raise a column of mercury in a U-shaped tube to a marked level, and to hold it at that level. It was not only a matter of holding your breath, but also of maintaining a given and steady pressure for at least sixty seconds. The really determined candidates went beyond the required minute; I was able to hold the mercury up for a minute and a half before I started to see exploding stars. The test clearly served no clinical purpose—my lungs had already been examined—but it did tell the doctors something about willpower and the determination to succeed. In that, it was a good test.

There were four or five units—or flights as they were called, of approximately thirty to fifty airmen each in the academic stream at any given time at ITS. Because of my previous musical experience in the high-school band, I was the drummer for our flight, along with another airman from Edmonton, Jim Reid. We alternated in drumming our flight on its mile-long march between the campus residences where we lived and the classrooms.

The late Senator Grattan O'Leary was once asked what he thought was the most beautiful sensation, the greatest emotional experience in life and his response was immediate: "Oh, the act of sex, of course, the sexual union of a man and a woman who care for each other." Although I agree with the late senator, I rank eating pretty highly as well. One of my great surprises in the Air Force was the quality (and quantity) of the food. The huge mess halls were spotless, and though the food was cooked in massive vats and on huge griddles measured in square yards, it was wholesome and appetizing. As we moved into units of smaller and smaller numbers from manning depot to ITS and into the flight training schools, the food got better and better. For example, for breakfast at ITS we had a choice of half a dozen kinds of dry cereal, bacon and eggs, or several kinds of porridge. Like most young men in good health, I had the appetite of a python on the prowl, and I made the most of my opportunities to eat. Such abundance was a substantial improvement over the family menus of the Dirty Thirties!

When we finished our ITS training, we were paraded and our respective futures were announced. The sergeant thundered the name of each candidate, followed by his new classification and posting. When the sergeant came to "Nielsen, Erik," he followed it with "pilot training, High River." I was not terribly disappointed, even though I had had my heart set on being a wireless operator and air gunner. I was determined that, if I had to be a pilot, I would be the best damn pilot around. To this day, I do not know whether that monumental, life-changing decision was made because I had done well in the mathematics and navigation tests, or because I had puffed for so long on that damn column of mercury, or both. For whatever reason, on January 10, 1943, I reported to No. 5 Elementary Flying Training School in the small Alberta town of High River.

At High River, we had the standard wartime living accommodations, H-shaped huts, each end occupied by thirty to fifty men, who constituted a flight. There were far fewer of us on the station than at ITS, because the number of trainees was determined by the number of airplanes that could take off and land on a grass field without pranging. The number of available flying instructors was also a limiting factor. The dining facilities were bright and spotless, and we were served with a wide variety of foods every day. The discipline was familiar as well. We marched to and from everything but the washroom: to and from mess parade, sick parade—whether voluntary or involuntary—flight parade, classroom parade, ground school parade.

Flying has always enthralled me, from my very first flight at High River to this day. The highest I had ever been before then was the eighth floor of the Tegler building in Edmonton, at the time the tallest office building in the city. The sensation I had on my first flight was that I had moved from ordinary life into a completely new dimension, and the sensation grew sharper the higher we climbed. As we soared into the sky, I felt detachment, absolute freedom to go anywhere, without hindrance; the air was mine to command. I remember this soul-lifting experience as though it were yesterday and any doubts I may have had about wanting to be a pilot vanished in an instant. I was hooked; it went beyond mere fascination to a love affair with airplanes that continues to this day.

The regimen was, apart from the flying, much the same: marching, drills, physical training, the inevitable parades, rifle drill, and standing guard duty in a sentry box. Each day was filled with intensive ground-school classes that concentrated on learning things so thoroughly and doing them so often that you could do them blindfolded. When you entered the cockpit you did not have to think about where the various dials, levers, buttons, and switches were; these matters had been studied, repeated, and drilled into you in class so often that they were stamped on your mind—and still are. Those who could not cope with this endless drilling left the flight.

Alberta seems to have produced more than the average number of pioneers in Canadian flying. My instructor came from Nanton. He was a civilian, as so many flying instructors were at the time. These civilian flyers applied to join the Air Force, and the Air Force, rather than sending them overseas, kept them in Canada to train pilots under the Commonwealth Air Training Plan. Reluctantly, they stayed, thinking they could work their way overseas later; fully half the instructors at High River were civilians, though they wore the Air Force uniform. Later, some of them became employees of the federal public service and to this day are having difficulty in claiming this early service as pensionable government service.

The chief instructor, who was instantly dubbed Tiny, was as big as a house. He had to be shoe-horned in and out of the tiny cockpit of the Tiger Moth, the frail-looking biplane that we used, along with Cornells, for flight training. The Tiger Moth was an astonishing craft, driven by a sixty horsepower engine: you could take off in a high wind after a very short roll, hurl it up into the air over the field, and, with the appropriate throttle setting, hold it there, stationary, against one of the chinook winds that came roaring in over the mountains. We must have looked, when pulling this stunt, like overgrown hummingbirds.

The flying course was just as well organized as the ground school. Everything was done by numbers; even the training sequences were described by numbers. If you were sent out to do climbing turns, that would be recorded in your logbook as 5 and 6; incipient spins would be 10A, and so on.

I soloed after eight hours in a Cornell, a low-winged monoplane powered by an inverted six-cylinder Ranger engine, which makes super use of what is known as ground effect—the air compressed between the mainplane (the wing) and the runway just before landing. Any fool could land a Cornell. It was a very safe airplane, but its very stability encouraged flying students to take risks. Even if you fouled up, you were confident that you could recover. If you took your hands and feet off all the controls, it would recover itself— well, most of the time. On one occasion I thought I would see how tightly the aircraft would "wind up" in a spin. After climbing to 8,000 feet I put the aircraft into a spin and kept it there. I started recovery procedure at 2,500 feet: full opposite rudder until the spinning stops. The spinning did not stop. I had the canopy open and was ready to jump when the spinning stopped, at 1,500 feet.

The more I flew, getting into advanced manoeuvres and aerobatics, the more deeply I fell in love with flying; I could not wait for the next flight. Even though I was in the military, I was in heaven. The war seemed very far away indeed.

I was hoping that I would pass out of High River to single engines and fighters, and many of the men in my flight followed that route. I was chosen instead for twin-engine training, and my record suggested that I was marked as potential material for training as a flying instructor, perhaps because of my clearly displayed love for flying, but more likely because flying instructors were in such short supply. Whatever the reason might be, I was determined that I did not want a career instructing others. I very much wanted to fly on combat operations.

My later life, both in law and the private sector and in politics— especially the House of Commons—depended upon precision, including precision in choosing words and in putting them together. That precision, combined with obedience and discipline, began with my paramilitary training at home with my father, whose Sam Browne belt and boots I had to polish along with the brass buttons of his uniform. I came from a household in which we all had jobs to do, and they had to be done by a certain time in a certain way. The application of highly disciplined habits became second nature to me and made the transition into the military environment that much easier. We had a saying in the Air Force, "Once is too often," meaning that your first mistake could be fatal. I carried those values into my legal studies and my legal practice. I also carried them into politics. Politics, however, is an environment where those admirable values can become a liability—indeed, a fatal liability.

After we finished at High River, we went to Curry Barracks in southwest Calgary, No. 3 Service Flying Training School. (The remains of the station are still there.) There we flew twin-engined Cessna Cranes, an airplane of wood and fabric construction. That is where the multi-engine flying and bombing training took place. The navigation training was conducted in the twin-engined Avro Anson. Just as the modern F-104 was known as the Widow Maker, the Cessna Crane, powered by two Shaky Jacobs radial engines, was known as the Flying Coffin by the students. Faithful Annie, as we affectionately called the Anson, was also known as the Flying Greenhouse—there were windows all around the aircraft. It was difficult to imagine so frail a craft flying in combat, as it did over Europe in the early years of the war.

Off in a corner of the complex was a school for training wireless and radio operators. They flew in the Fleet, a low-winged monoplane, a two-seater. At Curry Barracks, the flying situation was much more complex than at High River. Aircraft were constantly in the air, night and day, with a student and an instructor, or a student flying solo, and one was required to be more alert and careful, both on the ground and when flying. There were, inevitably, mishaps.

My second exposure to death was at Calgary. While waiting to take our turn in the aircraft by flights, we used to sit on benches in front of the five hangars, with our seatpack parachutes ready. To get to a parked aircraft, we had to walk across a busy apron along which aircraft were always taxiing in both directions. One day, Harmon, an airman in our course, started to walk across the tarmac to the parked aircraft he was scheduled to fly. How he failed to notice a Cessna Crane coming up on his left, I will never know, nor how the pilot of the taxiing aircraft failed to see Harmon. We watched horrified and heard the whack of the starboard propeller hitting Harmon in the small of his back. We knew instantly that it had to be fatal. We all ran out to the aircraft, which had been shut down immediately. Harmon had been thrown by the propeller to the aft end of the aircraft, under the tail. His intestines were visible. He was rushed to the base hospital, where he lived for thirty-six hours or so. A young man in the prime of life, a good student, but simply not alert enough. "Once is too often."

On another occasion we were sitting on the same bench joshing and talking, when a Fleet Fort with a radio crew collided with a Cessna Crane over the field. The Crane exploded and plunged to the ground in front of us; the Fleet Fort, with one wing severely damaged, landed safely. In all, there were five fatalities during my training at Calgary, and each one was a lesson, or should have been a lesson, to every one of us. The machines were as safe as the people operating them, and no more.

Our training at Calgary lasted from April to July 23, 1943, when we received our wings. By this time, we had logged about 120 hours of flying. Graduation was a big day. Some of us graduated as commissioned officers and others as noncommissioned officers, or NCOs. Graduates became either sergeants or pilot officers. At the time, rank really did not matter to me as long as I could fly. I graduated as a sergeant and had a party in the Palliser Hotel in Calgary, which my father and mother attended. Everyone had a girlfriend; mine came down from Edmonton.

There were some Norwegians training with us, and I remember one, who was behind us in training, getting very drunk at this graduation party and generally making all of us quite miserable. I was down the hallway when I heard voices raised in anger, speaking Norwegian—one of them was my father's. He had taken exception to the conduct of the Norwegian and was telling him so in his own language so as to make his message abundantly clear. The Norwegian took a swing at my father. It was the wrong thing to do. Father blocked the swing and nailed him with a short jab to the jaw. The man folded and slid down the wall.

A few days later, I was off on a troop train to Halifax, from where we were to embark for Europe. The old coaches had wicker seats which acted as a bunk all the way. Each time the train stopped, there would be a rush of uniforms, some brown, but most of them blue, to the hotel nearest the depot for beer. In some of the smaller towns, the hotels must have been cleared out of their entire stock. This routine was repeated all the way to Halifax.

That train ride was the first time that I had consciously taken stock of my country. The journey took five days in coaches pulled behind a steam locomotive puffing its way across the prairies, along the north shore of Lake Superior, across the unimaginable vastness of northern Ontario and the rugged shield of Quebec, to the valleys of the Maritimes. The size of my country was really brought home to me on this train journey.

When we arrived in Halifax, it was the first time I had seen an ocean, and the fragrance of the salt air was an entirely new sensation for me. We were assembled for our journey overseas in a huge manning depot reminiscent of the one in Edmonton, jammed with Canadian troops of all three services. Our ship, the *Queen Mary*, was in dock, and after strict instructions as to what we could and could not take, we arranged our personal affairs and packed our kit. We were allowed to take one kit bag only. This was standard issue, about sixteen inches in diameter and four feet long. Side webbing was used for odds and ends such as a shaving kit and toothbrush. We were required to wear our kit, which consisted of a small bag, a holstered revolver, ammunition pouch, and water canteen. That was it, no frills.

The day after we packed, we were boarded. I was awestruck by the size of the ship and even more so when I learned the number of troops on board at our sailing. When we marched up to the third storey of the building on the dock, we were merely on the level of the freight doors in the side of the ship. Her cargo on this trip consisted almost entirely of air crew and our gear, three or four thousand of us. The crew numbered about 1,200, so there were almost 5,000 people crammed aboard for this crossing.

Each of the luxury cabins had been fitted out with three-tiered pipe-frame bunks. Each cabin had nine bunks, and there was not enough floor space for all the occupants to stand up at the same time. To make it more interesting, three or four men also slept on mattresses on the floor. I could not tolerate such crowded conditions, and when I learned that it was permissible to sleep on the deck, I moved out forthwith. Unfortunately, so did several hundreds of others, so the deck was almost as crowded—but not as fetid—as the cabins had been.

That voyage was the only time during my service career that I could not eat the food. Huge vats of stew were placed on long tables running the length of the mess hall. We had mess kits, rectangular aluminum tins with flat bottoms and sides about two inches high. One was expected simply to dip the tin in the stew pot and scoop up a portion. The mess tin, thus filled, dripped with gravy and bits of stew while the owner looked for an open seat on the benches along the tables. The tables, benches, and deck were covered with stew after a meal like this, so I spent the rest of the time living on chocolate bars, fig newtons, and other cookies I had bought in Halifax. A dry canteen on the ship was open from time to time, and if I stood in line long enough, I could get chocolate bars and cookies to replenish my supply.

Our crossing was accomplished in just under four days—we travelled across the Atlantic at the phenomenal speed of thirty knots. That was a major achievement for any oceangoing ship at the time. The *Queen Mary* needed no surface escort; indeed, there was nothing that could keep up with her. The German U-boats, whose speed under water was eight to twelve knots, were hopelessly outclassed.

It was during that voyage overseas that I first became exposed to politics in an emotional way. Until that time, the closest I had come to politics had been during the Alberta provincial election of 1935, when I had accompanied my brother Gordon to the circulation office of the *Edmonton Bulletin* to pick up copies of the "extra" of the newspaper announcing the astounding victory of William Aberhart and his newly formed Social Credit party. I proudly announced that my father had voted for Aberhart, and my brother silenced me smartly. I learned then that there were some who preferred to keep their political affiliations to themselves.

On board ship, the men were not silent about their preferences. Indeed, the discussions were frequent and always noisy. There was considerable criticism of the Mackenzie King Liberals for the government's equivocal stand on conscription. At the same time, the troops blamed French Canadians for forcing the government to take the stand it did. There were many racial slurs against French Canadians, and an abundance of fanciful stories about them when they finally were conscripted. These stories were typical of the exaggerations of any soldiers, anywhere.

Although I did not take part in these discussions, they aroused my curiosity, largely because of the viciousness of some of the comments about Canadians who constituted 30 per cent of the population of our country. I also heard about the incident at Aldershot, where 5,000 Canadian troops had been assembled in formal parade formation to hear Prime Minister Mackenzie King speak to them. They removed their packs and caps and, along with their rifles, threw them to the ground and booed their prime minister. It had a profound effect on me.

I never forgot those heated and often violent shipboard discussions, and in London, while on leave, I visited the Conservative Club, out of curiosity. I was given the run of the library, and subsequently read the works of Bentham, Burke, and other political philosophers of their age. I became convinced that I was closer to Conservative tenets than any others. I would, then and now, categorize myself as a moderate Conservative, although that is certainly not the image I project. I became convinced that the principal tenet of Conservatism, namely that of free enterprise whereby the best government is the least government, was correct, but I believed too that society has an obligation to care for those who through no fault of their own are unable to work by reason of disability or because jobs simply are not available. To that extent, my beliefs were socialistic.

As a result of my reading and of the Canadian conscription issue, I became convinced that the King government was fundamentally dishonest, speaking out of both sides of its mouth at the same time—a trait epitomized by the famous phrase, "Conscription if necessary, but not necessarily conscription." I was ashamed as a Canadian that our minister of national defence, Colonel Ralston, had been forced to resign over the issue. In my view, his pro-conscription position represented the best interest of our country. That issue accelerated the formation of my political allegiances.

These thoughts were merely unformulated meanderings in my mind, of course, when the *Queen Mary* docked at Greenock, Scotland. I had been stirred, but I was far from politically knowledgeable or aware. Indeed, my principal emotion when we landed was one of relief that the days of crowded sleeping and the diet of chocolate bars and fig newtons had come to an end.

We disembarked to the welcome of an organization that I came to cherish very much indeed—the Navy, Army, and Air Force Institutes, better known as the NAAFI. There they were, as the ship was docking, hundreds of pretty NAAFI girls, with hot mugs of tea and loads of "NAAFI cakes" for the troops. We were marched from the dock to British troop trains a short distance away. I was happy to find them blessed with compartments—no wicker seats, but solid upholstery. They were fast trains, smaller than ours, and more comfortable. We were not told where we were going, but it turned out to be Bournemouth, on the south coast of England. It did not seem strange to me then, and it never has seemed strange in my political life, to be told only at the last moment what the destination was to be.

Bournemouth was a lovely city, and during the four weeks I spent there waiting for a posting, I attended my first classical concert, featuring the late Richard Tauber, the British tenor. In the interval of his concert, a banana—a rare fruit in wartime Britain—was auctioned from the stage for an enormous price for some wartime charity. During my stay in Bournemouth I also learned to play golf. So you will see that I had even more than the usual warrior's impatience to get going.

My first posting was to a Beam Approach Training (BAT) course. We were flying Oxfords, twin-engined wooden aircraft, similar to the Avro Anson. I was to take two more such courses before I flew operationally. It was all instrument flying, without any visual reference to the ground. Such training was also referred to as flying "under the hood" or "flying blind." Our flying skills were assessed and rated from time to time. After some ratings that were not particularly complimentary, I finally achieved a rating of above average. The delay in achieving this superior rating was no doubt due to some of my stupid boners, fortunately while under instruction. One such occasion illustrates the steely qualities possessed by a good instructor.

One of my instructors, a squadron leader called Farrell, had pioneered the art of navigating into enemy territory using a combination of British and German radio beams. Absolutely unflappable, he was. After a long session of beam-training exercises with him as my instructor, I was making a blind landing. I was concentrating on the approach to the runway and the landing; Farrell was sitting in the right-hand seat. My concentration on the instruments was so intense that I did not hear the loud, high-pitched blaring of the undercarriage warning horn, which sounded inside the cockpit if the aircraft wheels were still up when the throttles were retarded beyond a certain point. I was within twenty feet of the runway, just about to land, when the noise finally penetrated. I quickly opened the throttles and went around again. Farrell, who had known exactly what was happening, said, "By Jove, I was wondering if you were going to hear that horn." I often wondered whether he would have let me land with the wheels up.

My next posting, again on Oxfords, was to a unit that trained flying instructors. All of us were hoping that our training was leading to eventual posting to a combat squadron, but we began to get suspicious. Clearly, some of us were going to be selected as instructors. That was the last thing I had in mind for my own future. I knew by that time that no amount of pleading would change the minds of the personnel planners; some other method of wangling a posting to an operational unit had to be found. Another fellow in the same fix was a sergeant named Johnny Walker, from New Brunswick. We concluded that the only way to ensure a combat squadron posting was to convince our superiors that we would be hopeless as instructors. Now, England is a very foggy country, especially in the late fall, winter and spring. The terrain was also strange to us. Soon, Johnny and I were getting "lost" on an increasing number of our cross-country training flights. Each time either of us was "lost," we would land at a strange aerodrome and enquire about its location. The base officials would call our home air base and inform them that they had Nielsen (or Walker) here in an Oxford. We would ask for detailed instructions on how to return to base. The career planners were soon convinced that we two Canadians would be best shipped off to an operational training unit, and we were.

I flew my first operation against the enemy in the Wellington bomber, affectionately known as the Wimpy. (The Wellington, the largest twin-engined aircraft I had yet flown, was the transition aircraft between the lighter Oxfords and the heavy four-engined Lancasters and Halifaxes.) My first mission consisted of dropping propaganda leaflets over occupied Europe.

By this time I had acquired my crew of six, who with a few changes, stayed with me until the completion of my first tour with 101 Lancaster Squadron. The only changes were gunners. (The Wellington had a front gunner and a rear gunner.)

Our next posting was to a unit flying four-engined Halifax bombers—a Heavy Conversion Unit—in Lincolnshire. Here our training intensified, and we flew by night and day, familiarizing ourselves with the aircraft, its weapons, and, just as importantly, with each other.

While it was normal practice for Canadians to fly with Canadian units at this point in the war, some of us were sidetracked into Royal Air Force streams, and, once there, we stayed. Consequently, along with my crew, I was posted to 101 Squadron, an RAF special duties squadron flying four-engined Lancaster bombers. In my opinion, the Lancaster aircraft had to be the ultimate in heavy bombers of the day. It had a service ceiling in excess of 25,000 feet with a full load of bombs—22,000 pounds of various sizes, types, and weights. At that time, no other bomber carried a heavier load. By today's standards, such a load is nothing at all.

It was on 101 Squadron at Ludford Magna that we picked up the eighth member of our crew. Although the normal crew for the Lancaster was seven, we had an eighth member who was trained in wireless and radio techniques and was fluent in the German language. The 101 Squadron's aircraft were equipped with high-powered radio equipment that enabled the special operator to jam the transmissions of German fighter control centres, thus preventing German ground control from vectoring German airborne fighters towards our bomber stream. Not infrequently, the special operators were able to send out their own instructions to vector the German fighters away from the bomber stream. 101 was the only squadron in the entire Allied air forces that had this capability, code named Airborne Cigar.

The Airborne Cigar squadron operated whenever large numbers of aircraft flew on a mission against enemy territory. 101 Squadron aircraft were briefed to fly dispersed throughout the bomber stream at varying altitudes and distances so the entire stream could enjoy the protective benefits. That meant that the vulnerability of our aircraft was increased substantially over that of a standard squadron, which would more likely be briefed to fly at the same altitude.

With an attacking force of 800 to 1,000 Lancasters, Halifaxes, and Stirlings, we would fly to a central location in England, usually Reading, and then turn onto a single heading to proceed to enemy-occupied Europe. No lights were permitted, and radio silence was strictly imposed. On a dark, moonless night there would inevitably be some collisions between our own aircraft. These were chilling and tragically spectacular, since the bombs carried by the aircraft would go up in the collision with a single blinding flash, after which the pitch blackness of the night skies would once again close in.

In such a bomber stream, the leading aircraft would reach the coast of Holland while the tail end was still taking off from England. The stream would be seventeen to twenty miles wide and 10,000 to 15,000 feet deep, with Airborne Cigar aircraft dispersed throughout the length and depth of the stream.

In 1986, on my return to Canada from a meeting of NATO defence ministers, I stopped to visit 101 RAF Squadron, which is now a tanker squadron based at Brize Norton in England. While there, I discovered that during the short time it operated from early 1943 to the end of the war in May 1945, the squadron had 1,059 fatalities, the highest casualty rate of any squadron in the war. At any given time, the squadron had 2,500 supporting ground personnel (men and women), in all trades, from mechanics to weather observers to intelligence officers, supporting 250 airmen. There were thirty aircraft with crews of eight each. It was a rare mission from which the squadron returned without at least one aircraft failing to make it back.

On my fourth mission, over Kiel, the mid-upper gunner, a man from Bath, had a breakdown over the target. He just sat there babbling about his mother's candy-shop back home. Kiel was fiery red by the time we arrived, and, to use a common Air Force description, the flak was so thick you could walk on it. Quite a number of enemy fighters were up, but there was no dodging them; we were some distance back in the stream, and we still had to reach the target and drop our bomb load. There was nothing to do but wade into this. Nothing is more daunting than hearing the explosion of a bursting shell and moments later hearing the whump! of the pieces of metal flak hitting the skin of your aircraft. One piece of shrapnel lodged in the collar of my Mae West life jacket and another in my flying glove. I looked at the sky between us and the target and did not see how we could get through the veritable hail of flak without major damage or complete destruction. Nonetheless, we pressed on.

Moments after dropping our load of bombs, we had several more flak hits, as well as some damage from enemy aircraft. It was then that the aircraft was "coned" in the brilliant rays of enemy searchlights on the ground. Anti-aircraft guns are synchronized with the searchlights, so in seconds there was the drum beat of shrapnel pounding into us, piercing the aircraft skin and causing serious damage. We had to get out of that cone fast. The outer engine on the starboard side had been hit and I had feathered the propeller. We now had only 75 per cent of full power.

I decided to try a hazardous manoeuvre I had heard more experienced pilots talk about. Having lowered both wheels and flaps, I throttled off all power and simultaneously raised the flaps and wheels. The aircraft dropped like a stone. The stresses on the aircraft were considerable; rivets popped and a metal panel on the starboard wing ripped off. We were out of the cone, but we were losing altitude at an alarming rate. As if we did not already have enough on our hands, the starboard inner engine was hit and on fire. This was extinguished by the flight engineer, but now we had two engines down. I restored power to the two remaining engines and brought the aircraft under control at 10,000 feet. We had plummeted 13,000 feet.

Then a twin-engined Heinkel 110 fighter brushed by us—his wing tip seemed to pass between the port inner engine and the fuselage of our aircraft. While all this was going on, the crew were trying to get some sense out of the mid-upper gunner, who was not of much use to us at that moment, and the navigator was working out a course for home. The navigational equipment was powered by generators on the starboard inner engine, which was now shut down, so the navigator had to plot from his last known location and make his calculations by dead reckoning. This meant that I had to stay above the clouds so he could navigate by the stars. He brought us home, two hours late, but dead on target.

We were so late, in fact, that everyone at the aerodrome was sure that we had been downed. All the lights at Ludford Magna and the radio beam had been shut down. Fortunately, the cloud cover had dispersed and the ground was visible. But we had another problem. The hydraulics were powered by the starboard inner engine, which had been shut down. We could not mechanically lower our wheels. In addition, we had lost hydraulic fluid, and it was doubtful that there was sufficient fluid to lower the wheels by hand pumping. So, using another piece of hangar lore I had picked up, I told the crew to urinate in the hydraulics tank. That gave us just enough liquid to lower the wheels.

When the noise of our aircraft roared over the airfield, the runway lights were turned on and we landed without further difficulties. Our aircraft was a mess—peppered with flak holes, with most of the starboard fin, rudder, and stabilizer having been shot off.

At the conclusion of our tour, for his feat of navigation—he had hit the English coast within a mile of where he should have and, like a homing pigeon, had found the darkened airport thirty miles inland—our navigator was awarded the Distinguished Flying Cross. The engineer who had put out the fire in the inner engine was also invested with the DFC. Both were made commissioned officers. Our bomb aimer was also promoted to commissioned rank after winning the Distinguished Flying Medal. We had had our baptism of fire and survived. We survived because the long days, weeks, and months of training came to our aid when we needed it most. It may be easier to understand my respect for discipline when viewed in the light of incidents such as this one. If we could survive a mission like Kiel, we could survive anything except a direct hit by a large shell. We functioned even more closely as a team for the remainder of our tour. Team work paid vital dividends.

The exception, of course, was the mid-upper gunner. He was posted to a unit for those who had been classified LMF—Lack of Moral Fibre. LMF could be nothing more than an uncontrollable reaction to violent circumstances, as I am sure it was in this case, and need not have anything to do with cowardice in the face of the enemy. No one knows how he will behave under direct fire until it happens. Some people simply snap.

There were cases in which an individual or crew would deliberately avoid combat. Instead of pressing on to a tough target, they would fly out over the North Sea, drop their bombs, and return to base. There were two checks to detect this misconduct. One was the installation in every aircraft of a sealed camera that automatically took a picture of the target area when the bomb aimer pressed the button that released the bombs. The camera was inaccessible so that it could not be tampered with, and only the base intelligence officer could remove it. The other check, also installed in every aircraft, was IFF—Identification, Friend or Foe. This device, similar to a modern transponder, constantly transmitted a coded signal so that British radar could track the plane's flight path. The signal identified Allied aircraft, and if IFF was not on and operating, one stood a very good chance of being mistaken for the enemy and being shot down by Allied fire. Those two features, though they were not installed primarily to check up on the moral fibre of air crews, nevertheless provided a strong incentive for all of us to screw up our courage and press on.

The return from that first attack on Kiel was one of the more hair-raising of my tour, but not the strangest. That honor goes to another mission during which we were again badly shot up. We limped home very late—so late that the ground crew, convinced that we had been lost for good, rounded up all our gear, packed our kits, and even rolled up our beds to make way for a new crew. Everything was removed for storage and ultimate disposition. Even my revolver—which I never carried on flights—was gone. Upon our return very early in the morning, we had to round up all our personal kit. The ground crew were pretty sheepish, but we were so grateful to be back that we were able to laugh.

I was commissioned as a pilot officer soon after the first Kiel mission. The promotion required me to move out of the NCOs' quarters I shared with my crew. (Officers, NCOs, and other ranks were required to use separate living quarters and messing facilities.) I thought it was more important to the morale of my crew and the fostering of a team spirit for me to remain with them in the NCOs' quarters. I did so for several days until I was ordered into officers' quarters.

Some incidents from that time remain engraved in memory. One occurred during the first daylight attack of the war by Lancaster bombers. We were bombing the industrial sector of Essen, in the Ruhr Valley, the heart of Germany's industrial might. Just ahead of and below our aircraft I saw one of our planes drop its entire bomb load onto another of our aircraft, which must have been in its bombsight. The aircraft below was literally bombed out of the sky.

There were other, and happier, moments. Our aerodrome, Ludford Magna, sat in the county of Lincolnshire, about nine miles from the town of Louth, which boasts the fifth-tallest church spire in England. The spire soared 200 feet into the air and many of us, when we were sure we were safe from the scrutiny of our superiors, used to fly tight turns around it. That must have been quite a sight from the ground, to see the Lanc turning steeply around the spire.

We used to go to Louth for rest and recreation in the local cinema, the pubs, the dance hall, and the swimming pool. And it was in Louth that I met Pamela June Hall, who was eighteen and working in the post office. I bought more stamps than ever I sent letters, drawn to the breath-taking beauty of P.J., and I sparked her, as the English say, in an intense campaign, inviting her to the dances, the cinema, and the mess dinners at Ludford Magna.

Once, when I took P.J. to a dance at the station on the back of a motorcycle, the night turned so foul, and the roads so dangerous with black ice, that the commanding officer, Wing Commander De L'Everest, offered to drive us back to town. We accepted with gratitude. The night was pitch black, the wing commander had had a few, the roads were unmarked—naturally we became lost, and it took us considerable time to find our way first off the airfield and then to the highway to Louth. I had the perfect excuse for being lost—the wing commander was driving.

The normal tour of operations was thirty missions, but I saw no need to bring it to anyone's attention when I reached that number. I had done thirty-three before they caught up to me. At that point, I was told "No more," I was pushing my luck. Besides, I was told that it was time for me to rejoin a Canadian outfit. I felt sad about that, because I had enjoyed the international flavour of my crew and I wanted to stay where I was. Authority, however, does not normally consult the wishes of pilot officers; I was posted to a Canadian night-intruder squadron, which was equipped with Mosquito fighter-bombers. This was 406 Squadron, based at Manston in Kent, and commanded by Wing Commander Russ Banock, who after the war took on marketing for de Havilland aircraft and then became a private aviation consultant, a business which he still pursues.

From Manston, I was posted to a Canadian Spitfire wing at Heesch, in Holland. I reported in February 1945 to Group Captain Gordon McGregor, who later became president of Trans Canada Airlines, now Air Canada.

The war in Europe was rapidly coming to an end; the Rhine had been crossed, and it was clear that the Germans would soon be forced to surrender. One of my duties took me to Neustadt, in Germany, about twenty miles from Hanover. I flew the senior administrative officer of 126 Wing to Neustadt and helped to sort out the captured German air base there. It was the most beautiful base I had ever seen, with handsome buildings, a luxurious mess, underground fuelling facilities for the aircraft, and even a railroad to bring in munitions, fuel, and supplies. Because I knew some German, I was ordered to translate the instructions for firing up the main boiler on the base, but the technical jargon was too much for me. I was

assigned to more humble duties—filching wine from the extensive
German cellars and closing down the bordello on the base, whose
bewildered occupants had nowhere to go. They wandered off quite
disconsolate, I am sure, because they could not remain to greet our
airmen.

One night when I was orderly officer, we received a radio message
that a Junker 52 aircraft had requested permission to land. Accompanied by the orderly sergeant, I went out to the tarmac to meet
the German aircraft. The plane landed, taxied to where we waited,
shut down the engines, and Germans—some of them armed—began
piling out. It was like that circus act in which clowns keep coming
out of a tiny car. I have no idea how many emerged in all, probably
not more than a dozen, but certainly enough to overwhelm the
sergeant and me. I was just steeling myself to go down fighting
when a senior Luftwaffe officer marched briskly up, announced
"Alles kaputt" (Everything is finished), and handed me his automatic Walther pistol, butt first. I trust I did not show my relief.
I kept that pistol until 1985, when it was stolen from my house at
Quiet Lake in Yukon.

Before leaving Louth, I had proposed marriage to P.J. and she
had accepted, but we both thought it would be best to delay getting
married until the war ended. We wrote to each other frequently.
In the course of our correspondence we decided that we would not
wait for the entire war to end, but that as soon as the European
campaign ended we would marry. The European war came to a
close on May 5, 1945.

On May 1, I had heard that there was an aircraft returning
through Neustadt to England, and I asked the CO for an immediate
posting there to get married. He authorized the posting, but not
the permission to marry. For this, I had to apply in London, to
the office of Air Marshal Johnny Johnson, the ranking Canadian
officer in Europe. One of his subordinates, a senior officer, reluctantly granted this permission—shades of my father—and I rushed
back to Louth and P.J. We were married on May 3, 1945, in the
lovely old church there.

I was barely twenty-one, married to a beautiful girl, the proud
recipient of the Distinguished Flying Cross, which I thought would
ensure a future in flying. I was sitting on top of the world. Although
I did not know it at the time, my life was about to take another
dramatic turn.

Chapter Three

The Long Road to Yukon

There are hardships that nobody reckons;
There are valleys unpeopled and still;
There's a land—oh, it beckons and beckons,
And I want to go back and I will.
  Robert Service, The Spell of the Yukon

After P.J. and I were married, we left Louth for our honeymoon in Margate, on the southeast coast of England, just a short distance south of London. The trip across London, to change trains, was hectic—this was VE Day, May 7, 1945, and the streets were crammed with crowds cheering, singing, dancing, and imbibing. Our sympathy was with them, of course, but we did wish they would get out of the way and let us get to our train. We finally reached it, and arrived at last in a cozy little bed and breakfast of the kind so readily available in England. Two weeks of paradise, and then I reported back for duty at Louth to await my next posting.

I had no doubt that there would be a new posting, for I had made it clear for some months now that I wanted to make the RCAF my long-term career. I submitted a formal request for enlistment in the permanent Air Force and received formal acknowledgment, which reassured me. I marked time at Louth from May to August 1945, without a posting. Then, suddenly, I received orders to embark at Greenock on the *Ile de France* and to report to Debert, Nova Scotia. I was posted for conversion to Liberator bombers, which were the largest bombers on the Allied side, with a wingspan of 110 feet. I would be part of the Allied bomber force in the Pacific. We were about halfway across the Atlantic when we learned that the first atomic bomb had been dropped on Hiroshima. The handwriting was clearly on the wall, and I am one of those who believe that the second bomb, the one dropped on Nagasaki, need never have been dropped at all. The war was over, and I and all the rest

41

of the RCAF on board the *Ile de France* were notified that our services were no longer required. We were to report to the manning depot in Calgary for demobilization.

There were no exceptions made, and no screening was done. My protests to the officers on board that I had applied for the permanent force fell on deaf ears, so, after another long train ride across Canada—this time in greater comfort, since, as an officer, I was entitled to a berth at night—I was duly delivered to Calgary, and duly ushered out of the Air Force over my vigorous protests.

My personal records were not available, so there was no way to substantiate that I was an applicant for the permanent force. There was nothing for it but to accept my fate and start looking for a job, while setting the wheels in motion to bring P.J. over to Canada. I got the job a lot faster than I got my wife back—she did not arrive until August 1946.

The job I went to was in Edmonton. Just before joining the Air Force I had worked, briefly, in the drafting office of Northwest Industries, and they were obliged by law to accept me in my old employment. My first and only task there was to draw the elevator horn for the Ballanca aircraft. While I was there, I heard that the principal of the Edmonton Technical School was looking for someone to set up mechanical drafting courses for returning veterans, and I applied for and received that job. I stayed just long enough to set up the courses and brief my successor. Somehow, I did not feel I was cut out to be a draftsman, or a teacher, so I applied for employment as a pilot with what was then Canadian Pacific Airlines. I had already applied to Trans-Canada Airlines (now Air Canada) and others. I was anxiously waiting for a reply to my applications when, one day in February 1946, the afternoon mail brought a letter from the RCAF. Although they did not admit that they had made a mistake in demobbing me, my files had finally been put together and they invited me to rejoin the Air Force. It was too late that afternoon to report to the Edmonton recruiting centre, but when the office opened the next morning, I was waiting on the doorstep. I was sworn in and assigned orders to report to the Officers' Training School in Toronto.

The very next day, I heard from CP Air. They had accepted me for pilot training. Had that letter arrived forty-eight hours earlier, I would have become a civilian pilot and I would probably by now be flying a desk. There are a few politicians, I am sure, whose lives would have been easier had my career taken me along that fork in the road.

The Officers' Training School was located in what had once been the Eglinton Hunt Club in Toronto. It took three months of vigorous application there to learn all the administrative wrinkles one apparently required to function as an officer in the postwar RCAF: how to write a letter; how to compose—quite a different thing—a military memo; how to behave socially; how many calling cards to leave on the silver salver when one attended the Governor General's levee. All of it was interesting, and I attacked the work with enthusiasm, mainly because I could not wait to get out of there and get flying again. And, of course, the daily marching drills and physical training were high on the menu of activities.

Alas, when I was pronounced fit to be an officer again, I was not posted to a flying job. Instead, I was sent to take up administrative duties in Halifax. I was at the disposal of the officer in charge of Maritime Command, who decided that the best place for me was under the assistant judge advocate general. (The JAG office is responsible for the legal affairs of the military.) My boss in this new endeavour was Squadron Leader John Gellner, a man of outstanding character and intellect, who came to be one of the most influential men in my life.

Gellner was six feet tall, with slightly stooped shoulders and the habit of squinting his left eye when discussing a matter with others. He has a remarkable ability to isolate each element of a problem and analyse it before reaching an impeccably logical conclusion. He had been a doctor of laws in his native Czechoslovakia; he was an outstanding military man as well, blessed with abundant common sense. While at university in Prague, he foresaw the inevitability of global conflict, and just before the war broke out, he started, literally, walking west. He wound up in Italy and embarked on a freighter destined for South America—not because he wanted to go to South America, but because the freighter was the first available means of leaving Europe. His objective was Canada, where he intended to join the Royal Canadian Air Force and fight the Nazis, who had already seized the Sudetenland of his own country. When he finally made it to a recruiting office in Toronto, he had worn through the soles of his shoes and was walking on newspapers stuffed into the uppers.

He was accepted for pilot training and served in a number of flying postings, although he had no love of flying. He once confessed that it was a miracle that he survived his own ineptitude at the controls. Where his real ability lay was in administration, and he rose to the rank of wing commander before his retirement. This extraordinary man was my mentor; certainly it was he who pushed me into the study of law. Subsequently, he became a well-known writer on defence matters and political science and held an interest in a Toronto publishing company. Today, well into his seventies, he remains a vigorous and active man. Once, after his retirement, he came to Yukon to climb mountains in the St. Elias range. In fact, he met his second wife while mountain climbing in Europe, where he had written books on the subject.

John had little patience with my zeal for flying and was constantly urging me to "do something useful" with my life. He wanted me to apply to law school, since I seemed to have some aptitude for the work in the JAG office. At first, I was happy to do the work required of me, but I much preferred to be airborne every possible moment. I was a general list officer, a flyer, on the Air Force rolls. This meant that, whatever work I did for John, I was still required to fly a minimum number of hours each week. The Air Force practice flight in the area was at HMCS Shearwater, a naval air establishment and airport near Dartmouth, just across the harbour from Halifax.

Eventually, while remaining with the JAG office, I was posted to 101 RCAF Communications Squadron at Dartmouth. In addition to running practice flights, the squadron transported senior officers around Maritime Command, with occasional trips into the eastern Arctic: a latter-day executive air service for senior officers and other military and civilian VIPs. Most of the flying was with the old faithful DC-3 and the C-45 Expediter. The practice flying was done in Harvards, the model used to provide check rides for general list officers who had not flown for some time.

Finally, however, I succumbed to John's urgings and applied to Dalhousie University Law School. At first I had thought of applying for medicine, but the waiting list to register in that faculty was more than two years long. I checked with the faculty of law and discovered that they could admit me immediately. Since I had ample reestablishment credits provided under veterans' legislation, I enrolled in law.

Almost by accident I was embarking on a new career. Although I was doing court martial work for the Air Force, I had no intention of continuing in law. It was, I kept telling myself, simply a way to obtain more education, and I planned to switch into medicine after two or three years. I was able to arrange my lectures for the mornings, and I would attend lectures wearing a sweater, keeping my Air Force uniform hat and jacket in a locker. As soon as classes were finished, I would don my uniform and report to work at the JAG office. Every day I skipped lunch and worked late to make up for the time spent at classes.

Since Gellner was my immediate superior, he ensured that I was involved not merely in administrative matters affecting courts of inquiry and other such routine work in the JAG office, but also in courts martial, subject to the priority given to my studies.

There were two kinds of courts martial. One was summary, which dealt with minor offences such as drunkenness, minor theft, and so forth. The summary court martial was composed of three officers. The general court martial dealt with more serious offences, just as indictable offences are dealt with under the Criminal Code. Five officers sat on a general court martial, and they were judges as to fact, in much the same way as a civilian jury. Unlike a civilian jury in the Canadian system, however, they were also responsible for determining the sentence. In both kinds of court martial, the judicial adviser to the court was a judge advocate; at Maritime Command it was the assistant judge advocate general, John Gellner, or another officer qualified in law.

Courts were convened on the order of Navy, Army, or Air Force commanding officers in Maritime Command. Wherever the courts might be convened, whether it was in Newfoundland or in New Brunswick, I would be assigned some responsibility. Most frequently I was appointed prosecuting officer. Every court had a prosecuting officer and a defending officer. If the accused did not have defence counsel, one was named. It was not long before I was prosecuting the majority of the cases that came within the jurisdiction of Maritime Command and other service jurisdictions. My duties took me to military units throughout Canada. John Gellner was ensuring that I was adequately exposed to the legal environment. Gellner was one of only two legally trained officers assigned to the JAG branch in Maritime Command, so having an extra hand was advantageous for the Air Force and for me. I must confess, however, that my interest stemmed mainly from the admiration and respect I held for John Gellner.

One of the defence cases I undertook involved a man charged with theft from a fellow serviceman. There was no question that the offence had taken place, but the circumstances were such that I had the man examined by a psychiatrist, who was able to convince the court martial that this was a rare case of genuine kleptomania. The man was acquitted.

Some of the cases I prosecuted were quite ugly. One concerned an Air Force man who raped a girl in the base laundry at Goose Bay. As the evidence unfolded, it painted a horrifying picture of this poor woman, clad only in stockings and a garter belt, running through snowdrifts up to her hips trying to escape her rapist. He was convicted. I prosecuted more than one case of buggery in the Navy; in these cases, the accused often had civilian rather than military defence counsel. On occasion the counsel for these naval personnel was Roland Ritchie, who later became a justice of the Supreme Court of Canada.

Navy courts martial were distinguished by the custom of placing an officer's sword on the table with the blade parallel to the main part of the room. If the accused was found guilty, he knew it at once, because when he entered the room to hear the verdict, he saw the blade of the sword pointing at him. If he was found not guilty, the point of the sword was directed away from him.

During this first year of law school, I was flying, studying, and working on courts martial, all at the same time, while P.J. went to work for Simpsons. They soon recognized her unique beauty and had her modelling for catalogue and newspaper advertisements.

My triple life involved a lot of work. I had the full support of my superior, John Gellner, but just the same, there was the difficulty that I was supposed to be working full time for him. He would never have done anything improper, so he informed the air commodore of what he was doing, but very carefully never asked that worthy for permission to do it. As long as I made up the time, a blind official eye was turned to my studies. But the difficulty was that work in the armed forces is, officially, a parade, and to miss a parade is to commit a breach of discipline. While I had powerful sponsors, not everyone was receptive to the idea of letting me work and study at the same time. Thus it came about that, at the end of my first year, I was posted to Toronto and assigned to the recruiting office. My new commanding officer was Flight Lieutenant Bill Lee, who was soon to gain rapid promotion with Paul Hellyer and eventually become quite well known on the political scene.

That autumn, on October 26, our first son, Lee Scott, was born. Seven days later, when P.J. was barely out of hospital, I was ordered to Ottawa, seconded once more to the office of the judge advocate general and assigned to assist in the preparation of a new National Defence Act (which did not, in fact, pass Parliament until 1952).

The drive from Toronto to Ottawa was not a good augury. We stopped overnight at a rooming house in Trenton. Backing the car out of the driveway early the next morning, I strained the muscles on the left side of my neck. I could not straighten my head, and the pain was excruciating. I drove in this condition to the Trenton air base and visited the medical officer. He wanted to give my head and neck a sharp twist, but I was having none of that. Gentle massage partly eased the pain, and I finished the drive to Ottawa. The neck muscles eventually loosened, but the pain would return whenever I became overtired or tense. This continued until June 1986, when the problem mysteriously disappeared.

That pain was symbolically fitting for the Ottawa posting, which was in itself a pain. To begin with, my commanding officer, a man named McLearn, seemed to take an instant dislike to me because of my political views. I was becoming increasingly interested in politics and increasingly convinced that it was time for a change of government. McLearn, however, was one of those officers who believed that any member of the Air Force who was not a Liberal could not possibly be loyal. Needless to say, I was very unhappy under his command.

In the second place, our living conditions were pretty primitive, which was harder on P.J. and our baby than it was on me. I had started in the Air Force with the magnificent sum of thirty dollars a month as an aircraftman, second class, and had now worked my way up to about three hundred dollars, so the only housing we could afford was a cottage on the shore of the Ottawa River, at Crystal

Beach on Britannia Bay. We had water and electricity, but the only heat was supplied by a coal-burning stove in one room, which was far from adequate for an Ottawa winter, during which temperatures reached thirty below zero.

I applied for leave without pay, with a view to finishing my legal training. In this manner, I reasoned, I would be in a position to advance much more swiftly up the Air Force ladder of promotion. The leave was granted, but only reluctantly, and only after much lobbying by me and arm-twisting by John Gellner. Wing Commander McLearn was not at all helpful.

The leave, when it came, was accompanied by a posting back to Halifax. That was the one contribution of the Air Force towards easing my financial burden, since they paid for the trip back east. We moved into a small house in Dartmouth, on Joffrey Street, not far from the naval air base at Shearwater. This house was owned by friends of mine, a flight lieutenant and his wife, who invited us to stay with them and to share their new home to save money.

Expenses were paid for, in part, by our dog. In Ottawa we had purchased a German shepherd show dog, Acacia's Anxious, whom we called, naturally enough, Anxious. She produced litters of saleable puppies at regular intervals. There cannot be many Canadians who were put through law school in part by their dogs.

Those two years of studying law were difficult. My day began with a bus ride to the ferry docks in Dartmouth—this was before the bridge was built—a twenty-minute ferry ride, and then another ride, after a suitable wait, on one of the quaint Halifax streetcars of the day. It took about ninety minutes all told and in the winter it was often a frigid trip. To help out with the finances—I could not leave everything to Anxious—I drove a taxi at night and occasionally the Air Force would let me prosecute a court martial, for which I was paid. I received a veteran's reestablishment grant of about $120 a month, which was hardly generous; as well, every time I was paid by the Air Force for a job, that grant was cut off.

We started at Dalhousie with a class of about 150, of whom about 85 per cent were veterans. We lost many of them along the way. Fewer than sixty of us graduated. We were a mixed lot. There were hard-working plodders at one end of the spectrum, and at the other an ex-army type who sat at the back of the room with his chair tilted back, sipping from time to time from a bottle of Coke spiked with rum. I cannot recall whether he graduated, and I doubt very much whether he would remember either!

My first course in the law of equity began with the professor, William Hancock, giving us a long blast, all in Latin. Then he said, "That was the Magna Carta, from which sprang many of the rights we enjoy today." He went on to recite the prerogative writs in Latin: habeas corpus, certiorari, and capias which, he maintained, "were some of the reasons why law students should know their Latin." It was an impressive performance. He was a brilliant man, although terribly near-sighted: when he read from a book, he had to hold it so close to his face that he had to move it away again to turn a page.

At Dalhousie, as in most law schools, many of the courses were taught by full-time practitioners. They were, like us, a mixed lot. One of our visiting professors was a lawyer with a trust company, who was later convicted of embezzling trust funds. He taught, of course, the law of trusts.

We took constitutional law and torts (the law of negligence) from Vincent MacDonald. He was an intelligent Grit, if that is not a contradiction in terms, and was the architect of the treaty of union between Canada and Newfoundland, which was signed in 1949, my final year at law school. When MacDonald could not think of a word in the middle of a lecture, he would make one up. One day he spoke of the "dangerosity" of a course of action in a tort case. I thought it a very descriptive word.

James Lorimer Ilsley, who had been minister of finance in the King government and who left the cabinet to take up an appointment on the Nova Scotia Supreme Court, taught us taxation. W.R. Lederman, who later became dean of law at Queen's University, and still later appeared before the parliamentary committee on the Meech Lake Accord, was another professor.

I had and have a profound respect for intellects such as those of Gellner, Lederman, Hancock, and MacDonald. (Robert Stanfield is in the same league, as is, to a lesser degree and in his own field of expertise, Joe Clark, though obviously, the law was not his forte!)

Most of my professors were Grits. Lederman was a notable exception—I always held that he was too nice to be a Grit. Politics were important on campus, and, although I never had time for fraternities or other social pursuits, I did take part in the Moot Court and the Mock Parliament. In the latter, I was a natural for the sergeant-at-arms.

I became active in the Maritime Rights Party, whose ostensible object was secession of the Maritime provinces from Canada and union with the United States. The argument was that, under the current arrangement, everything produced in the Maritimes was shipped to central Canada for processing, and then the locals had to buy it back, at much higher prices. They were paying not only for the jobs created in Ontario and Quebec but for getting their own goods back. We were quite active in the 1949 provincial election (which the Liberals won), although we did not win any seats. My choice of the Maritime Rights Party indicated, I think, a willingness to challenge the political establishment.

There was also a federal election in 1949. It, too, was won handily by the Liberals, but not before the voting had been enlivened by the discovery by the auditor general that there were horses on the payroll of the defence department, and that significant amounts of money had been paid out for purposes that were never made clear. N.D. Murray, my criminal law lecturer, told us that having horses on the payroll was nothing unusual, and that during his stint in the army, as a lark, they had kept a ghost major on the payroll for months, not as a money-making scheme, but simply to prove how easily it could be done.

By the time that election came along, I had finished my law degree and returned full time to the Air Force as a general list officer attached to Maritime Command. While the campaign was on, there was a good deal of political talk in the mess, mostly in support of the Liberal government. I eagerly joined these discussions on behalf of the Conservative cause. I was told by a squadron leader to desist. I replied that I knew there was an unspoken rule to the effect that "Thou shalt not talk politics in the mess," but that I believed the rule should be applied to everyone, not imposed narrowly on one whose political beliefs did not happen to be Liberal. That blunt, almost rebellious, response to the squadron leader would prove harmful to my future career in the Air Force.

It was also becoming clear to me that my newly acquired law degree was not going to help my career either, since I was not transferred to the JAG office but was left on administrative duties. I therefore applied for a transfer to the security and intelligence branch. In due course this was granted, and my family and I were moved to Edmonton. Edmonton at that time had probably the most active S&I branch in the service, apparently because of its position as the headquarters of the northwest highway system and its juris-diction over the communications establishment in Whitehorse, which monitored Soviet radio traffic.

I had not been in Edmonton long when I realized that the law degree, which was to have helped me up the promotions ladder, was not benefiting me in my new duties. On the 1950 New Year's promotion list, a Czechoslovakian officer who had been in the Air Force for about four years—far less than I—was made a flight lieu-tenant, while I remained a flying officer.

When it dawned on me that I was not getting anywhere, I wrote to my immediate superior, requesting release from the Air Force. That request was denied, further up the line, by a group captain. Canada was now involved in the Korean War, and that meant the armed forces were on active service. At such a time, the group captain ruled, no requests for voluntary release could be entertained.

I was then posted to a course on censorship, organized by the United States military at Governor's Island in New York State. While there I visited my brother Leslie, who was working for the television networks centred in New York City.

Next I was posted to another security course in Ottawa. This time I decided to take action. I attended all the classes, but took no notes, and, at examination time, I returned a blank page. This unusual behaviour brought me an interview with Air Commodore Frank Waite, the national headquarters officer responsible for the careers of Air Force officers. He was a considerate man and had been instrumental in allowing me to pursue legal training. When I explained to him that I was determined to leave the Air Force, since I believed that my career was blighted, in part because of political antipathy, he tried to change my mind. When he saw that it could not be done, he approved my release. I returned to Edmon-ton to leave the service for the second time.

It was, despite my determination, a wrenching experience. From the age of eighteen, I had meant to make the Air Force my career, and it seemed to me that it was through no fault of my own that I was being compelled to leave after ten years. When I had gone through the final clearance procedures, I got in a cab and headed for our home in south Edmonton. Part way there, I suddenly had to tell the cabbie to pull over; I got out of the car and was violently sick.

Because I had intended to use my law degree only in the service, I had not articled, nor been admitted to the Nova Scotia bar, and therefore I could not practise. I had no immediate intention to practise, but I knew that I would eventually have to do so. Since I had always been intrigued by business, I applied for employment with the Hudson Bay Company in Edmonton. On the basis of one course I had taken in service management training, I was enrolled as an HBC trainee. My salary was even more minuscule than my Air Force pay.

In this job, I was given the task of doing an efficiency study of the meat department, where the employees wrapped cuts of meat in cellophane. An ordinary household iron was then used to heat-seal the package. I designed a goosenecked holder for the hot iron. The only motion now required was to run the parcel under the suspended iron, which saved a good deal of time. The process was later improved by installing heated plates in a much more efficient arrangement. The method is now widely used for meat packaging.

This gave me some satisfaction, but not, alas, any money, which we were going to need for a growing family. I would clearly have to increase my earning capacity by practising law.

I did some research to decide where I should go. I knew it would have to be in the northwest. I eliminated Edmonton and Calgary— I had never been comfortable in big cities—and narrowed my choice to Dawson Creek, Fort St. John, or Whitehorse. In the end, I chose Whitehorse, because of the unspoiled environment—it was my kind of country—and because there was only one lawyer then actively practising in town.

I embarked on Canadian Pacific Airlines' DC-3 service for a quick visit to Whitehorse. I spoke to the local judge, Jack Gibben, about being admitted to the Yukon territorial bar. There was a territorial ordinance that allowed the commissioner of Yukon to admit persons to the bar even though they were not members of another provincial bar (that is, even if they had not completed articles), provided they were otherwise qualified. Gibben thought I could be admitted under that rule.

Buoyed by these welcome words, I went to call on Yukon's sole practising lawyer, George Van Roggen, a splendid gentleman, but perhaps a little too fond of the grape at times. George told me some delightful stories. For example, when he first arrived in Whitehorse in 1949, he had stayed at the Whitehorse Inn, a hotel which was then owned by one T.C. Richards, who had won it in a gambling game. One of George's fellow guests was a prospector named Hardrock MacDonald. Hardrock had been out in the bush a long time and he was hungry for fresh food. He went to Burns's butcher store, then operated by the mayor of Whitehorse, who had just received a shipment of live chickens. Hardrock bought a couple of these, put them in a sack, slung them over his shoulder, and went back to the hotel, where he occupied a room down the hall from George.

Hardrock proceeded to get drunk and, while he was drinking, he plucked the live chickens. Soon the squawking chickens were naked except for the pinfeathers around their heads and necks, and Hardrock was so sozzled that he passed out. Later that night, he awoke to see two fiendish creatures like naked birds perched on the end of his bed. Hardrock slowly reached for his rifle, took careful aim, and blasted one of the chickens off the bedstead. The noise brought the hotel proprietor crashing through Hardrock's door, and the other chicken, taking advantage of the confusion, escaped into the hall.

In the meantime, George had been getting the best of a bottle of gin. When the commotion began in Hardrock's room, he stuck his head out his door, just in time to see a bare-naked chicken running down the hall. Quietly, George closed the door, went to the window, and poured the remainder of the gin into the night. He was—for a few minutes at least—on the wagon.

Talking to George, I realized that life in Whitehorse would be different from the well-ordered existence of an RCAF mess, but this in no way dampened my enthusiasm. I told George I was going to give him some competition. He encouraged me to come.

Following Judge Gibben's advice, I wrote to apply for admission to the Yukon bar, only to discover that the commissioner's legal adviser, N. Victor K. Wylie, did not see things the same way as His Lordship. He refused my request and told me I would have to finish my articles. N. Victor K. Wylie, I might add, was the assistant commissioner, and, by reason of his post as legal adviser, automatically a member of the Yukon bar. I represented potential competition. He was also, as it transpired, an active Liberal and intended to leave the territorial government to enter private practice in Whitehorse. None of these things, I am sure, was the reason for rejecting my request. In any event, it was clear that I had to return to Nova Scotia to complete articles and gain admission to the Nova Scotia bar.

We could not afford to move the family back to Halifax, so P.J. and Lee stayed in Edmonton, and I went on my own, to spend one of the loneliest and most frustrating winters I have ever lived through. I articled for a year with Gordon L.S. Hart, an active Liberal, but a first-class legal mind. (He was later elevated to the bench.) During that time, I had no income to speak of, so to earn enough money for us to live, I took a job "swamping."

A childhood friend of mine was driving for an Edmonton outfit called TransCanada Trucking. He invited me to swamp, which is the back-breaking work of wrestling large freight into and out of semi-tractor-trailers. I would swamp between Edmonton and Toronto, then hitchhike to Halifax, and go back the same way to Edmonton. This way, at least I saw my family now and then. In Halifax, I returned to taxi driving, and I even pumped gas to help make ends meet.

I finished my articles early in 1952, and was at once admitted to the Nova Scotia bar. I was ready for the move to Whitehorse, except that I had no money to pay for the move, let alone to set up a practice. I wrote to George Van Roggen, who was kind enough to write back assuring me of work once I arrived. All I needed now was my air fare. I went back to work at the Hudson Bay Company, to earn enough for the move and to tide over P.J. and Lee while I travelled north to get started.

I finally arrived in Yukon on February 6, 1952, the day King George VI died, but I was not admitted to the bar until April 15. In the meantime, N. Victor K. Wylie had quit his job as assistant commissioner and begun the practice of law. He became the competition to George Van Roggen, and I became George's partner.

When I stepped off the DC-3 from Edmonton, ready to go to work as a Whitehorse lawyer, I was decked out in the finery that seemed appropriate—blue pin-striped suit, dark overcoat, and a homburg. George and a friend of his were at the airport to welcome me. George gave my hat a look of disgust, his friend took it off my head, and the two proceeded to kick it to death. I have never worn a hat since.

It was, somehow, a suitable beginning for the boisterous adventure that was to constitute my early years in Whitehorse.

Chapter Four
Yukon Politics

No campaign in the Yukon was ever mild.
Martha Black, *My First Seventy Years*

When I arrived in Yukon in early 1952, the entire population of the territory was about 12,000 and the population of Whitehorse, which had not yet been named the capital, was 2,300—about 8 per cent of what it is today. My first impression of Whitehorse was that it was a town of shacks. Today, Whitehorse is a modern urban centre with many beautiful houses. In 1952 the northwest highway system—the Alaska Highway—connecting Edmonton and Vancouver with Whitehorse and Alaska was still being maintained by the Canadian Army. (A postwar agreement between the governments of the United States and Canada had given Canada control over the highway.) The biggest building in the town proper was the old Whitehorse Inn, which has since been demolished to make way for a bank building. In 1953 a federal government building was completed and the territorial capital was transferred from Dawson City to Whitehorse. The new building housed most of the government offices, including the post office and the courts. It was the first building in town to be constructed entirely of concrete and steel; parts of it were three storeys high and the remainder two and it covered an entire city block. Among the tar-paper shacks and log houses, it was as out of place as a duchess at a crap game. It also contained an elevator. There was one other elevator, a somewhat primitive affair, in the Taylor and Drury General Store, but the one in the federal building was the first such modern contraption in town.

There were no traffic lights, and no hard-surfaced streets, which made for extremely dusty driving in dry weather and mud in wet weather. Most of the town lacked water and sewer systems; a few households were lucky enough to be on the limited water and sewer system installed by the American army when they built the Alaska Highway in 1942.

That was an astonishing engineering feat. In nine months, 1,500 miles of road were constructed through some of the most difficult terrain to be found anywhere in the world. The road was built to convey aircraft and supplies to the Soviet Union, our wartime allies, and to link continental United States with Alaska in case of invasion from Japan. The last island of the Aleutian chain was, in fact, occupied by the Japanese during the war.

When I first arrived in Whitehorse and for several years thereafter, the Canadian Army was a considerable presence; the combined strength of uniformed and civilian personnel was in the order of 1,000 to 1,200 souls, nearly half the total population. All their offices and living quarters were in Takhini, a separate area of Whitehorse. The presence of the army establishment naturally enough contributed to the economy of the town.

In addition to the army, the Air Force operated a communications establishment and there was a Royal Canadian Air Force base of considerable size in an area known as Hillcrest. The Air Force then also controlled the Whitehorse International Airport. The combined military and civilian strength of the Air Force base was about 500 to 600, another major contributor to the local economy. After the military, the next largest employer was the White Pass and Yukon Route, a transportation group.

I found a house about six weeks after my arrival, and P.J., Lee, and Anxious soon joined me. (The house has since been replaced by the Royal Bank building.) The law office was next door to the house in a Panabode log-type building. Before I rented the house, George Van Roggen and I lived in separate bedrooms at the rear of the office building, which had a kitchen and bathroom. Our offices were at the front.

For the sake of privacy, the walls around George's office and my own went all the way to the ceiling, but the remaining walls were only eight feet high. George and I cooked our own meals, and it was not unusual for clients to be waiting while we finished our breakfast, with the aroma of frying bacon and eggs wafting throughout the building; nor was it unusual for our secretarial staff to arrive for work while one of us was still singing in the shower.

My law practice became my obsession, and I could easily devote sixteen or more hours a day to my work. During the Yukon summer, it was not difficult to go to bed at dusk and get up two and a half hours later in broad daylight. Unfortunately, in winter the reverse applied.

Shortly after I joined Van Roggen, he invited me to form a partnership with him. I accepted, and from 1953 we practised as partners until George left Yukon in 1958. George was, as one would expect with his political connections, Crown counsel appointed by the federal justice department to conduct all criminal prosecutions in both the lower and higher courts in Yukon. That work was fairly onerous. At the recommendation of Van Roggen, my name was placed on the list at the justice department, thereby qualifying me to act as prosecutor and to accept other federal counsel work. I was thus able to take much of the burden of Crown prosecutions off George's shoulders, and this led to some quite bizarre cases.

My first prosecution was a case in which I assisted George as his junior counsel. In the winter of 1952, two young men called Smith and Malmstrom, who came from the vicinity of Prince George, hundreds of miles away in British Columbia, had been drinking in the Whitehorse Inn tavern when they decided that they wanted to return to Prince George. Smith had a revolver in his possession. He called a taxi and he and Malmstrom entered the vehicle at the Whitehorse Inn. Smith said, "We're going to Prince George." The taxi driver, whose name was Caruso, was quite taken aback, recognizing at once that Smith was drunk. He tried with good humour to have the two men leave the cab. At this point, the taxi was proceeding down the street while Smith was arguing with Caruso and Malmstrom was trying to calm Smith. Caruso finally awakened to the reality of the situation when Smith placed the revolver at the back of his head and repeated, "We're going to Prince George." Caruso said, "I'll have to get some gas," and he pulled up to a garage. Smith warned Caruso not to try anything and, before anyone could come out to serve the gasoline, Smith pulled the trigger and killed Caruso outright.

Throughout the entire tragic escapade, Malmstrom had attempted to talk sense to Smith, and, having failed to do so, accompanied him in an effort to keep him under control. Smith and Malmstrom were tried separately, and Malmstrom testified as a Crown witness. The only reasonably sober eyewitness account of events came from him. Both George and I were satisfied that he was a truthful witness, but unfortunately for him, the law regarded him to be just as guilty of the murder as Smith, since they were both embarked on a common criminal purpose when the murder was committed by one of them. (For the same reason, the driver of the getaway car at a bank robbery would be as guilty of the murder of one of the bank tellers killed by one of the robbers.) They were both convicted and both sentenced to be executed. Smith and Malmstrom subsequently appealed, and the appeal court, on the basis that the jury was not adequately instructed by the trial court judge on the legal consequences of the drunkenness of Smith, reduced the sentence to manslaughter and sentenced the two of them to fifteen years each.

I also prosecuted a fellow in Dawson City whose name was Leo Devereau. This, like many tragic cases, occurred during the winter months in Yukon. Many of the woes that befall Yukon residents, either by way of violence or broken marriages, occur as a result of the long winters. I have never seen an analysis, but judging by the work that flowed through our law practice between January and March, a pattern of depression quickly emerged. Many attribute this phenomenon to "cabin fever."

Leo Devereau made his living by cutting and selling firewood. He had taken on another man called Smith as a hired hand. Smith had his own separate living accommodation. Devereau lived in a very small, narrow clapboard cabin, with room enough for a small woodstove and a few articles of furniture. Many of his belongings hung on nails in the walls, including his high-powered rifle. One evening, Smith was visiting, sitting on a wooden chair beside a small table. Devereau was sitting on his cot about six feet away, speaking to Smith, who was rolling a cigarette. Smith was about to wet the cigarette paper with his tongue when Devereau reached up behind himself, lifted his rifle from the wall, pointed it at Smith's head, and pulled the trigger. The shot was at such close range that portions of Smith's skull and brains were still adhering to the walls when the police arrived.

Since the killing was inexplicable, I felt very strongly that Devereau should be examined by a psychiatrist. (As the provisions of the Criminal Code stood in those days, however, this could not occur without the consent of the accused person.) The issue of insanity could be tried by a jury as a preliminary procedure. I convinced a jury that there was sufficient cause for Devereau to be examined. A psychiatrist was obtained by defence counsel—my old antagonist N. Victor K. Wylie—and a second psychiatrist was obtained by the Crown.

Devereau was found to be suffering from manic depression and paranoia. He maintained that the reason he shot Smith was that he feared Smith was going to attack him, even though there was no evidence to support this, and indeed evidence at the trial showed Smith to be quite a gentle individual with no history of violence. The charge of murder was stayed, and Devereau was detained at a mental institute under the condition that if the psychiatrists there ever determined that he was sufficiently healthy to release, the charge against him could be resurrected. He was, in fact, released about a year later, and I proceeded with the charge of murder. He was convicted and sentenced to two years. In my view the sentence was far too lenient for a crime of the magnitude of murder, notwithstanding the mental problems.

The sentence was appealed by the Crown at my behest. It was my first appearance in the Yukon Court of Appeal, which at that time was the British Columbia Court of Appeal in Vancouver. Although Devereau had been represented by counsel on the two previous processes, he rejected any representation at the appeal. The appeal was dismissed because between the time I had filed the appeal and the time I presented my arguments to the court, the Criminal Code had been amended in such a way as to eliminate half of the legal grounds upon which the Crown was relying to support its case.

The most vivid recollection I have of that appearance is that after I had cited legal precedents from Ontario, Nova Scotia, Quebec, and Saskatchewan, Chief Justice Cornelius O'Halloran interrupted with an exasperated, "Yes, yes, Mr. Nielsen, but do you have any precedents this side of the mountains?" I was flabbergasted; to me, the law was the law, wherever it was applied, but I had underestimated what British Columbians refer to as the effect of the mountains. They really do make a difference. Devereau had now gone through three trial processes: the pre-trial issue of his sanity, the murder trial, and the appeal. I thought he would consider himself fortunate, since his two-year sentence was now very close to having been served. But a fourth step was about to be taken in this remarkable case. Devereau, acting as his own counsel, filed an appeal against the original conviction, another trial process at which I appeared. To everyone's astonishment, the appeal court granted the appeal and ordered a new trial. My fifth appearance in the judicial saga of the Devereau killing, the new trial, was held in Dawson City, where the killing had occurred some two years previously.

The judges (three sat on the Court of Appeal) were, as required, different for each of these five court processes. Since the Yukon had only one judge, we drew judges from Alberta and British Columbia. The judge on the second Devereau trial was Jack Sissons, judge of the Supreme Court of the Northwest Territories and deputy judge of the Supreme Court of Yukon. Again Wylie was defence counsel, having been appointed by Judge Sissons. Devereau was once more convicted by the jury and was sentenced by Judge Sissons to serve one year. The conviction was for manslaughter, the judge taking into account the time Devereau had already spent in custody, some three years. With so many judges coming to the same conclusion with respect to the length of the sentence, I did not pursue the matter further.

Some time after that trial, I was in my law office in Whitehorse when my secretary came in to inform me that Mr. Leo Devereau was there to see me. She knew who he was, and asked, "Shall I call the police?"

I said, "No, don't bother, the man has served his debt to society and should be treated like anyone else." He came into my office, a small man, very wiry and thin. He took about thirty minutes of my time, during most of which he criticized the character, morals, and other standards of his own defence counsel, Mr. Wylie, and the various judges who had sat in judgment on him—those who had convicted him he roasted fiercely, but even those who acted in his favour he criticized. He also described how atrociously various policemen had acted. I was the only person about whom he had anything nice to say, and he praised everything that I had done. I was sufficiently concerned about the safety of Judge Jack Gibben, who had conducted the first trial, and who was still on the bench, that I called the police. I could not help but wonder about the sanity of a man who had shot another in cold blood, then castigated everyone who helped him but praised the only person who had tried to have him put away.

In another murder case, I acted for the defence. The accused was a native person named Jimmy Johnny. One day I received a telephone call from the RCMP detachment. I knew the officer who was calling. (By this time, I had an extremely good working relationship with all of the members of the RCMP in Yukon, having prosecuted so many of their cases and having worked with them so often.) He told me that Jimmy Johnny was charged with the murder of John Sunde, a huge man, more than six feet tall and weighing more than 200 pounds. Jimmy Johnny was about five-ten, 150 pounds soaking wet, but having spent all his life in the bush, he was very physically fit. John Sunde's body had been recovered from the Yukon River a considerable distance below Whitehorse. It had obviously been in the icy waters for some weeks. Police enquiries as to the last known movements of the dead man had led them to Jimmy Johnny.

I asked the policeman to tell Jimmy, a man I knew slightly, that I would act for him, but that I would not be over to see him unless I had to talk with him, and that I did not want him to speak with anyone else about the matters he was charged with—not the police, not his relatives, no one. If he did not heed me on that score, then I would not be able to help him and would not act as his counsel.

As it turned out I did not speak to my client until after he was acquitted. The police and Crown provided me with all the evidence they had, which was that John Sunde and Jimmy Johnny had been drinking wine in the old White Pass shipyard where the stern-wheelers were drydocked for the winter. The evidence showed that they had consumed a considerable quantity of wine.

At this time, there was no bridge across the Yukon River, and on the opposite bank, just below Whitehorse, there was a small community where Jimmy Johnny lived. I concluded that Sunde and Johnny had probably been crossing the river together in a rowboat late that evening, because John Sunde was going to spend the night at Jimmy's shack. An argument must have developed halfway across the river. According to the Crown, Jimmy at some point hit John Sunde over the head and face with one of the oars. (Sunde's face and head bore every evidence that he had been struck repeatedly.) I suggested that if there had been an assault on Sunde, it occurred on the opposite shore of the river. The Crown, picking up on that, advanced the alternative theory that the attack could have occurred on the Whitehorse side, and Jimmy Johnny could have taken the body out into the river and dumped it.

The six-man Yukon jury sat through six or seven days of a trial where, as a result of the cross-examination of the Crown witnesses, some very serious omissions began to appear, particularly in the way the police had conducted the investigation. They had seized the boat, in which there were considerable bloodstains, which had been analysed and found to be similar to John Sunde's blood. Mr. Wylie, who was prosecuting, had no intention of introducing the boat as evidence. I had the entire boat brought into court. On the middle seat, where the rower would normally sit, there was quite a pool of dried blood, and clearly outlined in the blood on the seat were buttock marks. I established through the cross-examination of police witnesses that upon his arrest, the police had seized Jimmy Johnny's clothes and put him in prison clothing; nothing further was done with the clothing he was wearing at the time of his arrest. I could not believe that the police had failed to subject Jimmy Johnny's clothing to forensic analysis, when there were obviously stains on them still visible to the jury. Were they blood? A man of Jimmy Johnny's means would be the owner of only one pair of pants until they were totally worn out, such was the poverty of the native population at that time. Therefore the stains could have been acquired at any time. Since the clothing had not been tested immediately, it was no longer possible to determine if the stains had anything to do with the crime.

That omission raised the biggest doubt in the entire case. Indeed, that single omission was enough to raise a reasonable doubt in the minds of the jurors that the police had the right man. The killing could have been committed by anyone. The two men had been drinking together—that was the extent of the Crown evidence. I called no evidence in Jimmy's defence, and he, naturally, remained silent. Jimmy Johnny was acquitted.

The case was unusual because of my decision not to speak to Jimmy before his trial. My fear was that because he trusted me, he might well blurt out compromising remarks and even perhaps a confession. I did not wish to be fixed with that knowledge, since without it, I would be perfectly free to advance any theory whatsoever to the court. If I had known something incriminating, I could not ethically advance any theory inconsistent with such knowledge.

Jimmy Johnny was grateful, of course. I did not charge him a fee (nor any other native person I defended on criminal charges throughout my twenty-seven years of active practice), but Jimmy paid me in his own way, by working on every one of my political campaigns thereafter.

Another case I carry clearly in my memory concerned a charge of rape. On this occasion, I was prosecuting. The complainant was a native woman in her early twenties. She had been invited by two fellows to a little one-room clapboard shack in Whitehorse for a drink. The three of them went to the shack and drank a lot of beer. According to the woman's testimony, her clothes had then been forcibly removed from her and, while one of the men held her on the single bed in the shack, the other had his way with her. She alleged that the pair had taken turns.

Corroborated by the fact of her "recent complaint"—that is, she went to the police at once—and by medical evidence obtained shortly after the alleged offences, there was a prima facie case for rape. Each of the accused was tried separately and each was called as a Crown witness against the other, notwithstanding the objections of defence counsel at this tactic. I argued strongly that it was either rape or nothing—that is, it could not be indecent assault (a lesser but included offence in a charge of rape under the provisions of the Criminal Code at the time), for the woman had not consented in any manner. The same circumstances and the same arguments were presented in both cases, but with an astonishing result: one man was found guilty of rape and the other of indecent assault.

On the second jury was Gordon Cameron, an aircraft engineer and part owner of Whitehorse Flying Services, who was later appointed Commissioner of Yukon. I knew him well enough to say to him, "Gordon, how in the world could you come in with a verdict of indecent assault?"

Gordon said, "I'll show you why." The police had taken pictures of every part of the interior of that single-room cabin. All of these pictures had been introduced in evidence as part of the case for the Crown. Gordon reminded me that the evidence of the complainant was that these men had forcibly removed her clothes. But the pictures showed a hook on the front door, on which were hanging female garments, including a pair of panties. Gordon said, "You tell me of a case where a woman is raped and, before running out to complain, picks up her clothes and hangs them on a hook behind the front door." It was even less likely that the two men would forcibly remove her clothes and then neatly hang them up. He certainly had a reason for "reasonable doubt."

It says something for the jury system that the second jury did not simply allow the first jury do their work for them, although the distinction, as far as the two convicted men were concerned, was somewhat academic, since they both received the same sentence—three years.

On yet another case in Dawson City, a charge was laid against the local madame of keeping a common bawdy-house. She was known as Ruby Foo, and she was defended by my old nemesis, N. Victor K. Wylie. It seems that an undercover police officer had been solicited by Ruby and the two of them had repaired to her quarters. The price was established, and he handed over the cash, which she placed in a box on the top of a chest of drawers in a sparsely furnished room that also contained a bed, chair, and washbasin. She then disrobed, at which point he identified himself and told her she was under arrest and was being charged with keeping a common bawdy-house.

She decided to defend herself and retained Wylie. I acted for the Crown. The policeman described the initial contact, their proceeding to her sparsely furnished bedroom, and went on to testify as to the details of the contents of the bedroom. Throughout his testimony, Ruby grew more and more impatient and fidgety. She could not wait to take the witness stand. She tried to speak even before she was sworn in.

"Now," said the judge, "please answer Mr. Nielsen's questions."

She blurted out in a thick French accent, "I just want everyone to know, it was *not* my bedroom, it was my *boudoir*." She was convicted despite her indignation. Years later she was still in Dawson and still going strong in her late sixties.

My legal career, fascinating and challenging though it was, was gradually being overtaken by politics. George Van Roggen was the key Liberal in Yukon, and it was largely his organizational efforts that got Aubrey Simmons elected as member of Parliament in 1949, representing both Yukon and the Northwest Territories. The riding of Yukon included the Mackenzie District of the Northwest Territories and covered more than 1.5 million square miles. Before then, the Northwest Territories had no separate representation in Parliament. Moreover, the remaining two districts of the Northwest Territories, Keewatin and Franklin, had to wait until I introduced a private member's bill, passed in 1962, before they received the franchise.

I did not take an active part in political organization until after the 1953 election, in which I became briefly involved on behalf of the Conservative candidate, George Black. He had been around for years, having been first elected in 1921. He became the Speaker of the House of Commons during the Bennett government, and was remembered for keeping a .45 revolver in his chambers. One of his favourite pastimes was taking potshots through the open window of his chambers at the rabbits on the lawn behind Centre Block.

In the late 1920s, George Black was going through a difficult time and had a serious quarrel with Prime Minister R.B. Bennett, after which he wrote a long denunciatory speech about the prime minister, which he intended to read from his place in the Speaker's chair. Bennett refused to allow this and demanded his resignation, whereupon George went charging back to his chambers to get his revolver. Fortunately, the House of Commons security staff had formed their own assessment of George's mental state and hurried to subdue him. In the course of the struggle, the pages of his speech, written on bright yellow paper, were scattered over the floor of his office. Medical assistance had already been summoned, and he was taken away and hospitalized. Dr. Maurice Olivier, parliamentary counsel, arrived on the scene and, with admirable foresight, salvaged the sheets of the speech.

Because George was hospitalized indefinitely, his seat was declared vacant, and his wife, Martha, contested the Yukon by-election as an Independent Conservative. She won handily and became the second woman to be elected to the House of Commons (the first was Agnes Macphail in 1921). Martha served for the remainder of that Parliament and ran again in the next general election, in 1935. She again won handily. By the time the 1940 vote came around, George was healthy once again and ran on his own account. He was victorious in 1940 and 1945, but then was defeated by the Liberal, Aubrey Simmons, both in 1949 and in 1953.

I became involved in the August 1953 campaign because Black was losing so badly to Simmons. Gordon Lee, a local businessman, had been a George Black supporter, but he had decided to run for the Social Credit party, even though they had no organization in Yukon. Black was in his seventies by now, and very much showing his age. It was obvious a month into the campaign that there were only two active candidates, Simmons and Lee, and that Simmons was far ahead. I decided that, as a dedicated Conservative, I could not stand by any longer.

There was no such thing as a Conservative organization. There were those who supported George Black and there were those who did not and that was that. I visited George in his home on Front Street in Whitehorse (now the site of the McBride Museum) and offered my services. George was in the kitchen with half a dozen of his old cronies, some of whom were well into the sauce, even though it was still morning. This was his campaign committee. I also met Martha Black for the first time. I found her a charming, delightful lady. At one point, when no one else was listening, she took my hand and said, "Mr. Nielsen, why don't you run?" She knew that George should not be running at his age.

I joined the campaign very late. I discovered immediately that there were no campaign funds. I could not rob my partner of my time, nor could I afford to pay the expenses of travelling with George on the campaign. I phoned Progressive Conservative headquarters in Ottawa and spoke with Doug Rowe, the son of Earl Rowe, MP for Dufferin-Simcoe. I had never met him, and knew no one at headquarters. I identified myself and described the situation in the riding. I said that if something was not done, and soon, the Conservative candidate would run a very sorry last. Rowe thanked me; he had heard nothing from the riding. I told him that I was prepared to devote time to the remaining weeks of the campaign, but that there were no campaign funds.

Rowe said, "Well, what do you estimate it will cost?" I had no idea. He estimated, at this late stage of the campaign, the sum of $5,000. He said, "I'll send it to you, but I would not send it to George Black." They knew George's habits and feared it would be consumed in liquid by his cronies. I put the money into a trust account, and, after ordering some printed advertising, we hit the trail.

That campaign was based primarily on the waste and extravagance of the Liberal government, and the integrity of George Black and of Progressive Conservative leader George Drew as opposed to Prime Minister Mackenzie King. One of the pamphlets published by national headquarters was entitled "The case of the gold-plated piano." There was also a pamphlet by Donald Fleming called "Why I Am a Conservative."

I had what I thought was the bright idea of printing party leaflets and, taking a page out of my Air Force propaganda-leaflet-bombing days, dropping the leaflets over Whitehorse from an aircraft. I did the flying and the leaflet-bombing myself.

People did not really know anything was going on in the Conservative campaign until these pamphlets began to rain down out of the sky over Whitehorse. George Van Roggen was having a drink in the Whitehorse Inn with Jim Hannah, another active Liberal, when somebody brought one of these pamphlets in from the street. George immediately went out and saw the leaflets fluttering down from above. He told some nearby children that he would pay a penny for each one of the pamphlets they and any of their friends brought to him. The children immediately mobilized dozens of others to pick up the campaign literature. Thus George paid a penny to destroy each pamphlet it had cost me about a dollar to put there. I appreciated being outwitted by my own partner and spent the remaining budget for advertising with greater care.

My strategy having "bombed" in Whitehorse, I immediately departed with George Black for Discovery Day celebrations, a festival held in Dawson City. George was to speak at Minto Park during the height of the festivities. I drove my new car over a toll road from Whitehorse to Stewart Crossing. (Before Diefenbaker's Conservative government had the three bridges constructed over the Yukon, Pelly, and Stewart rivers at Carmacks, Pelly Crossing, and Stewart Crossing respectively, these rivers were traversed by ferry during the summer months and by ice bridges during the winter months.) That was quite a journey. By road, the distance is approximately 320 miles, and because of the nature of the road and trails, the trip took about ten to twelve steady hours. George Black had a case of MacEwan's ale in the car. I did not drink at all, but by the time we reached Dawson, late on the night before the holiday, George had polished off the entire dozen, and was ready for bed. I took him to his room in the Penguin Hotel, undressed him down to his red longjohns—I had never before seen red longjohns on anyone in August—and put him safely to bed. He was so sozzled that I was sure he would have a nice long uninterrupted sleep. I was famished, so I went in search of a cafe.

There was a cafe under the Penguin Hotel, with a long U-shaped counter surrounded by stools. There were three men across from where I sat. One of them, a man in his fifties, was dressed in what I immediately recognized as an RCMP standard-issue shirt. One of the men sitting beside him called him Kirk, and as soon as I heard the name, I wondered, could it possibly be the man whose legs I had tripped over in Fort Norman when I was four years old? I went over to him and said hello. I told him I had noticed that he was wearing an RCMP khaki shirt, which I had seen every day of my life. He said, "Yes, I was in the RCMP." I asked him his name and he said, "George Kirk."

I said, "Do you recognize me by my lip?" He thought that was a strange opener, and I told him my name. He said, "Oh my God, you're Niel's boy." Thus I met, thirty-one years after the event, the man whose name my father had mentioned every time he described to me the circumstances of my scarred lip.

Kirk told me that he had been a corporal at the RCMP detachment, at Old Crow, where he served for several years beyond the normal posting. When the RCMP offered him a promotion to sergeant in a southern location, he requested that he be allowed to stay at Old Crow as a corporal. It was there that he served his final years in the RCMP. After his retirement, he decided to get into the business of river transportation between Dawson City and Old Crow. (River transport was still a major form of transport in Yukon. The stern-wheelers ran until the rivers were bridged by the Diefenbaker government; one of the last stern-wheelers, the *Klondike*, ran until 1958.)

After dinner and my reunion with George Kirk downstairs, I returned to check up on George Black in his room. Midnight had come and gone and George's bed was empty. I visited everything that was open in Dawson City (that did not take me long)—no George Black. I understood that George knew the people of Dawson very well, since he had been a lawyer, commissioner, and Yukon MP there for years. I was not worried that he had met with foul play, but I had lost my candidate, who was, the last time I saw him, in his cups.

I went to bed, and got up early to look for George, who was due to make a public speech at two that afternoon. I almost went door to door. By noon, all the bars and establishments were going full steam, but no one had seen George Black. I was making my enquiries as discreetly as I could, and I was about to give up. In fact, I had already called the organizers at Minto Park to report that George was not going to be there. They said they understood. They understood better than I did.

I came upon George in a house from which there seemed to be a lot of jovial sounds emerging. I knocked on the door, and it turned out to be the home of a delightful, elderly couple who had a magnificent garden. I asked if George Black was there. Why certainly, he was in the kitchen and, of course, had been drinking all night.

All those hours and all those dollars spent to get George Black to Dawson City to make a fifteen-minute speech—down the drain. Still, he was able to make many personal contacts in his own way. We left the following day. Clearly there was more to this political campaigning than I had anticipated.

On election day, I was at George's home with all his cronies. The tally of the votes had George coming in a very bad third. Even he realized that his political career was finished. He and Martha urged me to run the next time.

I said, "No, I won't do that, but I will help build a Progressive Conservative organization and organize a candidate search."

Although I was determined not to seek election myself, I was equally determined that the serious deficiencies encountered during the campaign just concluded would be overcome. In particular, there were many abuses of the election laws. No wonder the Liberals had won. They had everything tightly sewn up with their control of the election machinery. Because of the limited number of polling stations, a good organization could exercise total control and intimidate people. The entire Yukon riding was a rural polling division, in which anyone could be sworn in at the polling station, whether he or she was properly eligible or not. Enumeration was not essential, and abuses in the swearing-in process were rampant. In the 1957 election, for example, we would prove at least twenty-two cases of duplicate voting; most were truckers who were sworn in by Liberal campaign workers at different polling stations along the Alaska Highway.

Something else that disturbed me was that the entire village of Old Crow, where there were more than 280 Canadian citizens, most of them native people, did not even have a ballot box or polling station. They simply did not exist as far as Yukon election officials were concerned.

I was determined that we would never again have such a disorganized and ineffective campaign, but I never dreamt that during the next one, in 1957, I would be the candidate.

Chapter Five
A Reluctant Candidate

*Nothing improves a politician's manners like an
election.*

Sam Slick

The years between 1953 and 1956 were spent largely in establishing
a law practice, building my own clientele, and generally injecting
some administrative organization into the practice, which by now
was growing quite rapidly. In those years as well, our second son,
Rick, and our daughter, Roxanne, were born. My law practice often
took me to different parts of Yukon, a vast territory of 207,000
square miles, much of it inaccessible by road for a good part of the
year. It was not yet served by any radio network, although there
was a volunteer station in Dawson City and another in Whitehorse.
Telephone services existed in Whitehorse, Mayo, Dawson City, and
Watson Lake, and in a few other communities on the main line and
along the Alaska Highway. The same applied to electrical energy;
the only hydro came from an old plant operated by Yukon Consolidated Gold Corporation, near Dawson City, and another operated by Yukon Electrical Company near Whitehorse.

When my court or other legal duties took me outside Whitehorse,
I did not waste any opportunity to make new acquaintances and to
assess the political climate of the many communities I visited. Thus,
when I began organizing seriously in 1956, I did not start from
scratch.

There was no doubt that there would be a federal election in
1957. The custom of calling an election every four years had been
honoured for so long that it had almost acquired the force of law.
Bearing that in mind, and my determination after 1953 never to
permit the Progressive Conservative party in Yukon to repeat its
poor showing, I knew that a good deal of planning, travel, and
organization had to be done in the year leading up to the election.

71

When the 1957 election was called, Yukon would be ready, if I had anything to do with it.

One of the early friendships I formed was with a man named Wilfrid Desrosiers, known to all as Curly. He was an ebullient, gregarious individual, always smiling. He had come to Yukon in 1942 as part of the civilian construction crew on the Alaska Highway. He had been born on a railway train 100 miles north of Winnipeg, and his birth certificate noted, as his place of birth, Mile 100. In Yukon, I met him as a big game guide and outfitter, along with his wife, Belle. Curly has been dead for many years, but Belle, highly admired and respected throughout Yukon, is still going strong in her sixties; still climbing mountains and putting many a youngster of twenty-five to shame in the process. Belle was the daughter of Buck Dixon, a member of the Northwest Mounted Police, who had been posted during the gold rush days to a place called Burwash Landing, about 210 miles north of Whitehorse, on the shores of Kluane Lake. This was where Belle was born.

The outfitting and big-game hunting season in Yukon opens in early summer and extends to the middle of October. After the season is ended, most big game guides pursue other employment. Some winter in southern Canada or even in climates far warmer. Curly and Belle, however, normally stayed in Yukon. Curly and Belle became my early and fast friends well before I became active in politics. Between the two of them, there were few people in Yukon who were not known to them and who did not like them.

Curly began travelling with me during my political organization trips in the fall of 1956. We visited every community, including all of the native settlements. Curly was at home everywhere and helped me to identify at least one and often more residents who could represent Progressive Conservative interests, and actively recruit others. I followed up this initial contact with regular visits and steady written communications. Every person contacted this way knew that he or she was part of a growing political organization.

There was a widely held belief in the territory that the Liberal government in Ottawa had forgotten Yukon and that a change was necessary to obtain the same basic services that were enjoyed by communities of a similar size in southern Canada—telephone services, roads and bridges, radio service, education, and housing. For example, even though the Canada Mortgage and Housing Corporation legislation legally applied to all of Canada, it was clearly not being applied in Yukon and the Northwest Territories. Improvements in housing were therefore very difficult to achieve. (That was to be one of the first changes brought about during the first Diefenbaker government, at my urgent insistence.)

The city of Dawson still had some very colourful characters, men and women who had settled there during or soon after the gold rush days at the turn of the century. Alec Adams, Harry Lehman, Black Mike Wenige, Hardrock MacDonald, High Pockets Butterworth, Digger Cook (the undertaker)—these were some of those aging Yukoners I met in 1956. Early in 1957, I attended a political meeting in Dawson, at which I was to be the principal speaker. It was an extremely well attended meeting for Dawson, with about forty souls there to hear me. Harry Lehman was there; he had walked the seven miles from his claim on Bonanza Creek in minus-forty-degree weather to attend, and he afterwards walked back. That is a measure of his dedication to the Progressive Conservative party. I never had enough nerve to ask him if he thought my speech was worth it.

Wherever Curly and I went, we were greeted by friendly people, and it did not take us long, particularly in the Dawson area, to recruit supporters, most of whom became my lasting friends. Some are still alive. The story was the same in the native communities. Friendships were formed and have lasted to this day, particularly with the older native people. (I did not have the opportunity of developing that kind of relationship with the younger native people. Their views are not unlike those held by the average young Canadian of today, in part because of the infusion of massive amounts of capital, which has radically changed the lifestyle of the Yukon native. The political party now most active among the native people is the NDP.)

During the early organization days in 1956, when Curly was travelling with me, my approach in the communities was pretty well always the same. I would seek out the local restaurant around dinner time, when workmen and others were bound to be there. Nine times out of ten Curly would be recognized by someone. If a local party representative was not in evidence, I would simply stand in my place in the restaurant, raise my voice, and inform everyone of my name, where I was from, and that I was seeking help in organizing the Progressive Conservative party in Yukon. Was there anyone who could help? More often than not a volunteer either indicated there and then that he or she was interested, or one would wait until after most people had left and then come over to me. That is how most of the team was recruited outside Whitehorse.

On one occasion, in Destruction Bay, an army maintenance camp about 160 miles north of Whitehorse on the Alaska Highway, I made my pitch in the restaurant and was met with dead silence. After waiting quite a while, Curly and I decided this visit was going to be a total failure, and we left. Within seconds, someone was on our heels. He said his name was George, and that he was a committed member of the Social Credit party. He was not interested in becoming a card-carrying member of the Progressive Conservatives but, in true Yukon spirit, he said he did not like the silent treatment we had received in the restaurant, so he would be happy to help us to build a party in Destruction Bay. He did the job so effectively that we did well in every election in Destruction Bay thereafter.

Watson Lake had three restaurants. I made my pitch in each of them, but this time I announced that I would be speaking at a public meeting in the community hall at eight o'clock that evening. The community hall was simply the lobby of the curling rink, very recently constructed. At eight, Curly and I showed up. There were only three others there, Johnny Friend, still very active in Watson Lake, his business partner, Hugh Peet, and Hugh's wife. There was not much point in my making a speech to three people so Johnny suggested we spend the time curling. We did just that. I had never curled before.

Johnny Friend's conversion to the Conservative cause was unusual, as was everything about this blunt, bearded man. He had for a long time been a Liberal, and an effective one. There was scarcely a soul along the Alaska Highway and in a good portion of northern British Columbia who had not been helped at one time or another by Johnny Friend. If ever a man was aptly named, it was he. A generous bachelor, he placed no limits on what he would do for anyone in trouble, and it used to be said in Watson Lake that Johnny had loaned more cash up and down the highway than the Bank of Montreal had in Whitehorse. A pretty good man to have on your team.

One day Aubrey Simmons, the Liberal MP, came to Watson Lake. While there, he did not find the time to have a chat with Johnny Friend. In addition to his boundless generosity, Johnny has a fairly good-sized ego, and he could not forgive Simmons for not speaking with him. He thereupon tore up his Liberal membership card, bought a Progressive Conservative membership card, and never looked back. Johnny has attended more than one national convention of the Progressive Conservative party in Ottawa.

After he had attended a few of my meetings over the years, Johnny pretty well knew every one of my views and was familiar with my speeches, so he began to doze off towards the end of meetings. During the 1979 campaign, he was in the third row at our public meeting at the community hall in Watson Lake, and he had fallen asleep. Johnny is a chain-smoker of cigars, and his cigar had burned quite short. I did not usually disturb him when he dozed off, but on this occasion, smoke came curling out of his nest of whiskers and I had no choice but to shout in the middle of my speech, "Johnny, Johnny, you're on fire!" That drew the attention of the audience, who roused Johnny and put out the fire, which had spread deeply into his beard.

My very first political meeting, at which I made a speech, was held in the second storey of an old community hall at Keno City, Yukon. Keno City is about 250 miles north of Whitehorse, part of the United Keno Hill mining community. The leading Liberal there was Masa Sakata, a Japanese Canadian, who owned and ran the only cafe in town. I lost no opportunity in reminding Masa of the Liberals' treatment of Japanese Canadians on the west coast of Canada during World War II. I do not think those reminders finally changed his loyalty, but I am sure he gave us his vote on more than one occasion. At one point Masa said, "Well, the Liberal government has been in office a long time; it's like a pair of socks—when they're worn too long, they have to be changed and washed."

At this meeting in Keno, he was there, in the front row. The hall was "crowded" with about fifteen citizens. I spoke extemporaneously, and followed my speech with a question period. I was not paying any attention to the passage of time and was astonished when I looked at my watch. The audience was just as surprised that three hours had gone by so quickly. Of course, apart from the bar in the hotel, there was no other local entertainment. Subsequent meetings were managed so that I spoke for a maximum of thirty to forty minutes and then answered questions for as long as the audience wished.

One of the many things I learned about during those early trips was mining, the most important economic activity in Yukon. My first contact in the mining community of Calumet was a very nice couple, Bob Mason and his wife, Olga. Bob was a shift boss who had started mining at about the age of twelve in the coal fields of Nova Scotia. (His first job was walking along the drifts and picking up chips of wood and rubbish between the tracks of the tramways over which the ore cars travelled in and out of the mines.)

My introduction to underground mining was thorough. Bob took me into every nook and cranny, every stope, every drift in United Keno Hill Mines, which extended some 1,400 feet below the surface. Eventually I visited all fourteen levels, climbing, crawling, following Bob Mason through the most confining stopes, shafts, and other underground mining structures. I will never forget those experiences, which were, at Bob's insistence, repeated each time I visited Calumet. He said there was no way to meet the miners and gain any idea of what they were doing unless you met them "at the face." For a cheechako (Yukon slang for greenhorn) and a person who spent hours behind a desk, it was quite an eye-opener for me.

At Calumet I stayed in the bunkhouse with the men and shared their meals, though I had been invited by management to stay in the guest house for officers and visiting executives from Toronto. The hoist man at Calumet, Harry Venechuk, was a committed socialist, but at Bob's urging attended my first political meeting in Calumet and then became quite committed to me as my friend and consequently to the party. Harry and I exchanged Christmas cards and letters for years after he retired.

During that early organization work I also visited the placer mining gold dredges of Yukon Consolidated Gold Corporation near Dawson City. Huge three- and four-storey-high machines scooped out yards of gold-bearing gravel from a creek bed, using a chain of huge metal buckets. The gravel was washed inside the dredge and the "tailings" were discarded out the rear on a conveyor belt. The mounds of gravel that these dredges left behind after passing over a producing creek are still evident today, although largely overgrown and re-vegetated.

The mining areas had heavily supported the Liberal candidate in the previous two elections, and indeed there was a strong Liberal nucleus in each of the mining communities. The task in those communities had to be to try to confine Liberal support to their hardcore. The Liberal movement was so well embedded that it would have been unrealistic to try to remove it entirely. We succeeded in establishing strong organizations in each of the communities, which, in later campaigns, won the day for us, although sometimes by a very narrow margin.

It was as a result of my underground experiences and familiarity with the work of miners that I began taking an intense interest in labour law. I had been exposed to the subject at Dalhousie, but it was not until I viewed the actual activities of miners, their work environment, their lifestyle, and the relationship of miners with management that I took a real interest. I took an interest also in the union movement and felt extremely honoured when I began to receive invitations from the union executive at Elsa to attend their smokers. Normally no one but union members was admitted. I was subsequently made an honorary member of Local 924 of the International Union of Mine, Mill and Smelter Workers in recognition of the work I did in representing Yukon miners' interests as their MP. The union itself was later absorbed by the United Steelworkers during a massive takeover at Sudbury, which was preceded by many raids in mining communities throughout Canada.

All of that was still ahead of me when, during the closing months of 1956, I was combining the task of organizing the party with that of searching for a candidate. I had reviewed the old nomination papers of George Black to help me identify Conservative supporters. I realized later that many Liberals had signed his papers, but before I discovered this, I found myself approaching Liberals to run for the Progressive Conservative party. I struck out with such well-known Yukoners as Bud Fisher, Howard Firth (whose father before him had an insurance business in Dawson City), and Gordon Cameron.

Finally, I identified a grocery store manager with whom I had become acquainted through my law practice. His name was Jim Smith, and he had recently moved from the town of Atlin, in northern British Columbia. I was impressed with his ability to talk non-stop. He expressed a keen interest in running as the candidate, and I obtained from him his commitment to run when the election was called in 1957. I informed party headquarters in Ottawa of this good news. We now seemed to be in pretty good shape. We had the beginnings of a broadly based organization in place, an organization by no means trained in such matters as scrutineering and polling-day procedures, but one that had lots of enthusiasm. And we had an affable candidate who had an excellent reputation, and since everyone had to buy groceries, he was widely known. He said he was Conservative and gave every evidence of being a winner.

I was told by the national director of the party on the telephone that I was "expected to attend" the national convention in Ottawa in December 1956. I had not planned to go, and I wrote to Doug Rowe accordingly. However, he left me feeling that I would be a deserter if I stayed away. I therefore recruited a local chartered accountant, David Porter, along with George Black and myself and our newly committed candidate for the convention.

Until that time, the only prominent politicians I had met had been Liberals, persons such as Vincent MacDonald and James Ilsley. At the convention in Ottawa, I met Doug Rowe for the first time. I also met headquarters personnel from whom I gleaned much precious information on canvassing, scrutineering, and the like to take back with me for training those who would be working on the campaign. I also met Alvin Hamilton, and we became fast friends. (The Roads to Resources program that opened the North was the brainchild of the resolutions committee on which Alvin and I were members. Indeed, that policy came mainly from the two of us.)

Seeing a political convention for the first time would be exciting for anyone. For me it was doubly so as I was now part of this great national political movement and was meeting people I had only read about in newspaper articles, men like John Diefenbaker, at that time at the height of his vigour, power, and eloquence. We spoke of the North, and although normally he would have passed on quickly to the next person to be greeted, he had a fairly lengthy exchange with me. He was impressed that we had a delegation of three from Yukon (Jim Smith had not yet shown up). Ours was the first northern delegation to put in an appearance at a national convention, and that counted for something. (I did not really get to know Diefenbaker until after the 1958 election when, for the first time in history, a Canadian prime minister visited north of the 60th parallel.)

I also had a brief but pleasant exchange with Davie Fulton, the man we had come south to support. And I met the third candidate running for the party leadership, Donald Fleming. Fleming was very remote, and I never did get to know him, although I have always respected him for his undoubted abilities in the field of finance.

George Drew, the out-going leader, was visibly ill; his political career had obviously come to an end. We had it in our minds to replace him with Davie Fulton, but once we heard John Diefenbaker rolling out those magnificent phrases, full of scorn, humour, and anger, we changed our minds, and so did the rest of the convention. Diefenbaker was an easy winner, and he became our party leader.

Most of my time at that convention was taken up on the resolutions committees, and the one I was active on was the resources committee. That is where I met John B. Hamilton, John Pallett, and many others. Dalton Camp was also active there and it was with him that I first raised the issue of Roads to Resources, but he was listening with a leaden ear; I could tell that while he was giving the appearance of politeness, he was not really taking it in.

Jim Smith had still not arrived, and I was increasingly worried. Eventually I received a telegram from him. He was in Calgary. He had stopped off there to have a business discussion with Bruce Sung, who held the principal interest in Tourist Services, the company that owned his grocery store. It turned out that Bruce Sung was about to build a supermarket in Whitehorse and had asked Jim to manage it. Jim had accepted the offer and reneged on his commitment to be our candidate.

I was pretty gloomy when I left the convention on my way to Toronto and Yukon. We had a very short time left to find a candidate. It was going to be difficult.

I returned to the job again, and so did others. Armed with the information we had picked up at the convention, we once again travelled around Yukon holding seminars for the supporters we had organized. By the time that second swing of the territory was completed, the Yukon Conservative organization was not only in place in every single community in that vast area but it was trained and eager to put its newly acquired skills into practice, in the election we all expected for the summer of 1957.

But we had no candidate.

On the way back from Ottawa, on the suggestion of a Yukoner who had been helping me in my political organization efforts, I had stopped long enough in Toronto to attend a meeting in the Royal York Hotel with a number of Conservative supporters, many of them in the mining industry. In that room were Colonel Cockeram, a former MP, F.M. Connell, then the principal of ConWest Exploration, and Nick Gritzuk, who was an engineer heading a transport company for United Keno Hill Mines. These mining people wanted to see bridges over those northern rivers, access to the territories, and better communications. They wanted to see a change in the government in Ottawa and a change in the candidate in Yukon. As we talked, I was enthusiastic about our chances with the organization, but I had to tell them that we had lost our candidate, and I showed them Jim Smith's telegram. F.M. Connell said in his deep, gravelly voice, "Well, Erik, I guess you'll have to roll up your sleeves and run yourself."

I said there was no way I could do that; I had a growing family of three young children and a budding law practice. I simply could not take the time nor find the money to do it.

Colonel Cockeram piped up, "How much do you need?"

This came at me right out of the blue. I said, "Your offer is most generous, being open-ended like that, but I do not want to run. I will try to find a candidate, but if I change my mind about your generous offer, I will be in touch with you."

"That's fine," he said, "but the people in this room will make sure you have the necessary funds to run, and you should think very seriously about doing so."

When I decided to run, I did need the money. It was not a gift or a grant—today I probably could have obtained a grant of some sort—but a loan, a demand note which I made in favour of Colonel Cockeram for $15,000. The demand note was accompanied by his statement, "Look, you pay me back when you can." When he died a short time afterwards, I had not paid anything on the note and his widow, whom I had never met, told me that I should see the trustee of her husband's estate. The trustee presented the note and demanded payment in full, forthwith. I had no difficulty classifying him as a Liberal! So I borrowed from the bank and paid off the Cockeram debt. I have not been out of debt since. That was my fiscal introduction to politics.

It could have been avoided had I been able to find a candidate, but as the election came rushing upon us—it was set for June 10, 1957—it appeared that Aubrey Simmons would be returned by acclamation. With all the work that I and others had done, it would have been almost a betrayal to the new organization to allow that to happen. We all believed that the Yukon Liberal candidate had a substantial edge and would likely win by a comfortable margin, but to give it to him without a struggle was wrong. It can be truthfully said that the candidacy was going begging, and I did not at all relish switching from an organizer-manager, but in desperation and with the approval of other party organizers, I offered to run as the candidate.

I determined that Jim Smith would not get off scot free and I asked him to be my campaign manager. He agreed, but during the two months of the campaign he rarely showed up. I like to remember him as the only one of my campaign managers who managed a losing campaign.

It was difficult for me being a partner of the principal Liberal in Yukon, and I did not want George Van Roggen to think that I was betraying his best interests. I had several long talks with him before announcing my decision to run. The proposal I put to him was that Yukon was getting nowhere with the sitting member. Simmons was a typical politician, always friendly and polite, but he never made a constructive move. I knew that Aubrey had told George that any time George wanted to run, he would step aside, so my proposal to George was that he tell Aubrey now was the time. He did not come back to me for some time, so we met again on the subject, away from the office. We drove around Whitehorse, and up and down the highway, talking all the while. I was urging him to run, and I told him I would look after the practice and keep it going if he did so. He thought about that for two days and then decided he would not do it.

I asked him, "Did you speak with Aubrey Simmons?"

"No," he replied.

I said, "Okay, I'm going to run then."

The results of that election are history. The national Conservatives upset the Liberal regime that had ruled the nation for twenty-two years. And in Yukon, much to our surprise, primarily because of our organization and also as a result of our new approach, we won the election by fifty-nine votes before the service vote was counted. When that came in, the net result left the Conservatives the losers by sixty-four votes. However, the organization was so well trained that when we called for the scrutineers' records, which were meticulously kept in all polls, we turned up many irregularities. We did this by calling a meeting of scrutineers from every poll and assembling in the ballroom of the Whitehorse Inn. There were about fifty-five or sixty of them. One person read voters' names from a master list, while every scrutineer from each poll checked the lists to see whether the name called had voted at one or more of the sixty polls. The operation took us nearly eight hours, but it would have taken six to eight weeks any other way. That process identified 681 voting irregularities, more than enough to comply with the controverted election laws, which required proof of at least as many irregularities as the margin of victory. Among other irregularities, we found that twenty-two voters had voted twice. The easiest way to do this, as I had already observed in 1953, was for travellers on the Alaska Highway to drop in to more than one polling station on their way.

The results of our scrutineers' reports went to Ottawa, with my strong recommendation that we contest the election in court. I was sure we would win a by-election. Prime Minister Diefenbaker did not have a clear majority and one seat would make a difference. But my real motive was to clean up the Liberal-dominated, sloppy election procedures extant in Yukon. Ottawa headquarters sent George Shaw, a lawyer from Annapolis, Nova Scotia, who was one of George Nowlan's key organizers, to investigate. I spent several days with him, and took him to Dawson City, where he spoke with party supporters. I showed him the evidence, and he attended several meetings with our organizers and left behind some valuable tips. He submitted a favourable report and Ottawa finally agreed to the court case.

I sent the list of irregularities and the names of the individuals whom we were alleging had cast irregular votes to the counsel appointed by national headquarters, Gowan Guest, who was to become prominent in Conservative circles. He proved to be excellent counsel. The trial of the issue was held in early October of 1957. Of course, before this there was the recount to go through, and George Shaw helped with that. We knew it would not change anything, but it had to be disposed of before the trial. It did not take the court long at all to find in favour of my petition and the election was declared null and void. The Speaker of the House declared that the seat for Yukon riding was vacant. As a courtesy, Simmons was informed beforehand, and resigned his seat.

All that remained now was for a by-election date to be fixed. It was my view all along, and that of the vast majority of the organization, that we should act at once. After the court judgment and Simmons's resignation, there was a high degree of resentment against me and against the Conservative party in Yukon—we were considered poor sports. National headquarters was reluctant to agree to an early vote; I rather suspect that the planning for the election of early 1958 was already well under way. However, the prime minister made the decision, and polling day was set for December 16, 1957.

Here we were campaigning again, less than six months from the last federal election. By this time, our organization was probably the most experienced one in the country, and it functioned with meticulous ease. We won the by-election by 148 votes, far fewer than might have been expected, so the "poor sports" reaction was obviously widespread.

Throughout these rather arduous campaigns, with all the travelling that was entailed, in which Curly was my almost constant companion, we slept in bunkhouses in the mining camps, or in the homes of native friends, and had our meals in the cookhouses of mining camps and restaurants. It was simply not practical nor desirable for P.J., with two babies and a young son, to be out campaigning with me. Throughout subsequent elections, it became the norm for me to do most of the campaigning by myself.

During that by-election, we had help from Alvin Hamilton, who was a big hit in Yukon. He was extremely well liked and he did not come only to Whitehorse; he travelled to the outlying communities with us, and the people took to him for his friendly, down-to-earth demeanour. We also had a visit from Marcel Lambert, then parliamentary secretary to the minister of defence. Marcel, from Edmonton, looked very out of place in Yukon with his blue pin-striped suit, dark overcoat, and homburg (shades of me on my arrival in Whitehorse five years earlier). George Hees and Mabel Hees were visitors, too.

The successful skills of our party organization were put to use once again in February 1958, when the prime minister called an election after the famous "hidden document" debate. That meant the third federal election for us within eight and a half months, and by the time of that election, on March 31, it would have been impossible to find as sophisticated and expert a team of organizers anywhere in Canada as we had in Yukon.

That election gave us a majority of 607. I had entered upon a parliamentary career, quite by force of circumstance. I did not intend it to last long, certainly not for almost three decades, but I was already in the grip of events quite beyond my power to control.

Chapter Six

Moving the Elephant

It is not easy nowadays to remember anything so
contrary to all appearances as that officials are the
servants of the public.

Sir Ernest Gowers

The by-election that first put me into the House of Commons occurred on December 16, 1957. The writ was returned to the Speaker in early January 1958, and I was off to Ottawa to be sworn in with Alvin Hamilton in attendance. But I did not go immediately to my desk in the House of Commons. Instead, I spent several days watching the daily proceedings from the East Gallery, wondering why I was there. This delay turned out to be part of Prime Minister Diefenbaker's strategy, that I would not take the Yukon seat until the right moment. He was quite a showman in his own way.

Eventually, on January 20, 1958, I was marched into the Green Chamber with the prime minister on one side of me and on the other Alvin Hamilton, minister of northern affairs and national resources. I was the new boy, representing a victory over the shoddy practices of the Liberals. The symbolism was clear a few minutes later when debate was joined over one of the most extraordinary motions ever to come before the House of Commons.

Lester Pearson, the new Liberal leader—Louis St. Laurent had resigned as leader after his party's defeat in 1959—had been presented with a remarkable new strategy by Jack Pickersgill, who had been the right-hand man first of Mackenzie King, then of St. Laurent. In my opinion, Pickersgill was one of those politicians who let a brilliant mind be overpowered by a helium-inflated ego and an overbearing arrogance. Just before the 1957 election, he declared, "It is not merely for the well-being of Canadians but for the good of mankind in general that the present Liberal government should remain in office."

85

When the new minority government of John Diefenbaker rejected this advice, Jumping Jack, as he was often called, prepared for Pearson a motion that cited a gloomy economic future, which it attributed to seven months of Conservative mismanagement, and called on the Progressive Conservatives to resign office and to transfer power to the Liberals, without the awkward necessity of an election. The motion concluded: "And in view of the desirability at this time of having a government pledged to implement Liberal policies; His Excellency's advisers should, in the opinion of this house, submit their resignations forthwith."

The arrogance and stupidity of the move were breath-taking. Diefenbaker had been waiting for just this moment. He rose in the House to reveal the contents of the "hidden document" that would plunge us almost at once into another election.

This confidential document, entitled *Canadian Economic Outlook for 1957*, had been prepared under the direction of Mitchell Sharp, then associate deputy minister of trade and commerce. Contrary to the optimistic public posturing of the Liberals during the election campaign, it painted a gloomy—and, as it turned out, accurate— picture of a looming recession. This advice had been studiously ignored by the Liberals when setting their pre-election budget. The document was brought to the attention of Diefenbaker by Patrick Nicholson, a sympathetic journalist, and the Chief took obvious pleasure reading the damning paragraphs into the Hansard record while the humiliated Liberals squirmed and bellowed. Jumping Jack's strategy had backfired.

Diefenbaker was in magnificent form. Pearson, on the other hand, was clearly embarrassed; the Chief referred to his participation in the ensuing debate as being "about as nourishing as homeopathic soup made from the shadow of a pigeon that had starved to death." When the CCF opposition demanded that Diefenbaker table the document, he replied with glee, "I rather welcome that suggestion. I could not have tabled it unless requested."

In ringing tones, he thundered, "You turned a deaf ear to the elderly ... to the poor ... to the unemployed." Diefenbaker drove home the legacy of economic incompetence left by the Liberals. He even drove that wily and skilful debater, Paul Martin, into a grumbling whine: "We did not say we would cure unemployment."

Diefenbaker shot back: "You concealed the facts. That is what you did."

That was my first introduction to the animated debate of the House of Commons. It was a magnificent example of a now almost extinct tradition. The standards of debate were extremely high then. There was no modern sound system whereby operators could electronically control members' microphones, turning their voices on or off as the operator might choose; there was no automatic cut-off of all members' comments whenever the Speaker rose. Participation was spontaneous and decorous. The rules were there, but were adjusted to accommodate spirited debate. When that occurred, the chamber was filled, and so were the galleries, including the press gallery. Today, that spontaneity is no longer there. During important debates there are seldom more than twenty-five or thirty members in their seats, and the galleries are seldom occupied except during Question Period. That is the one hour of the day when the chamber and the galleries are both filled. The members of the press gallery, if they follow the House proceedings at all, do so on television and not from their seats in the gallery. Question Period is certainly not the reason for the existence of the House of Commons, but it has become so. This sorry situation is the result mostly of the changes brought about by the electronic age.

My electrifying introduction to the House was followed in eleven short days by the dissolution of the Twenty-Third Parliament. Diefenbaker had the issue that he wanted to go to the country with, and he knew that he could move from a minority to a majority government by doing so. We were back to the hustings again.

The next general election, on March 31, 1958, resulted in the Diefenbaker landslide of 208 members (up from 112), including fifty from the province of Quebec. There were so many Progressive Conservatives in the House that for the first time the rump—the benches directly to the Speaker's left—was formed by the NDP, who had been reduced to only eight members. Those eight were led by Hazen Argue, now a Liberal senator. The forty-nine Liberals (down from 105) were led by the Four Horsemen of the Apocalypse, as they were dubbed by Public Works Minister Howard Green: Lester Pearson, Lionel Chevrier, Jack Pickersgill, and Paul Martin. They kept the Liberal party alive and well in the House during those four years in opposition, and they also inspired Liberals throughout the country by the calibre of their work in the House. Everything they did, of course, was geared to regaining office but in the meantime, Pearson often referred to his forty-nine-member caucus as "we few, we happy few, we band of brothers." (No one in my hearing ever called the Conservative caucus a band of brothers!)

The debates were punctuated with many amusing moments. Once, when we were engaged in a debate in the House on the subject of wheat, leading up to a vote of confidence, the prime minister took a dominant role in the discussion—something seldom seen any more—and he aroused Pearson's anger so much that Pearson, even though he had already spoken, tried to re-enter the debate. He was ruled out of order by the Speaker, since a member cannot speak twice in the same debate. Pearson sat down, utterly deflated, and dropped his notes on his desk in front of him. Paul Martin, who sat beside him and had not spoken in the debate—he knew nothing about wheat—scooped up Pearson's notes and spoke for some forty minutes without once mentioning the word "wheat." When the Speaker brought him to order on the rule of relevancy, he retorted that the Speaker had perhaps failed to recognize the sophisticated refinements that he was bringing to the debate on this complex subject.

On one occasion, a Conservative member from Saskatchewan was fast asleep in the House. Gus Henderson, an elderly Alberta Conservative, sent him a note that read, "I dropped by to have a chat with you. Sorry you were asleep. JGD." When his neighbour woke him, he read the note and looked up in astonishment at the prime minister, who knew nothing of the matter.

On another occasion, when Paul Martin was holding forth, Gus Henderson sent a note over to him. We all saw Paul, as he was speaking in the debate, take the note from the page and read it without interrupting his verbal flow. He then placed his right hand on his top vest button and slowly, as he continued speaking, ran his hand down his vest buttons to his belt, and, still speaking, ran his fingers farther down, over his fly. When his fingers reached his fly, a sickly grin of relief spread across his face. The note had said simply, "Paul, your fly is open."

It was in my early days in Parliament that Robert McGregor celebrated his thirty-fifth year in the House of Commons. McGregor, an elderly construction contractor from Ontario, had participated actively in committees and attended the House regularly. He was evidently a good constituency man, for he continued to be re-elected.

But he never once spoke in the House. On his anniversary, Pearson rose to pay tribute to McGregor, followed by Prime Minister Diefenbaker, who also lauded McGregor's service. Neither mentioned his extraordinary record of silence. McGregor responded with a twenty-five-word speech of thanks. The next day, the *Ottawa Journal* blared, "Blabbermouth McGregor Speaks!"

In those years, my work was devoted to improving the sad neglect not only of Yukon but of the Northwest Territories as well. I was on the doorstep of Alvin Hamilton, minister of northern affairs, and of the prime minister on every possible occasion. Although I seldom spoke in the House or in caucus, I spoke up as often as possible in the Department of Northern Affairs and with the relevant ministers. For the most part, they cooperated handsomely. Funds for road improvements were made available; three major bridges and several minor ones were constructed during that first full term between 1958 and 1962; and the telephone system was brought into the twentieth century by the establishment of a microwave system along the Alaska Highway. The CBC assumed responsibility for the volunteer radio stations in Dawson City and Whitehorse and, with the installation of low-power relay transmitters, expanded the network throughout Yukon and northern British Columbia.

I also succeeded in having the legislation governing Central Mortgage and Housing (predecessor of Canadian Mortgage and Housing Corporation) amended to allow Yukoners and residents of the Northwest Territories to obtain mortgage money.

The bridge constructed over the Yukon River at Whitehorse made residential housing lots available in the newly created subdivision across the river and resulted in a veritable housing boom between 1958 and 1963, during which the communities of Riverdale and Porter Creek mushroomed. The tarpaper shack look of Whitehorse gradually disappeared, and it became a modern, good-looking city.

When I first went to Ottawa, I was the perfect example of an idealist. I did not believe that the system was corrupt, and I did not believe that public servants were anything less than totally honest. I was not so naive as to believe that there were no dishonest persons in the world, including some politicians and some bureaucrats; but the general run of those in positions of power, I thought, were persons of probity and honour. By the time the 1963 election rolled around, I was rapidly becoming the country's number one cynic. The incident that caused me to change my views completely had to do with the building of a school at Old Crow.

When I first visited Old Crow, the isolated community in northern Yukon that had been denied a ballot box for so long, the only schooling available was provided in a small, one-room log cabin. The lighting throughout the long northern winters was supplied by Coleman lanterns. It was gloomy, dark, and dull, and when there were twenty-five or thirty young scholars confined in that space, the stink was appalling.

Such conditions would never have been tolerated in a southern community, and I failed to see why they should be tolerated in this largely native community. I therefore set to work to get a new school for Old Crow. After discussion with the native leaders, we thought that a new school should be large enough to accommodate twice as many students, to allow for growth. The people of Old Crow were eager to pitch in and work on the project themselves.

There was no difficulty in obtaining the support of the minister, who already knew the prime minister's views on the living conditions of northerners. Officials in the Department of Northern Affairs were instructed to plan the building of the school. Several months went by, and one day I visited the department to see how the plans were coming along. I was ushered around by the assistant deputy minister and introduced to the man in charge of the engineering branch. He showed me plans for a veritable palace of a school, with about eight classrooms, a laboratory, and living quarters, which included two- and three-bedroom suites for teachers. In all, the cost was approaching $400,000.

We had done our own estimates. A friend with experience in construction and I had worked out the probable cost of a two-room school with attached living quarters for one teacher. We had blended into our calculations the establishment of a portable sawmill which would put normally unemployed native people to work to supply the timbers required for building. The entire cost we came up with was $45,000.

"That is far too much money for far too much school," I told the bureaucrats, and, after some intense debate, they shaved about $75,000 off their estimates. But the project was left substantially as the bureaucrats had planned it. I urged them not to build the school at all rather than to waste such a huge amount of money. But, like Frankenstein, life had been breathed into the project and it could not now be stopped by a non-bureaucrat.

It did not end there. Old Crow is on the Porcupine River, and during the summer the normal transportation route there was aboard George Kirk's freighter, the good ship *MV Brainstorm*. The freight travelled as far as Dawson City, where it was loaded onto the *Brainstorm* and down the Yukon River to its confluence with the Porcupine River at Fort Yukon, Alaska, and from there up the Porcupine to Old Crow. The bureaucrats in Northern Affairs, however, decided that all of the construction materials, including such items as heavy Gyproc sheeting, were to be flown into Old Crow by chartered aircraft. This would be enormously expensive. (Our original plan called for an interior of locally harvested logs, common to many houses and public buildings in the North.) When I discovered the amount of freight that the bureaucracy intended to fly in, and the cost of it, I was absolutely astounded; I could not believe that the department would allow such a massive waste of taxpayers' dollars. Although I did not bother Alvin Hamilton with my continuing complaints about the school's design, I felt compelled to speak to him about the enormously costly and entirely unnecessary air freight. I had told his officials that they would have between May and September to move materials to Old Crow by river barge. Although none of them had been to Old Crow, they responded that the ice on the river system did not break up until mid-August and froze again in mid-September. No matter how often and how strenuously I told the mandarins that they were wrong, they would not accept my advice, and they pressed merrily ahead with plans for the use of air freight.

When I pressed the point with Alvin, he became impatient with me. "For heaven's sake," he said, "the river's only open for a month."

"Alvin," I replied, "they're lying to you. The river usually breaks up during the third week of May and does not normally freeze again until late October. Take it from me, I live there."

Alvin said, "I'm afraid I have to accept the advice of my experts."

I could not believe that Alvin, of all people, would have been so enslaved by the bureaucrats, but the evidence was plain. I thought there was still one chance. I said, "Look, if I send a telegram to

Chief Charlie Able at Old Crow, will you take his advice as to the time of break-up and freeze-up?"

"Go ahead," Alvin responded.

Chief Charlie must have thought I was mad when he read my request. I urged him to respond immediately, and he replied, "Break-up mid to late May. River freeze mid to late October."

Elated, I laid his reply before Alvin. After reading the telegram, Alvin looked at me, and then he said, "Well, Erik, the matter has gone so far now that I have to accept the advice of my bureaucrats."

The result was that the local air charter operator, Great Northern Airways, and an air charter service from the Northwest Territories were very busy that summer flying construction materials over the open Yukon River to Old Crow.

To this day I do not know if this perverse and expensive course was followed because of blind bureaucratic stupidity, or simply to prove that no one, no minister, MP, or local expert, was going to tell the Ottawa "experts" what to do.

That bitter experience showed me that the bureaucracy was a stubborn, immovable elephant; the elephant could not even be moved by the mahout—the minister who, in theory, is the elected authority in charge. I began to suspect that Alvin, whose integrity and determination I respected, could not possibly be alone.

I gradually learned that with every project I wished to bring to fruition, whether it was something major like the Roads to Resources program, or a lesser matter such as building a bridge, I not only had to gain the support and approval of the appropriate minister, I had to develop tactics to get those projects approved and designed without running into the serious problems that I had encountered with the Old Crow school. In short, I had to learn how to move the elephant, and I did. After the Old Crow school fiasco, I seldom if ever took a project idea directly to the minister, nor to the deputy minister, nor to the assistant deputy. My most successful tactic was to inject the idea at about the level of the chief assistant to the assistant chief and wait for it to seep slowly upwards, giving it a prod from time to time if necessary. Although this method was somewhat more time-consuming, by the time the idea reached the top, it had acquired bureaucratic authority and departmental approval and became the child of the minister as soon as he announced it. Since my concern was to get the project on the rails and the job done, I did not care who took the credit for the idea.

It remained for me only to congratulate the minister on being so familiar with the needs of the people in my constituency as to have produced such a brilliant solution to the problem. That approach stood me very well indeed throughout my tenure as a member of Parliament.

To work effectively for Yukon, I required two things: an effective approach to the bureaucrats, and the support of the prime minister. I came to know John Diefenbaker for the first time during his 1958 visit to Yukon.

That trip was enlivened by, among other things, the account by Charles King in the *Ottawa Journal* of the catching of what he called "the $10,000 fish." This was the cost attributed by King to the catching of one lake trout by the prime minister in Big Kathleen Lake.

The trip was not all that elaborate by modern standards of prime ministerial travel, but by the perceptions of that time, the planning seemed to be extensive. I believe that the Privy Council Office simply asked the Canadian Army to take control of the planning. Any lavishness was due to the army's idea of what was appropriate for a prime ministerial fishing-stop. They arranged for a huge marquee to be erected on the shores of Big Kathleen Lake, surrounded by several smaller tents jammed with supplies. A chef was supplied by the army and a marvellous luncheon spread laid on in the marquee for dozens of invited guests (including the press) to go "fishing" with the prime minister.

When I planned this part of the trip, I expected the expedition to include myself, my close friend Rolf Hougen, and a few others, perhaps half a dozen people in all, which is what Diefenbaker desired as well. But the army expanded the project until we had a small convention in the wilderness, including the usual brigade of journalists. It was a good thing Diefenbaker did not have to catch lunch for everyone. It was a windy, cool day, and the prime minister, with considerable determination, patience, and skill, eventually managed to land a very respectable lake trout, for which he was duly pilloried in the press.

During this trip I took advantage of every opportunity to inform the prime minister of the living conditions of Yukon residents compared to those in southern Canada—the lack of telephone service, roads, bridges, and electricity. I reminded him of the resolutions passed at the leadership convention at which he was elected, especially the Roads to Resources program. I detailed the housing problem for him and told him of the appalling conditions in which the native people were living—people who had supported me through three tough campaigns. Coming from Saskatchewan, the prime minister was not unfamiliar with hardship but he was nonetheless impressed by the particular harshness of the northern environment.

I told him that there were some people in Yukon who argued that the territory should declare war on Alaska, lose the war, and apply for aid under the Marshall Plan, as a result of which we would obtain assistance much sooner than we would ever get help from Ottawa.

I told him about Old Crow, and he was incensed when he learned that the residents of that isolated community who ordered supplies by mail, had no post office, so they put American stamps on their letters and sent them downriver to Circle City in Alaska, whence they travelled through the American postal system. One of Diefenbaker's first actions when he returned to Ottawa was to order the postmaster general to establish a post office in Old Crow.

During that visit, Diefenbaker was given the key to the City of Whitehorse by the mayor, Gordon Cameron. (He was one of those I had tried to recruit as a candidate, thinking he was a Conservative. He later did convert and has remained a Progressive Conservative ever since.) About 1,500 people came from all parts of Yukon to hear the prime minister speak on that occasion, a number well in excess of the adult population of the city.

Anything is possible once the prime minister becomes involved. On that trip, Old Crow was the beneficiary. That village had an inadequate school, no medical facilities, and poor housing conditions. The conditions at Old Crow in 1958 were the same as conditions in Fort Norman in 1929. During the first Diefenbaker government, we managed to move the elephant far enough to establish, besides postal services and the new school, a nursing station and new housing.

That trip had other benefits for Yukon. Dawson City, long a colourful but undeveloped tourist centre, became the focus of federal investment to preserve its historic heritage and to encourage the tourist industry. The Dawson loop was declared a site of national historic importance, and buildings such as the Grand Palace Theatre became tourist meccas. The entire restoration of Dawson City to refashion it as an authentic turn-of-the-century gold-rush community came from that early visit—although with some complications.

To allow the producing mines to better get their ores to market, bridges were built over the Stewart, Pelly, and Yukon rivers. Roads were built as part of the Roads to Resources Program. The Dempster Highway, which gives access to the North Slope and the Mackenzie Delta, was begun in this period. (Pearson sneered that this highway was "going from igloo to igloo" and that we were spending money "like drunken sailors" on the project. The highway took well over a decade to build, but one of the "igloos" was the Beaufort Sea and another was the North Slope.) The road contributed to the development of one of the largest-known petroleum reserves in the world, off the coast of Yukon and Alaska, and set the stage for the future exploitation of the Beaufort potential.

Whatever his other weaknesses, in that first term Diefenbaker delivered to northern Canada in spades. He sincerely believed in the northern vision others were so quick to ridicule. He did not simply create the vision for political purposes; he held a genuine belief that the 40 per cent of Canada north of the 60th parallel was a vast storehouse of resources needing only proper facilities and amenities to allow the development of its riches for the benefit of the nation as a whole—a conviction I hold to this day.

But it was on that first trip, too, that I began to see some of the flaws in his personality and character. I saw an overwhelming ego and a vanity that I thought would cause most people difficulty. During the Big Kathleen Lake fishing expedition, Diefenbaker asked me about the December by-election that had first elected me to Parliament. I explained that the only real difficulty was the charge of being poor sports by forcing the by-election in the first place. Then he said, "Well, did you have any trouble in March?" He left me in no doubt that he believed that I had been elected on his coattails and that I really owed my victory to him. It may well have been the case; his popularity was a factor in that victory, but modesty might have prevented him from making a point of it.

In later years, the traits I noticed on that trip were the ones that got him into trouble, both when he was in office and when he was Leader of the Opposition.

Diefenbaker was riding high in the polls at that time, and there was no reason why he could not have maintained that popularity for some time. The Progressive Conservative party, however, seems to suffer from what I call the prima donna syndrome. There are, in every Conservative caucus, almost as many prima donnas as there are members. But only one prima donna at a time can lead the caucus. There were too many other self-appointed candidates for the post to permit caucus stability, and Diefenbaker's ego would not let him understand or deal with the problem (a common failure of prima donnas). He saw leadership only in terms of himself and lacked the capacity to share any of his authority by taking others into his confidence. A successful leader must be able to work well with others, even when that means, as it often does in politics, submerging the expression of his own ego.

A prima donna like Diefenbaker comes to believe that so many people vote for him because of his superb qualities as an individual. It follows that he must be the best-liked, nicest, most beautiful person in the world. Freud once opined that all human beings seek to be the most desirable companion. Few believe they have attained that goal, but most of the few seem to turn up in politics.

Diefenbaker coveted the prime ministership as much for the fact that it fed his vanity as for the power it conferred on him. He wanted people to know he had that power—I suppose there is nothing odd in that—but given his ego he not only expected his will to prevail, he expected people to like it. Usually that is asking too much.

That combination did not sit well with the likes of Doug Harkness, Leon Balcer, Davie Fulton, Donald Fleming, and George Hees. They, too, had the syndrome in varying degrees; it was inevitable that they would first chafe and then rebel under Diefenbaker's leadership, and inevitable that he would never understand why they did so. It would be oversimplifying to say that the syndrome was the sole cause of the erosion of loyalty that eventually led to Diefenbaker's downfall—there were other factors—but the Chief's flawed personality did contribute substantially.

I therefore returned to Ottawa with a much clearer idea of my leader and of the tasks that lay before me. I returned to the capital alone. Two of the children were still babies, and I had to make some important personal decisions. Should we move to Ottawa? What should I do about my law partnership? Would our income be sufficient? I was entitled to draw the full salary of an MP—

$8,000, plus a $4,000 tax-free allowance for travel, telephone, and other expenses. During my first year in Parliament, I went considerably further into debt (I still owed Cockeram $15,000) as a result of the meagre remuneration. In travel alone, I spent well over $5,000, flying the old DC-3 and DC-6B between Whitehorse and Ottawa.

It was impossible for me to meet the expenses of being a member of Parliament. Had I not maintained some income from the law practice, I would have sunk even more deeply into debt than I did. However, I soon had other things to worry about besides money.

Chapter Seven

The Flying MP

To combat may be glorious, and success
Perhaps may crown us; but to fly is safe.

William Cowper

There were in those days no set times for Parliament to convene and recess; the parliamentary workload was established by the government, and the House sat until the government's program was completed. If the opposition chose to become entrenched and bloody-minded, as was its wont, Prime Minister Diefenbaker's solution was to extend not only the hours of sitting—at one time the House was in session from 11:00 a.m. until 11:00 p.m.—but also the days of sitting.

As the heat of the summer rose, so did the tempers of the MPs. The combination usually resulted in a rapid dispatch of government business, so that the House would recess some time during July. As soon as that happened, I was off to Yukon and my family.

Upon arrival in Yukon, I would engage in my law practice to supplement my income and would travel widely to visit my constituents and maintain contact with the party organization. I would visit Dawson City, usually on the Discovery Day weekend, travel the loop, and visit placer-miner camps to renew acquaintances and pass the time of day with some of the old-timers and others on the creeks.

I also caught up on the stories about what had happened during the winter. One such story concerned Phil, a placer-miner whom I used to visit. As did many old people there, he lived alone in his cabin on the "lay" of ground. One winter, he had not been heard from by his neighbours for some time. When they went to look, they found Phil frozen in his cabin. He had died of a sudden heart attack, fallen to the ground with his limbs asprawl, and frozen that way. The RCMP arranged for the removal of Phil's frozen body to the custody of the local undertaker.

In most Yukon communities, there was not the volume of business to justify a resident professional undertaker, so the task usually fell to a local citizen who volunteered—or was volunteered—to do the work. In Dawson City the job had fallen to a chap named Fred Cook. He did not care for the distasteful chore at all and often hit the bottle when he knew that he was going to have to perform the duties. Because of this work, Fred came to be known as Digger Cook. Digger's place of business was one of the smallest clapboard shacks in Dawson City, but it was scrupulously neat and tidy. There he would prepare the corpse for burial.

For the most part, Yukoners died intestate and with very few assets. Their estates were looked after by the public administrator for Yukon, a federal official who would pay all funeral expenses for a fixed fee. The standard rate for embalming and burial in Dawson City was $250, but because of the condition of Phil's corpse, with its limbs frozen in various grotesque attitudes, Digger Cook thought that the straightening process was worth an extra $50. This the public administrator refused to pay. So Digger refused to bury poor old Phil, and there was a sort of Mexican standoff between the two. Phil had been transported to Digger's little mortuary in February. The impasse continued through March and most of April, with Phil still frozen on the mortuary table. The temperature rose in April, and since Digger had no refrigeration facilities in his place, he put the corpse in the community freezer, where the locals stored their meat and game. The locals naturally became quite annoyed at the continued presence of frozen Phil and soon began to complain. So did Digger Cook. His wife wrote me a letter about the standoff. I knew that a direct appeal was unlikely to move the bureaucracy, so, after informing the department officials of the situation, I called Richard Jackson, a reporter with the *Ottawa Journal*. The story appeared on the front page of the *Journal* the next day, under a banner headline.

The instruction from the Department of Northern Affairs to the public administrator in Yukon to cough up the extra $50 for Digger Cook was issued at once, and frozen Phil was finally straightened and laid to rest in Dawson City cemetery. He was not the first nor the last miner living alone on the gold creeks to die and freeze in such a fashion. Indeed, Robert Service wrote of many such incidents in his poems.

My friend and co-Conservative Johnny Friend was elected in much the same way as Digger Cook to serve as undertaker in Watson Lake, the southernmost Yukon community on the Alaska Highway. Johnny also looked after the grading and maintenance of the streets in the community. One winter, a man had a fatal accident on the highway about twenty-five miles south of Watson Lake. Johnny, as the local tow-truck operator, was called by the RCMP to tow the car, complete with its frozen contents, into town.

Johnny was not skilled in the art of undertaking, and he had no idea how to straighten the arms and legs of the dead traveller, who had died and frozen in a sitting position holding the steering wheel. The options were to provide a warm enough environment for the corpse to slowly thaw, or to straighten the limbs and bury him quickly. Johnny opted for the quicker route. So it came about that a visitor to his garage early one morning was startled to find Johnny with a body on the floor of his garage. He had placed it underneath the blade of the grader he used to clear the roads; he would lower the blade onto one limb at a time to straighten it. There are, indeed, strange things done...

During those early years, while recognizing that it was next to impossible to set up an additional home in Ottawa, P.J. and I thought we might be able to be together in the summers at least, so one summer we drove our station wagon all the way to Wakefield, Quebec, near Ottawa, where we had rented a spacious summer house on the Gatineau River. We spent a very happy summer there. The children discovered garter snakes and many other forms of life that do not exist north of 60. However, the expense of living in the south for even that short period confirmed that, for the time being at least, it was financially impossible to maintain two residences, or to have my family with me.

There were three commuting options. I could drive all the way from Whitehorse to Ottawa, which took eight to ten days, three of them on the Alaska Highway. Or I could fly from Whitehorse to Edmonton and take the train to Ottawa from there. Every MP was entitled to a railway pass for himself and his family, so that option was cheaper than driving all the way. The third option was to fly all the way from Whitehorse to Ottawa, a very expensive proposition in those days. Only the portion from Whitehorse to Edmonton was covered by expenses. Therefore I travelled mainly by car or train.

Before amendments were made to members' services and allowances, telephone calls, telegrams, and other forms of communication were paid for by each member—that was what the tax-free allowance was for, but it could not begin to cover the expense of keeping in touch with a Yukon riding.

I was careful not to incur costs that would further prejudice the fiscal stability of my family, but it was inevitable that a fair portion of the budget would be eaten into by expenses incurred either in carrying out government business or keeping up the political organization in my riding. (In those days, there was no reason to expect that any honest person would ever become wealthy by getting elected MP.)

By the time the first Pearson minority government was formed in 1963, however, when I had been an MP for more than five years, the supplementary income from my law practice provided enough to establish a permanent residence in Ottawa. Even better, the practice was growing sufficiently to allow the purchase of a single-engine Cessna 180 aircraft, which I used mostly for business commuting in Yukon but which I could also use to commute between Whitehorse and Ottawa.

This provided not only transportation but a renewal of my first love, flying. It is difficult to describe how much I enjoyed the flight from Ottawa to Whitehorse in a float-equipped airplane, as the broad sweep of the nation unfolded below.

Before one of these trips to Yukon, I told John Diefenbaker that P.J. and the children were accompanying me across the country. He insisted that I stop in Prince Albert on the way, to meet the mayor and other Progressive Conservative supporters.

One brilliant sunny afternoon we landed on the North Saskatchewan River near Prince Albert. As I taxied towards the dock, I saw a large group of people waiting for us on the riverbank. They were gaily dressed in bright summer finery, whereas I was in bush clothes—khaki shirt and trousers and waterproof Greb boots—and P.J. and the children were dressed for comfort. As we came up to the dock, about twenty people moved out onto it. The dock began to sink. One lady dressed all in white—hat, dress, high-heeled shoes—was carrying a large bouquet which she probably meant to give to P.J. She was advancing on us when I disembarked and told her rather brusquely, "Get off the dock!" This must have seemed unfriendly, but just then the dock plunged a little and half the crowd got a good deposit of muddy water on their shoes. We managed to tie up, and we had a pleasant chat with everyone once they had retreated to the riverbank, and then went on our way. Diefenbaker himself did not put in an appearance—he was in Ottawa—although his brother Elmer was on hand.

My usual refuelling stop in Saskatchewan was near Saskatoon, where I made arrangements for someone to meet me at the river with aviation fuel. The first time I went there, with no arrangement made in advance, I landed on the river and taxied to the shore close to a large building above a thirty-foot embankment. As I walked up the embankment and towards the building, I noticed several men working about the grounds, all of them dressed just like me in khaki clothes and bush boots. The building turned out to be a hospital. I asked a nurse if I could use the telephone, and she said, "Certainly." I called the flying school, which agreed to truck some fuel down to the river. Then I struck up a conversation with the nurse.

She said, "I haven't seen you before."

"Oh," I said, "I'm just travelling through."

"How are you travelling?"

I explained that my airplane was parked on the river.

"Oh, yes?" She had a very odd expression on her face.

I returned to the aircraft to wait for the fuel. The chap who eventually arrived from the flying school told me that I had landed at the Saskatchewan mental hospital. It's a wonder I ever got out of there!

It was in that same Cessna 180, in late April 1963, that I and my family were travelling from Whitehorse to Dawson City to attend a Kiwanis dinner, at which I was to speak. Although my pre-flight weather briefing had been for clear flying all the way, about forty miles south of Dawson City, near Gravel Lake, we ran into heavy snow. I decided to turn back the way we had come, where I knew the weather was clear. Unfortunately, the snowstorm was moving more rapidly than we were, and it was now just as bleak behind us as ahead. By this time we were about 300 feet above the ground in very hilly terrain, and the visibility was getting worse and worse. We could not safely proceed, so I decided to land on the highway.

I found a long, straight stretch of road and made an approach with full flap, which allowed me to approach at a low speed, about fifty miles an hour. By the time the wheels touched ground, the speed was down to about thirty-five miles an hour. It was a fine, classic precautionary landing, until about 50 yards down the road. The road was covered with wet slush, and there were two high windrows of snow left by the graders on either side.

The Cessna was equipped with self-cocking wheels, a feature designed for student flyers in crosswind landings. If the student erred in not straightening out the sideways drift in the touchdown, the wheels would cock automatically, and although the plane might be crabbing sideways, the wheels would take it straight down the runway. That feature was to be my nemesis, for, even though the plane was proceeding straight down the road, in the slushy snow on the semi-frozen ruts, the self-cocking wheels took a turn to the left. We hit the snowbank on one side of the road and the airplane flipped onto its back. This broke the main spar and the back of the airplane. It was a complete write-off.

We were all hanging upside down in our seatbelts. I looked around, and miraculously, no one was even scratched. Then, in the eerie silence, ten-year-old Rick complained, "Gee, Dad, I thought you said you were going to land on the highway."

We got out of the airplane as quickly as possible. The road maintenance man at Gravel Lake, who lived nearby, was soon on the scene and took us to his home. P.J. was quite shaken up, but since no one was hurt, I telephoned Dawson City and the Kiwanis came to pick us up. We made the dinner in time, I made my speech, and we returned in due course to Whitehorse.

I made a point of not flying my own plane on campaign trips. Much as I loved flying, I reasoned that I could not manage the total concentration required for safe flying when I was thinking about politics. Fortunately, I always had enough friends in the flying community either to donate their time or to persuade their employers to provide employee pilots for me. Most of the travel in the early campaigns had to be done by aircraft, because there was no other way. In the winter, for example, Old Crow is still accessible only by air.

Another occasion when we found ourselves in a predicament requiring a highway landing was on the return flight from a campaign trip to Old Crow. I, of course, was not flying; the pilot was

George Landry. We had two passengers: Joe Netro and his wife, Hannah, from Old Crow. We ran into the large, wet snowflakes of a storm. We had just passed Parkinson's Strip, an airstrip deep in the rugged Ogilvie mountains northeast of Dawson City. I had urged George to land there, but did not insist, and he continued into the storm.

Eventually, we could not fly any farther in that weather. The visibility was deteriorating when we reached Chapman Lake, nearly 100 miles up the Dempster Highway. George looked over the section of road upon which he would have to land. It was covered with about ten inches of snow; deep for a Cessna 180 to cope with. There was a small wooden bridge at the end of the landing run. Such was George's flying skill that he made a perfect landing on the road, coming to rest about fifteen feet from the end of the bridge. We stayed overnight at the maintenance camp at Chapman Lake and carried on by car the next morning.

During winter campaigns, it was best not to stay overnight in the remoter communities, since it is extremely difficult to start an airplane engine in forty-five-below weather. If there was no other course, the pilot would have to drain the crankcase oil into a pail that we carried in the aircraft, remove the battery, and take pail and battery indoors for the night. In the morning, the engine would be covered with a canvas tent and warmed with a plumber's pot underneath. When the frost was off, the oil would be replaced and the heating continued until the engine was warm enough to start.

The exigencies of winter travel meant that some of our political visits had to be short. At Old Crow, where the intense cold always made restarting the engine chancy, the pilot would stay with the plane while I went into the village and talked to as many people as possible. We would be on the ground from ten or eleven in the morning until two or three in the afternoon—that is, the daylight hours in the northern winter. The pilot would warm up the engine from time to time while he waited for me to finish visiting the village. Somewhat different from campaigning in Rosedale or Westmount.

Air travel allowed me to get around my riding and to make sure I was in on anything that happened. During the Pearson minority government, when John Turner was parliamentary secretary to the minister of northern affairs, Arthur Laing, he accompanied the minister on a visit to Yukon. Laing was to visit Mayo and United Keno Hill Mines at Elsa, north of Whitehorse. I did not want these two Liberals touring my bailiwick without me, so I offered to help. Arthur did not take me up on this, but I thought I should go along anyway. I flew to Mayo in a Beaver to welcome them there. Laing did not seem overjoyed to see me.

I knew John Turner quite well, since he was practising with the law firm of Stikeman Elliott in Montreal, and his firm and mine had some clients in common. He seemed to want to visit with me, so I said, "Well, if you're fed up with this formal tour, why don't you fly back to Whitehorse with me in the Beaver?" John said he would be delighted.

There is a gravel bar in the Stewart River, known to anyone who has flown in and out of the river on floats. I taxied along the river until I had enough room for a safe takeoff run—it did not have to be a long distance in a Beaver. I lifted one float out of the water on the takeoff, a common practice to get airborne more quickly, and skimmed along on the other float. The gravel bar came up very quickly and passed right under us. This was not unusual, but John thought it was, and thought that we had had a very close call. He mentioned it to me again not long ago. The only real danger he faced was from Arthur Laing, who was not pleased at the desertion of his parliamentary secretary. As far as I was concerned, the weather was good, the flight uneventful, and I had a pleasant visit with John.

To keep my hand in, and because Great Northern Airways, the local charter firm, was having trouble getting pilots with DC-3 experience, I flew for them as much as I could when the House was not in session. I continued to fly all types of aircraft for them until the company went into receivership in 1974.

Any visitor to Whitehorse airport will notice a DC-3 aircraft weather vane, with the registration CF-CPY, standing on a pedestal. It was one of the airplanes I flew for Great Northern, and I was in it when it made its last flight. Joseph Langlois, a GNA pilot, was the captain on that occasion, and I was first officer. The cargo was a load of meat for Inuvik—the plane was so full that we had to crawl over the cargo to get into the cockpit. On the takeoff run, it is the responsibility of the first officer to follow through with the left hand behind the throttles and take over whenever the captain decides he wants both hands on the control column. Normally, the captain will open the taps, as we say, and advance the throttles about halfway to get the aircraft rolling, and then transfer his right hand to the control column to ensure control for takeoff. As soon as the captain takes his right hand from the throttles, the first officer continues advancing them until takeoff power registers on the instruments.

We had reached that stage on our takeoff run: the tail of the plane had left the ground, and we were almost at takeoff speed; in another two or three seconds we would have been airborne. At this point, the starboard engine caught fire. The routine sequence to meet that kind of emergency is to shut down the fuel through the mixture control, retard the pitch and the throttle, and actuate the fire extinguisher. We did this and Joe brought the aircraft safely to a halt. Had we taken off with that load, there is no question that we would have crashed. Although a DC-3 is a good flyer on one engine at altitude, in those conditions we would not have maintained altitude, and we could not have turned back to the airport to land.

There were many miserable aspects to hauling freight by air. One of the most troublesome was the transportation of forty-five-gallon fuel drums full of gasoline or diesel oil into remote areas for heavy-duty equipment. Many exploration companies used the winter months to fly the fuel into camps that would be operating in the spring and summer, since heavy loads could be flown onto the frozen surfaces of nearby lakes. (This requires some careful judgment; on one such exercise, a Hercules aircraft went through the ice. It is still on the bottom of Baker Lake, near Whitehorse.)

Most of my fuel hauling was done during the summer recess from the House of Commons, and I did not have to contend with cold weather. A pilot hauling fuel with a Beaver would usually have a swamper along, whose job it was to help load and unload the barrels, which weighed 450 to 500 pounds each. On one fuel haul, into Swim Lake, near Cyprus Anvil Mines, Great Northern asked me to take forty-five drums of fuel in—alone. The Beaver can handle 1,500 pounds at a time. It took fifteen trips of fifty minutes each way to bring in the forty-five drums. A lot of flying and a lot of hard work.

Each barrel had to be jockeyed into the Beaver and then worked around: the barrels had to be in exactly the right configuration to get three of them aboard. They had to be unloaded the same way.

Because of the heavy load, the aircraft's floats would ground in the shallow water some distance from shore. To do the unloading, I had to use long poles as a ramp. I hacked these from the spruce forest with an axe, limbed them until they were smooth, and notched them so they would grip the plane's doorframe. Then each barrel was tilted onto its side and rolled out the door. Gravity and the poles steered it ashore. There were only four inches of clearance past the wing strut, so I prayed that each 500-pound barrel would miss the strut and not drop onto the float. That would have crippled the aircraft, and would have cost about $6,000 to repair.

The flying was delightful, the work back-breaking, but at the time it seemed well worth it, even if it was not the usual employ of an off-duty MP. Not that I was ever really off-duty. I often met Yukoners in remote camps and talked politics with them. Sharing bunkhouses with the workers did not do me any harm when the campaigns warmed up again. They knew I knew how to work, even if they did not know that I got only ten dollars a flying hour as a token payment for wages.

Chapter Eight

The Diefenbaker Parliaments

*"What is a Caucus-race?" said Alice; not that she
much wanted to know, but the Dodo had paused as
if it thought that somebody ought to speak, and no
one else seemed inclined to say anything.*

*"Why," said the Dodo, "the best way to explain
it is to do it."*

*First it marked out a race-course, in a sort of
circle ("the exact shape doesn't matter," it said),
and then all the party were placed along the course,
here and there. There was no "One, two, three, and
away!" but they began running when they liked,
and left off when they liked, so that it was not easy
to know when the race was over.*

Lewis Carroll, *Alice's Adventures in Wonderland*

My life in Yukon was quite a different matter from my life in Ottawa,
and I often wondered what some of my colleagues in the House of
Commons would have thought had they been able to see me wrestling fuel drums off an airplane in the bush, or bedding down in
a bunkhouse or native tent, or scrambling over a cargo of meat in
a DC-3, or appearing in the Supreme Court to argue a case.

I lived two very different lives in two vastly different worlds.
Pioneer standards applied north of 60—deals were sealed on a hand-
shake, self-reliance was the daily gauge of living, and personal honour, integrity, and loyalty were highly prized. These were not the
standards, as I discovered by bitter experience, that applied in
Ottawa.

Although I have spent, and still spend, much of my time in
Ottawa, where I have made many friends and achieved some prominence (notoriety?), I have never really been at home there. The
reasons become clear in contrasting the Ottawa scene when John

Diefenbaker was prime minister with the scene when we moved to the opposition side of the House of Commons.

Polling day for the election of members to the Twenty-Fourth Parliament was on March 31, 1958. It was the third election within eight months in Yukon, and there was never any doubt about the outcome. The efficiency of the organization in Yukon guaranteed that a Progressive Conservative would be elected.

After the writs were in, I again made the long journey to Ottawa. I was assigned an office on the fifth floor of the Centre Block of the House of Commons, next to the cafeteria. Rather, I was assigned part of that office by our party whip, Elston Cardiff (he was later replaced by John Pallett). I had to share with another MP, since there was no such thing as the generosity of space that exists today. My office mate was John Pratt, whose riding was Jacques Cartier-LaSalle in Montreal. He was known to me as the author and star of *The Navy Show*, from which came the hit song "You'll Get Used To It." He had a highly developed sense of humour.

Our office was divided so that his desk faced one wall and mine faced the other. He kept a sign on his desk that read "Ici on parle franglais." When he had visitors, I would have to leave the office and roam the halls, to make room for them; similarly, if he had something confidential to discuss with a constituent, I had to make myself scarce. He would accommodate me in the same fashion, though I had very few visitors.

There was no such thing as an individual secretary for each member; we had to rely on the secretarial pool on the lower level of the building. When services were required, even for something as simple as correspondence, someone from the pool was sent along, and often it was a different secretary each time—a very unsatisfactory state of affairs. I had to keep up my law practice, because I could not afford to live on the parliamentary stipend, but managing such a practice from 4,000 miles away was very nearly impossible, in the straitened circumstances in which I found myself, without adequate secretarial help. Therefore, I hired a secretary in Ottawa. That meant another desk in an already crowded office. Her desk was next to mine, and she shared my view of the blank wall. She also had to join me in the corridor when John had confidential business to conduct.

In 1963, when conditions were improved for members, we were each allotted a secretary, but by this time my legal secretary was well established. This meant that our small office had to accommodate five souls: two MPs and three secretaries, with five desks in all. It was slightly crowded.

It was a major accomplishment in that Parliament, getting to know 208 Conservative MPs and becoming familiar with the committee system. In that term, I did most of my work in committees. A check in the Hansard index for 1958 under "Nielsen, Mr. Erik (Yukon)" reveals only eleven entries, beginning with my speech seconding the Speech from the Throne (by tradition, the seconder is a new MP) and ending with my comments on amendments to the Yukon Act, which brought about a number of reforms in the administration of the territory. (These reforms included broadening the powers of the commissioner to borrow or lend money, a necessity to implement new low-rental housing, road construction, hospital services, and the like. I said in support of change, "I feel that it will do a lot towards achieving provincial status and autonomy eventually for the Yukon." Today, such status is further off than ever, and perhaps rendered impossible by the Meech Lake Accord.)

The sparse record of Hansard does not reflect the extent of the work I was doing in committee, nor the amount I was learning about the machinery of government, with the help of some of my caucus colleagues. One of the first members to advise me was J.W. Murphy, from Lambton West, in Ontario. He was chairman of the Standing Committee on Lands, Forests and Waters. His best advice to me was "never throw anything away, put everything in writing, and always make a copy" of anything I wrote. I thought that advice was very sound and I followed it. Consequently, after thirty years, I have a thorough record of all my activities and communications.

In that first Parliament, I developed a great admiration for Howard Green, who was minister of public works when I first took my seat in the House, and later became secretary of state for external affairs after the sudden death of Dr. Sidney Smith. I do not believe there was a soul in Ottawa who did not respect the high degree of honesty and integrity that Howard Green displayed at all times. I sought his advice often on matters that touched ethics and the standards that should be maintained by MPs, and always received sound advice, which I followed. In my later years in Parliament, I often harkened back to that advice.

Alvin Hamilton, minister of northern affairs and natural resources, was another of my early mentors, and we renewed the friendship that began over the Roads to Resources program conceived at the 1956 leadership convention. He certainly was the key minister who unlocked doors in Northern Affairs, although even he was often undermined by the entrenched bureaucracy.

My particular problems as an MP were quite different from those of most members because, in Yukon, the federal government also acted as the provincial and municipal authority. Local autonomy in those days was unheard of, and as a result, the range of problems was much wider than in a provincial constituency. In order to have a new sewer or water system installed, for example, we had to have the direct involvement of the federal government. For solutions to these problems I often worked with Howard Green. Justice Minister Davie Fulton, Agriculture Minister Doug Harkness (who later became defence minister), Labour Minister Michael Starr, Fisheries Minister Angus MacLean—all wore provincial or municipal hats in connection with Yukon affairs, and all had to be lobbied to obtain approval for projects. Transport in the North was always a major problem, and Transport Minister George Hees, who was most effectively approached through Mel Jack, his capable executive assistant, was another of those with whom I found myself working. George was one of the first federal members to visit Yukon during that Parliament. The defence establishment in the territory meant that I also worked with the defence minister, first George R. Pearkes, V.C., a former Canadian Army major-general, then, after he was named lieutenant-governor of British Columbia in 1960, Doug Harkness.

I had to get to know all these ministers, and quickly. Some were much more effective than others, but all, in the end, were dependent to a greater or lesser measure on the bureaucracy. Therefore, in addition to dealing with the ministers, I had to apply Nielsen's Golden Rule for Moving the Elephant.

It is significant, I think, that Prime Minister Diefenbaker, on his first visit to Yukon, pledged that the policy of the Progressive Conservative government was to meet the legitimate aspirations of Yukoners to become a province if they should so desire. In a public address in Whitehorse in 1958, the prime minister expressed the hope that by Canada's centennial year, 1967, Yukon would be Canada's eleventh province. (That progressive attitude ceased abruptly when Pearson became prime minister in 1963 and has not since seen the light of day save for the brief months of the Clark government.)

I kept fairly busy during those first four years. The House of Commons was vastly more exciting (and better populated) than it is today, and the committee work was far more concentrated. The level of debate and the quality of the speeches in the House were superior; the good debaters and the good speakers were a constant topic of discussion among members of all parties. When one of the better speakers was expected to engage in the debate, there would not be an empty seat in the Commons chamber—nor in the press gallery. When Arthur Maloney delivered his speech in the first capital punishment debate, it was standing room only, and there was many a tear shed during the delivery of his twenty-minute speech on one of the most emotional topics of the day. I did not agree at all with the stand he took (he was opposed to any form of capital punishment), but I was mesmerized by the quality of his oratory.

Debates took place in the atmosphere of a free spontaneous exchange—sometimes a violent, clashing exchange—of views. Yet always, even during the most violent debates, decorum was maintained. There was little of the raucous heckling that seems to be the order of the day since the installation of television and electronically controlled microphones on members' desks. (This behaviour, intended to entertain home viewers, has nothing to do with debating; sometimes the shouting reaches such a level that no one can be heard, not even the Speaker.) Until this change, the sound system consisted of a number of microphones suspended from the ceiling, with muted speakers on members' desks. The system was sufficiently sensitive to carry a normal speaking voice to all corners of the House. Heckling, which is bound to occur in any Parliament, could be voiced and heard without any need to shout. Nowadays, if the microphone at a member's desk is turned off, he or she must shout to be heard.

The modernization of the sound system and the invasion of television have destroyed the fundamental purpose of the House of Commons as a meeting place for elected representatives to make decisions. Even the most important of matters are now debated with seldom more than thirty members in their seats, even during debates over bills involving billions of dollars, attendance is maintained at a bare quorum. When huge sums are being spent, or crucial decisions being made, we should expect not only a vigorous, high-quality debate but the attendance of at least three-quarters of the MPs.

Another aspect of this decline has been the gradual disappearance of the prime minister and leaders of the opposition, to say nothing of cabinet ministers, from the debating process. It is rare indeed now for a government leader to take part in anything but Question Period and a few set-piece occasions in the House. In the Twenty-Fourth Parliament, it was common for the leaders to engage in debate, but gradually that custom has disappeared. What is the point of a prime minister or an opposition leader coming to the House to lead an important debate on an important issue if he is always greeted by loud, boorish heckling? I would be the last to advocate that the House of Commons should be run like a Sunday school. The House is a forum for the vigorous exchange of views, but there is no reason why those exchanges must be reduced to name-calling contests.

Diefenbaker was a great orator and a great debater, and the House of Commons was often enthralled by the verbal duels that took place between him and Lester Pearson, M.J. Coldwell, Tommy Douglas, and David Lewis. Though I admired these skills greatly, I was seldom close enough to the prime minister to tell him how much I enjoyed his performances.

Even in caucus, which is supposed to be an intimate meeting of members and cabinet ministers, there was seldom any opportunity to speak with the prime minister about personal or even constituency matters. Picture if you will a meeting of 178 MPs, all trying to put their views and riding matters forward to thirty cabinet ministers, including the prime minister, within the space of two or three hours each week, and you will understand why my first four years as a parliamentarian brought me no more intimate a knowledge of our prime minister than when I first met him.

I had had no intention of seeking a career in politics when I first agreed to run for office, and the three election campaigns of 1957-58 had given me no opportunity to make long-term plans. The four-year term at last offered me the time to reflect and choose someone to replace me so that I would not be required to run again. However, during the closing months of that Twenty-Fourth Parliament, cracks began to show in the government. Some of the decisions that were taken were undermining party unity not only in Ottawa but throughout the country, and Yukon was no exception. Decisions such as the one to discontinue the production of the Arrow aircraft, although directly affecting business in Ontario, had a profound effect on political support in Yukon. Disunity was surfacing more and more within our caucus, where expressions of lack of confidence in the party leadership were being heard more and more often.

Legitimate criticisms were being voiced; indeed, there are some remarkable similarities between the Progressive Conservative caucus of those days and some of the events that are occurring today. I suppose the rational explanation is that while a party is enjoying a honeymoon with the electorate, the members themselves are happy, because they bask in the security of knowing that they in all probability will be re-elected. When members begin feeling insecure about their re-election, they become restive in caucus. In my view, that is regrettable, since it reflects an attitude more concerned with the selfish interests of the individual than with the best interests of the party and consequently of the country. It has always been my view that if it served Canada and the party better to endorse an unpopular policy or position, though it would mean the loss of the Yukon seat in Parliament, that would be the proper course to follow. I recognize that I am in a substantial minority in holding that view, but that has always been my approach.

I must say that in exercising this philosophy I was careful at first not to propound it needlessly, for it could have cost electoral support if constituents thought that their member of Parliament would not respect the majority opinion in the riding on any given issue. I therefore exercised due care in voicing these views until the death of my wife, P.J., in 1969. After that, I came to the conclusion that there were more important things in life than getting re-elected, and I felt free to express my opinions, however unpopular, in public. To my astonishment, I found that if anything, this helped me at the polls. The moral to be learned from this is that hypocrisy is not essential to get elected.

The election of 1962 gave birth to another minority government and another short-lived Parliament, and it was during these ten months that I had the opportunity to form an in-depth assessment of the character of Prime Minister Diefenbaker. As unrest in his ministry and in the caucus had increased, the cracks had begun to show in his personality. His stubbornness, his pride, and his supreme ego stood him in poor stead in dealing with the kinds of problems that confronted him, and that were growing almost daily. The more active the cabals, the more aloof he became; the more serious the plotting against his continued tenure, the more icily he ignored these disloyal activities. He refused to confront the problems by trying to convince his detractors of the folly of their ways; instead, he relied totally on his standing as prime minister of the country. That fact alone, he seemed to think, would insure that there would be no disloyalty. He treated the ills that beset the land, from rising unemployment to a serious breach with the Americans over defence policy, as if they were nothing more than terriers yapping at his heels.

When we look back today, we can see that much of the damage that was done had more to do with appearance than reality. In the midst of the 1962 election, for example, it became necessary to devalue the Canadian dollar from $1.02 U.S. to 92.5 cents U.S., a move that enormously improved Canada's trading position because it made our goods much cheaper on international markets. This change, which was overall a positive one, became a subject of endless wrangles among cabinet ministers as to whether the devaluation should have taken place, whether the dollar should be pegged or allowed to float free, and at what level it should be set. The public was left with the impression that cabinet was in total disarray. The financial pundits leapt in with pronouncements that the change would be very harmful to Canada, the Liberals took up the refrain with their famous "Diefendollar," which looked like Monopoly money, and an intelligent policy was made to appear foolish and panicky.

The governor of the Bank of Canada, James Coyne, propounded his own economic theories, which were quite at odds with the government's position. The proper course was to secure his dismissal, but this too created a split in the cabinet, daily leaked to the press, and Coyne became the hero of the media. Again, a perfectly clear course of action became bogged down in factional squabbling that left the people of Canada with the impression of a government gone awry.

Similarly, the disagreement about North American defence policy (a policy on which, in my view, the prime minister was quite wrong) became a day-by-day round of speculation about who was leaking what from the cabinet, who disagreed with whom, and how strong were the anti-Diefenbaker forces within the party. The prime minister ignored all this, but the foundations of his support were being seriously eroded.

These were some of the incidents that demolished the Diefenbaker majority and led to the 1962 minority government, but very little was learned from these lessons. As Parliament staggered from day to day and the government drew necessary support from the Social Credit party, the activity of the cabals within the party grew ever more frenzied; the scent of blood was in the air, but Diefenbaker went on behaving as though everything would come out right.

In the end, inevitably, the government lost a vote of confidence in the House of Commons, and we were plunged into another election. Immediately following the defeat on the vote in the House, with the election set for April 8, 1963, an extraordinary caucus meeting was held, a two-day affair intended to "clear the air." It was held in the Railway Committee Room, a long, high chamber on the first floor of the Centre Block, which was jammed with 116 MPs, as well as senators and senior officials.

At that meeting, the leaders of the party let their hair down. Like most backbenchers, I had nothing to say. Most of the speaking was done by members of the cabinet and some senators, some of whom had already resigned. The discussion was astonishingly frank; I was astounded by some of the criticisms of the government I was hearing from ministers for the first time. It constituted an open confession to caucus of a total absence of cabinet solidarity. On that first day, with Diefenbaker mostly silent, the tension was so great that I was expecting an explosion at any moment, but it did not come until the next day.

On the second day the accusations started flying. Some of those who had left the cabinet now began to have their say, among them Doug Harkness, who had resigned over defence policy, and Léon Balcer, who had accepted a cabinet post, but who could not accept Diefenbaker as party leader. The caucus deteriorated rapidly into chaos, and I felt absolutely sick about what I was seeing and hearing from these leaders of my party. I wanted to do something about it, I wanted to make Davie Fulton and George Hees and others of similar inclination, who had served with Diefenbaker and who seemed to be bent on undermining his authority, realize what they were doing to our party, what they had already done to a government that had been elected with the greatest majority in history. Now they were putting the funeral touches on that effort.

Suddenly, Angus MacLean, the minister of fisheries, delivered an impassioned plea for unity. This was the Angus MacLean that we all knew as a quiet, unassuming man, never raising his voice or showing emotion; now here he was with tears streaming down his face, trying to pull these ministers together. He was doing just what I had wanted to do and in a far more effective way than I could ever have done. He carried an enormous amount of respect in caucus, but, while I am sure he touched every heartstring there, he failed to reach the reason of those who were hell-bent on pursuing their destructive course. If Angus's words, delivered so emotionally, could not pull things together, nothing would.

After he had finished speaking, George Hees and Davie Fulton came up with their familiar old line—we were doomed to defeat in the election unless we had a change in leadership. Then Senator Grattan O'Leary, known as "a silver-tongued orator," jumped up on a table and made another plea for unity. Grattan was absolutely superb. When Angus was speaking, he was the only one in tears, but when Grattan finished, many members were openly wiping their eyes. When caucus concluded that day, the press outside were quickly aware that something momentous had happened. They were treated to the astonishing sight of George Hees striding out of the caucus with his arm around Diefenbaker, proclaiming his undying allegiance to party unity.

"We're going out to lick the Grits!" George thundered in cheerleader fashion. "We're going to go into this election and give them hell!" He withdrew the statement made earlier in caucus that he would not run again. He told us, "I'm not going to be the one to be blamed for losing an election because of disunity in the party. All for one and one for all."

The next day, he sent Diefenbaker a letter announcing that he was no longer a Conservative candidate. I realize that the Christian thing to do would be to find it in my heart to forgive him, but I cannot. It is my view that if it had not been for Hees and Fulton and Balcer, the 1962 election would not have resulted in a minority government, and the 1963 election would never have taken place. Diefenbaker would have been prime minister for a dozen or more years.

More importantly, the party would have been in office long

enough to put some kind of Conservative face on the country. Although the Diefenbaker government in five and a half years accomplished much—from Roads to Resources to the Bill of Rights—it did not accomplish any lasting changes in the fabric of our country.

Unless two things occur, that is not going to change. There must be, first, a return to a more conservative philosophy by the Progressive Conservative party itself and, second, enough time in office to consolidate change. The health of any democracy relies on alternating political forces being in office, each long enough to affect the direction of national progress to the point at which the electors are able to make a value judgment about whether the nation should continue in that direction or choose a different political party with a new direction.

One of the difficulties of the Diefenbaker approach was that there was no discussion of major government decisions in caucus. It was more or less a "like-it-or-lump-it" approach. The Arrow issue was never raised in caucus before the government decision was made, any more than the question of nuclear arms or the devaluation of the dollar—all matters that gave us considerable difficulty on the hustings.

I have always believed that in our parliamentary system a government has a right to expect the loyal support of government measures by caucus members. The quid pro quo is that the member of caucus has the right to make his or her views known to the government before a decision on a matter is taken. Public service employees are invariably informed (and properly so), since they must prepare the discussion documents for cabinet that form the basis of the decision-making process. (The decision to cancel the Arrow, for instance, required the preparation of voluminous cabinet documents containing enormous amounts of data. The advice of the chiefs of staff of the Canadian Armed Forces was also obtained.) The practice of governments "consulting" caucus members after decisions have been made does not satisfy what I feel to be the members' fundamental right to have a say in policy formation.

The decision to cancel the Arrow and to reject the Bomarc missile warheads aroused discussion in caucus, but the MPs had no idea that life-or-death decisions were being made. The Arrow was discussed, but we had no inkling that a decision was about to be made to kill the project; Bomarc missiles were discussed, and nuclear policy vigorously debated, but we did not know until it was too late to contribute, that government policy had been determined and was about to be implemented.

It is not unusual for members of Parliament to learn of government decisions by reading the newspapers. It is a common belief that MPs know everything that is going on in government, but, in fact, the public may be better informed on many matters than the members.

In my twenty-nine years as a member of Parliament, it was my observation that the practice of governments did not change. It was also my observation that once an MP becomes a minister, that belief in a member's right to be heard before decisions were made is quickly cast aside as the minister seeks refuge in "cabinet secrecy" or "cabinet solidarity."

Often matters were raised in caucus and supported by successive members who spoke to the matter in a manner which made compelling sense, and which should have been adopted as the position of the government. But, since the decision had already been taken, it was as though a minister would be committing the gravest possible sin if the decision were to be abandoned in light of the far more sensible policy suggested by the views of caucus. This happened over and over again, most often to the detriment of the government of the day and, even worse, to the detriment of the country.

I found the caucus in the Diefenbaker government not so much different from that of the Clark government or indeed of the Mulroney government. Perhaps it is not surprising that all of them suffered from a level of internal bickering and back-biting of the kind that Robert Stanfield alone was able to avoid. *Plus ça change, plus c'est la même chose.*

I saw Diefenbaker twice during that short Parliament. Once was to tell him of my resolve not to run again—a decision I should have reached in 1962, and did not. He appealed to my sense of loyalty to stay with the party while it was going through trying times. I, of course, did so.

The other occasion gives a better insight into how Diefenbaker worked. It had to do with the Dawson City Festival, which was part of the federal government's program to encourage tourism in Yukon. No one would think twice about undertaking that sort of program today, with the plethora of subsidies that are available from taxpayers' money, but in those days, it was regarded as an utter waste of tax dollars.

Jack Pickersgill led the charge on the event in the House of Commons, ridiculing the restoration of what he called "Arizona Charlie's place" (the Grand Palace Theatre in Dawson had originally been owned by a man named Arizona Charlie Meadows). The reopening of the Grand Palace was to be accompanied by a show organized by Tom Patterson of Stratford Festival fame, featuring entertainers such as Bert Lahr, who had played the lion in *The Wizard of Oz*. This company was to perform a musical called *Foxy*. The show had been advertised all over the continent, and thousands of people planned to attend. Everything was going along fine until suddenly the money ran out, and props and players were stranded in Vancouver without the cash either to get to Dawson City or to turn around and go home. The money to pay their way had all been properly voted and approved under the aegis of Walter Dinsdale, who had become minister of northern affairs by this time, but Diefenbaker, in response to the heckling in the House of Commons, had suddenly cut off further funding.

I went to see Walter at his office in the Langevin Block and he showed me his letter of resignation to the prime minister. He felt that Diefenbaker had lost confidence in him, and the $50,000 involved in this festival (the last of a much larger sum that had all been approved and spent) was just the latest sign of this. I was much more concerned about Walter's determination to resign than I was about the stranded actors, and I spent a good hour or so talking him out of it. If he had resigned, that would have been another blow to unity in the party and cabinet, and Walter, an excellent member of Parliament, would not have run again.

When I had Walter settled down and knew where the real trouble was, namely the prime minister's concern that he would be ridiculed on the campaign trail for spending so much money on the festival, there was nothing to do but seek a personal audience with him. His offices were in the East Block. I will never forget going over there. I am amazed to this day that I was able to get an appointment.

Without even mentioning Walter's problems, which I do not believe have ever been mentioned publicly to this day, I was shown into the Chief's office and he heard me out politely. He did not say no in so many words, but there was no mistaking his rejection of my remarks. He was not going to change his mind. He ran through the political reasons for Pickersgill's stand and said we were becoming the object of national ridicule by proceeding with the restoration of what even he was now calling Arizona Charlie's. I continued to argue for funding, reminding him of the political consequences of leaving these internationally known entertainers stranded in Vancouver, for the sake of $50,000.

He was having none of it, and he was becoming short-tempered at my temerity. He stood up behind his desk. I remained seated, even though my boldness gave me some qualms. When your prime minister stands up, it is quite rude to remain seated. He became even angrier, and his voice rose a notch or two. He continued with his criticism of the northern affairs department for having thought of the idea in the first place. I continued to argue about the need for these funds. By this time his jowls were really shaking and his face, while not entirely red, was getting pink. He walked from behind his desk over to the door of his office—at which point I finally got up. He waited by the door for me to leave. I did not leave, so he walked out into his outer office. There, waiting to see him, was Davie Fulton, one of the five ministers who made up the Treasury Board. Once Diefenbaker had left the room there was no point in my staying, so I went into the outer office. I thought I had been defeated, and I could see some real problems not only in my own riding but nationally. I was about to make myself scarce. I said hello to Fulton, and just then Diefenbaker said, "The Treasury Board is meeting now, and if you can convince them, you can have the money."

I thought, "My God, I've won."

I did not know where the Treasury Board was meeting, but I found out in a hurry. It was just down the hall. I put my case to Donald Fleming, Waldo Monteith, and Mike Starr. Fulton explained to them what the prime minister had said. They very quickly approved the money. Now there was a question of getting the cheque issued. By the time we had the cheque drawn in proper form, Donald Fleming, who as finance minister had to sign it, had already left for the airport. An official was dispatched by cab to track him down, and Fleming signed the cheque on the wing of the airplane that was waiting to take off.

This crisis nearly cost the prime minister one of his cabinet ministers and one of his members of Parliament, for there was no way that I could have held my head up again in Yukon had the prime minister allowed the Dawson City Festival to fold before it started.

Chapter Nine

The Education of an MP or, the Making of a Cynic

Hon. L.B. Pearson (Leader of the Opposition): Mr. Speaker, may I ask the Prime Minister whether in view of current reports, he contemplates any further changes to the ministry?
Right Hon. J.G. Diefenbaker (Prime Minister): Mr. Speaker, I do not know what the current reports are that have been turned out by the Liberal propaganda factory.
Mr. Pearson: A supplementary question, Mr. Speaker: May I ask the Prime Minister if he considers the press, radio and television a Liberal propaganda factory?
Some hon. members: Yes.
Mr. Diefenbaker: Mr. Speaker, I consider the inspiration to be Liberal propaganda.
Some hon. members: Oh, oh.
Some hon. members: Hear, hear.

Hansard, February 5, 1963

During the Diefenbaker period, as a backbencher I learned how the governmental system works in practice as opposed to theory. I learned that projects are not achieved by common sense and decency, or because they are in the national interest. I had entered politics because I thought that the ills of Yukon and of the country could be cured in short order by the application of a good dose of ordinary common horse sense and by the application of logic and reason to problems. I was gradually disabused of such beliefs and over the years from 1958 to 1962, my ideals slowly metamorphosed into disillusionment and finally crystallized into a deeply held cynicism about the whole process.

I suppose it began with my early attempts to obtain the simplest things for the Yukon—for instance, my attempt to get a school built at Old Crow at a reasonable cost to the taxpayer.

National issues were treated the same way. That was the case with the development of the supersonic interceptor jet called the Avro Arrow, a technological wonder that was cancelled in 1959, after the expenditure of $310 million, notwithstanding the fact that anyone with a scintilla of understanding of the air industry could recognize the Arrow as one of the most outstanding aircraft in existence. We were told at the time that it would cost half a billion dollars to produce 100 jets, which in today's terms is peanuts. The cancellation was a dreadful mistake—14,000 employees of A.V. Roe were laid off and the aircraft industry in Canada suffered a devastating blow. I instinctively believed that at the time, and hindsight has convinced pretty well everyone else.

The government's stand on the Bomarc anti-ballistic missile was another mistake. Canada had accepted an arrangement with the United States under which we would acquire American Bomarcs as part of the North American defence system and build bases for their deployment. Then a decision was taken to reject the missiles themselves, because they carried nuclear warheads. The shameful hypocrisy of a policy whereby Canada could acquire the bases but not the warheads had far-reaching consequences. It split the party, caused the resignation of Defence Minister Douglas Harkness, a fine, decent man, kept Parliament in an uproar (the epigraph for this chapter is taken from the proceedings the day after the Harkness resignation), and revealed what could only be called costly stupidity on the part of the government.

Other such frustrations were common. For instance, a bill was prepared that would have established an Indian claims commission to resolve all the outstanding native claims in Canada. (Sound familiar?) A process to deal with these claims had come to an abrupt halt in 1924 for no known reason. The cause was taken up again, in the name of decency and fairness, by the Diefenbaker government, with the Indian Claims Commission bill. However, this bill was volleyed back and forth in caucus and never saw the light of day.

I was slowly coming to understand that it takes years to accomplish even the simplest task. One would think that in this enlightened age there would not be any doubt about the right of every Canadian citizen to cast a vote in a federal election; I could not believe it when I encountered resistance to this fundamental right.

During the 1957 and 1958 campaigns, I studied the rights of native people to vote, along with the Indian Act and the Canada Elections Act. I discovered that the Canadian citizens in the districts of Keewatin and Franklin had never had the franchise. They were not included in any electoral district. The electoral district of Mackenzie, to the west, covered a huge area surrounding the Mackenzie River as far north as Tuktoyaktuk, but the eastern Arctic and the High Arctic were omitted from every electoral description and map. In those two vast districts covering almost a million square miles, there was not a single ballot box to serve the thousands of Inuit Canadian citizens who lived there or the hundreds of white citizens: officers of the RCMP, weather observers, members of Canada's armed forces, exploration company employees, prospectors, and their families: all Canadian citizens, and all voteless.

I thought it would be a simple matter to correct. I would inform the government of the fact, and the oversight would be rectified immediately. So I spoke up in 1958. Nothing was done. It was like dropping a rose petal down a well and waiting for the splash. When I finally realized that nothing was going to be done—that justice and common sense were not reasons enough to provoke action—I decided to introduce a private member's bill to give these Canadians the vote. I thought that bringing the matter to the attention of the public (especially to the attention of members of the House of Commons, who would immediately understand the issues involved) would lead to a quick solution, that the government would be embarrassed into acting. So, in 1959, I introduced Bill C-55, which called for the franchise to be extended to all Canadian citizens in the Keewatin and Franklin districts of the Northwest Territories.

Not only did the government display utter indifference—perhaps the matter was of such little consequence to the government that indifference was to be expected—but other members of Parliament were equally unmoved. Even the media paid scant attention to this upstart who kept harping on the rights of all Canadians to vote. I continued lobbying, more and more vociferously, until, well over two years later, the government began to show some interest.

Towards the end of 1961, it became apparent that there would be an election the following year, and I thought that if the bill were ever going to be successful, the time was now. Therefore, rather than asserting, as I had previously, the right of Canadians to vote as the chief reason for the government to support the bill, I pointed out to the administration the kudos that would come their way if they appeared as the champions of democratic rights, the government that finally took action ignored by previous Liberal governments. The strategy worked, but the bill had to be advanced as a government measure, not my own. By then I did not care whether it was my bill or a government bill, so long as the franchise was extended. The bill finally passed as C-14 on March 2, 1962—almost four years after the expression of a simple idea, one that no one in a democratic society could decry, and just a month before an election was called.

By the end of the first Diefenbaker term in 1962, there was not very much that the government did that I did not view with suspicion. An idealist will seldom question motive, because the idealist takes a proposal advanced at face value and assumes that it has been presented in good faith. Certainly that was my approach when I entered Parliament. On the other hand, the cynic questions everything; questions not only the basis of any and all proposals and theories but the motivation behind them. And indeed, it has been my unhappy experience both in and out of government that the cynic is more likely than the idealist to be right.

Time and again, the government has chosen the course that will either (a) lose the fewest number of votes in the next election or (b) gain the greatest possible number of votes in the next election. Other considerations need not apply.

Later, when I was a member of the government, I sometimes went so far as to say in cabinet that if the decision under discussion was going to go the way it was headed, my colleagues should realize that all they were doing was buying votes. Such an observation was usually met with cold, resentful silence, but no one questioned the truth of my assertions.

Another reason for my conversion to cynicism was my exposure for the first time to the ultimate political power circles in the country. I was able to observe the manner in which the levers of power were operated, both collectively and individually, and came to understand that, while in theory a political party is based on the notion of shared principles and beliefs, the fact is that too often the motivation is opportunism and greed for power. As the Diefenbaker government was increasingly beset by economic problems, it was castigated for unemployment levels that rose to 6 per cent and inflation that topped 5 per cent. Split by internal divisions, it quickly became a battlefield of warring camps, each led by someone driven by personal ambition and greed, rather than by principle. I had always understood that although there might be a strong and vigorous difference of opinion in a cabinet, ultimately the members would pull together as a team, and that those who opposed a point of view that was eventually carried by the majority would forget their differences and move on to the next problem.

Not so. Grudges were carried long after a minister lost a battle in cabinet. Such grudges went beyond the natural human reluctance to admit defeat, because most of the ministers who remained resentful harboured ambitions for power. Everyone seemed to think he could do a better job of being prime minister than the man who had been placed in that position by the people of Canada, John Diefenbaker.

This was true of Davie Fulton, who acted as if he believed himself in every other way superior to Diefenbaker as the leader of this country. There is no denying that Fulton, a Rhodes scholar, was prime material for the nation's top job. The only problem was that the position was already occupied. Another who believed he was head and shoulders above Diefenbaker was Donald Fleming. Again, he had a superb intellect, but also a grossly distorted appreciation of his net worth to the country.

Another minister who for many, many years held the belief that he should be prime minister was George Hees. Eventually the light of George's unceasing ambition was dimmed by his advancing age. When he was well over seventy, he finally confined his desires to being a mere cabinet minister. He chose not to run in the 1988 election. In my view, George was never one of our towering intellects.

Léon Balcer, the MP for Trois-Rivières from 1949 to 1965 and a former national president of the party, was not so much ambitious for himself as anxious to pull Diefenbaker down. He was bitterly opposed to the prime minister personally and rejected his One Canada policy out of hand. He was so opposed to the Chief, in fact, that the moment the 1956 leadership convention results affirmed

Diefenbaker as party leader, Balcer and his wife stalked out of the convention hall. This did not prevent him from accepting the port-folio of solicitor general (and he later became minister of transport); he merely used his position to conduct a campaign against Diefenbaker.

There were, of course, excellent cabinet ministers, although they were a minority. The best example of one who had no extra-ter-ritorial ambitions and displayed a remarkable degree of humility in power was Howard Green. He treated everyone as an equal. He had no pretensions, shunned ostentation, and always treated the taxpayer's dollar as if it were his own—an honest politician, of which there were few in his time and even fewer today.

When one examines the disparate characters in the Diefenbaker cabinet, it is logical to come to the conclusion that, in large measure, this disparity was a principal contributor to the internal strife that dogged the Diefenbaker years. Of course, given his stubbornness, as the number of his critics increased, so did Diefenbaker's deter-mination to defend himself. It was a battle fought surreptitiously, a battle of leaks and hints and back-alley betrayals.

The civil service certainly did their bit to add to the chaos, in a form of guerrilla warfare, by deliberately frustrating the wishes of a particular minister in the hope that it would be seen as prime ministerial interference. This appeared to be the case in cabinet, as observed from my position as an MP; it was certainly the case within party circles.

The party officials were aligned to the various factions within caucus and cabinet, so that some party members supported the views of Davie Fulton and Léon Balcer and others the views of Donald Fleming, George Hees, or Alvin Hamilton. When each of the major players has his own cheering section within the party hierarchy, it is not easy, to say the least, to work together as a single team.

Perhaps the staunchest Diefenbaker supporter was Allister Gros-sart, who ran the Diefenbaker campaigns and was named national director of the party. His loyalty to Diefenbaker never wavered. I did not know him before 1957, but later I came to know him well, and I am satisfied that he never uttered a disloyal statement about Diefenbaker. On the other hand, Flora MacDonald, who was then the office manager at Conservative headquarters and supposedly functioned under Grossart's direction, did not share his convictions nor his loyalty to Diefenbaker, as either leader of the opposition or prime minister.

On one occasion, I delivered a paper in caucus on the subject of legislation introduced by Prime Minister Pearson which would have allowed the opting out of any province from national cost-sharing programs. The legislation was designed for Quebec, and I felt it ran counter to the constitutional practices of our country and would substantially contribute to national disunity. There were some in caucus who wished to support the Liberals on this issue, among them Fulton and Balcer, and I prepared a paper of some length, which took about half an hour to deliver, arguing against that position. I decided copies of my paper should be circulated to caucus members so that they could follow my closely reasoned constitutional position. There were copying facilities available in the House of Commons, but since my paper concerned confidential caucus matters, I asked Flora if copies could be prepared at party headquarters. I emphasized the confidentiality of the paper and explained that it was intended for distribution only to caucus members. The job was done and, as promised, the original and all copies were returned to me. When I received them, though, I reconsidered the wisdom of distributing in printed form that which, in fact, would become part of caucus discussions, which are strictly confidential. I therefore destroyed all the copies, keeping only the original.

It became obvious, however, that at least one extra copy had been made, since it found its way into the hands of Peter Newman and the public media and was used to spread the internal disagreement in caucus into the public arena. Although the leak could have come from anywhere, I was aware that by this time Flora was no fan of Diefenbaker. Indeed, there was no reason to believe that loyalties were any less divided in headquarters than they were in caucus.

It was a very distressing time for all of us who thought that everyone should be loyal to the party and hence to the leader and, even more importantly, to the prime minister of our country. The ordinary citizen observed a higher standard of loyalty to the prime minister, I am sure, than did many active members of our party, who ought to have been the first to maintain allegiance.

Meanwhile, the party leaders in various provinces and regions were aligning themselves with the developing factions. In the years leading up to the election of 1962, I estimated that—party leaders aside—90 per cent of the party members, the ordinary people who made it run, wanted the leaders in cabinet and caucus to settle their differences and get on with the job of running the country. After 1962, when we were returned with a minority, the internal strife continued and grew, until, in 1967, it became so overwhelming that we were forced to call a leadership convention.

New factions developed, and one of these, composed mainly of western Canadians, but with a good sprinkling of support from the Atlantic provinces and Ontario, urged me in 1967 to enter my name for the leadership convention. I declined.

It was in this atmosphere of intrigue, dissent, and disloyalty that Dalton Camp was able to operate and, eventually, to triumph, if what he did can be called a triumph. I first met Dalton at the 1956 leadership convention, when he turned a deaf ear to the suggestions that came pouring out of the resolutions committee. Others, among them Alvin Hamilton, party whip John Pallett, and John Hamilton, who later became parliamentary secretary to the prime minister, were all sincere politicians who encouraged me to go further and continue to develop new ideas. But Dalton, although he did not overtly oppose these suggestions, and indeed seemed to support them, dismissed them out of hand. He was the first to hear of the Roads to Resources plan from me, he told me what a good idea it was and then he forgot all about it. It was Alvin who took it up and helped to push it through. My first assessment of Dalton Camp was one of insincerity and I have not had any reason to change my mind.

It is clear that, with Diefenbaker as with me, Camp said one thing in face-to-face meetings and quite another when the meetings were concluded. He accepted a position as party president, which demanded his loyalty to the leader, and then went about plotting the downfall of his leader.

It remains a mystery to me how, given Camp's record, Conservative leaders can continue to place their trust in him. Robert Stanfield placed great trust in him, I presume because Camp had been closely associated with Stanfield's election victories as premier of Nova Scotia, but I cannot understand how Stanfield would not suspect that a man who was capable of undermining one leader might do it again.

The position is the same with Joe Clark. As a young Conservative, he campaigned actively against Diefenbaker and was aligned with the Camp forces. And yet, when he in turn came to be leader of the party, he continued to place total reliance on Camp and his views. Clark is an extremely intelligent man and a very astute politician, but, knowing that Camp traduced a leader once, I do not understand how he could rely on him not to do it again.

Similarly, Brian Mulroney not only relies on Camp's views and opinions but he ensconced him in the Privy Council Office with the rank of deputy minister, thereby putting him into the ranks of the civil service, who must be resentful of this intrusion into their inner sanctum, notwithstanding public statements to the contrary.*

To me, it is a simple fact that a person who is capable of disloyalty once is capable of disloyalty again. The only two times Camp ran for Parliament, he was defeated; perhaps ordinary voters picked up something that Conservative leaders missed.

The situation in which we found ourselves as the Diefenbaker leadership came under continuing attack was ideally suited to someone like Camp, and it must be admitted that Diefenbaker's style lent itself to his kind of submerged attack.

There are three options for a member who disagrees with a course of action taken by his government. In the years of the Diefenbaker government, when I became so disillusioned, I conscientiously considered those options. The first, if you hold your views deeply enough and they are directly at variance with a position taken by the government, is to align yourself with a political party whose views are closer to your own. That is, you cross the floor. Winston Churchill did this twice, and of course there are many Canadian examples. The second option is to resign from the party and sit as an independent. The third option is simply to accept the disillusionment as a fact of life, and retire completely from politics.

This third course recommended itself to me on more than one occasion, and I conveyed my views to Diefenbaker; each time, I changed my mind at his urging and stuck with the party. Not until 1968 was I finally reduced to writing down my intention not to run in that year's election. However, I was compelled to reconsider by the circumstances of the 1967 leadership convention and the persuasive request by Robert Stanfield to give his leadership a chance.

*Camp resigned in June 1989.

The option that ought not to be available, in my view, is the one in which the member who disagrees does nothing, says nothing, and then uses his position to undermine the leadership. That is a form of treachery that, unfortunately, is all too common and all too successful. It was that kind of behaviour that led first to our demotion to a minority government in 1962 and then to our defeat on a confidence motion on the subject of defence policy in 1963.

Ironically, it was when we moved into opposition that I found myself doing my most effective work as an MP.

Chapter Ten

Scandal Time: The Rivard Affair

Mr. Favreau: On a point of order, Mr. Chairman—
Some hon. members: Oh, Oh.
Mr. Favreau:—I do not know why any matter
concerning the contribution of political funds would
be discussed on the occasion of the consideration of
my estimates.
Mr. Skoreyko: There are a lot of things you do not
know.

Hansard, November 23, 1964

In 1958, Diefenbaker brought back with him 208 Conservative members, the Social Credit party was wiped out completely, and the CCF was reduced to a rump of eight members. The official opposition consisted of a mere forty-nine Liberals. The opportunities for a new Conservative member to contribute in the House of Commons and elsewhere in Parliament were few and far between. In debate, and in Question Period, every intervention by a government member delayed legislation by lengthening the debate, which was already made long enough by opposition members, whose objective was to slow down the government's legislative program. By 1962, the internal divisions rending the Conservative party contributed to the return of a minority Conservative government. Now the problem was worse, since the opposition seemed more determined than ever to make the effective functioning of government impossible, and the backbenchers' contributions were neither sought nor desired (until the time came to count their votes).

That short Parliament lasted until February 1963, when yet another election was called for April. That resulted in the first Pearson administration, a minority government. As a member of the opposition, I suddenly found I had plenty of opportunities to engage in debates and other proceedings of the House. I took full advantage of these opportunities and I believe my stepped-up activities contributed to the effectiveness of the Conservative opposition, with the result that I was called upon with increasing frequency by the leaders of caucus to assume responsibilities in the House and in standing committees.

At the time of our transition to the opposition, I was, however, nowhere near the inner circle of advisers to John Diefenbaker. These were confined at the time to members of the stature of Angus MacLean, Waldo "Monty" Monteith, Michael Starr, George Nowlan, and of course Gordon Churchill, our opposition house leader. The whip during the early opposition years was Tom Bell. (Of these, MacLean, Monteith, Nowlan, and Churchill have all passed away and only Michael Starr is still enjoying good health.) All of these men played a prominent role during the turbulent party divisions over the continuation of Diefenbaker's leadership.

When I was on the government side of the House, silence was golden, but silence was worthless to an opposition member. One of the results was a constant watch for government abuses in such matters as conflict of interest or patronage, which government members are rather shy about bringing to official notice.

One of my earliest forays into the use of this new freedom involved Jean Chrétien, who had come into the House of Commons for the first time in the 1963 election. He remained a member of his law firm, which was not uncommon for lawyers who were sitting members (I had done so myself), but his firm continued to act as counsel for Central Mortgage and Housing, a Crown corporation. In my view, then and now, that constituted a conflict of interest, and I said so.

The most glaring example of patronage came to my notice when one day I received a "plain brown envelope" (these are communications from public employees who wish to remain anonymous but who believe that they have important matters to disclose) containing an inch-thick list of Liberal party supporters who were to be given hiring preference for post office jobs. A patronage list.

Without informing anyone that I was in possession of the document, I raised the matter in the House. I asked Postmaster General Azellus Denis to produce his patronage list. Denis indignantly and vigorously denied that any such list existed and averred that all postal appointments were made on the basis of proper competitions conducted by the public service. I pressed the matter, and was joined in my attack by the NDP, notably by that party's new leader, Tommy Douglas. We insisted that Denis produce the patronage list.

The denials continued despite the mounting pressures, until I finally pulled from my desk the bulky list of eligible appointees. I held it aloft and said, "Why is it that the postmaster general continues to deny the existence of this list, when I have it here in my hand?"

At this, Denis leapt up, red-faced and angry, shook his finger across the floor at me, and shouted, "You stole my list!"

(Shortly after that incident the prime minister, who had sat blushing through much of the grilling of his postmaster general, moved Denis on to the final resting place of most long-serving Liberal parliamentarians, the Senate of Canada.)

From 1958 to 1963, we had maintained our family home in Whitehorse, with my wife, P.J., holding down the fort with our three children, and me commuting between Whitehorse and Ottawa to discharge my responsibilities as a member of Parliament and to supplement that income by continuing with my law practice in Yukon. However, when I decided to run in 1963—and was subsequently re-elected—the question of residence had to be considered anew, since our two youngest children were approaching school age. My wife and I decided to make Ottawa our major residence, and so we moved there, into an apartment at first, then into a rented house, and finally into a house of our own.

Parliamentary life is extremely hard on any family, particularly if the spouse remains at home to raise the family. The strains imposed not only by the long working hours of a conscientious MP but also by the nature of the work are enormous. Much of the stress is occasioned by the member's political opponents, who often make statements deliberately calculated to undermine the character and integrity of the member, to the distress of his loved ones.

P.J. was not particularly well suited to withstand the ravages of this kind of emotional stress, which was to contribute significantly to her death. Statistics show that the survival rate for any marriage is fifty-fifty. I would estimate that the mortality rate of politicians' marriages is much worse because of the environment in which the career politician functions. Given the high divorce rate of politicians, any person seriously considering a political career should study these odds with the greatest care and consult his or her spouse before deciding to enter politics. In my view, there are few pursuits in life that place more stress and strain on a marriage and family relationship than that of a politician.

It is not surprising that my own marriage became one of the casualties, but I was utterly unprepared for the tragedy of the death of my wife.

The unleashing of the destructive forces was the infamous Rivard Affair. I want to make it clear, for the record, that the proper solution to what became one of the nastiest affairs in Canadian political history lay from the beginning in the hands of officials of the Pearson administration, and, had Justice Minister Guy Favreau taken prompt and decisive remedial action, matters would have worked themselves out in quite a different way.

I knew nothing of Lucien Rivard when I was invited, one day in 1964, to have lunch with a person who worked on the Senate side of Parliament. (It has always been assumed, by journalists especially, that my original informant in the Rivard Affair was someone in, or employed by, the RCMP. After the matter was exposed in the House of Commons, I was visited by two RCMP investigators, who naturally wanted to know the identity of my source. I told them the truth, which was that I had never discussed the case with any member of the RCMP or anyone employed by the force. That was difficult for them to accept. It was just as difficult for members of the media to accept, and I was not believed. But it remains the simple truth.)

My informant was a young man who was working as an aide to Senator Wallace McCutcheon. That young man is now a senator himself—Lowell Murray. I undertook then not to reveal his role while any of these matters were current. That was twenty-five years ago. Murray did not have the details, but what he told me was profoundly disturbing. He had learned that a Canadian named Lucien Rivard, who was at that time in Bordeaux Jail in Montreal, was awaiting extradition to the United States to face charges of trafficking in narcotics, chiefly heroin. Rivard had offered a bribe of $20,000 to the lawyer acting on behalf of the American government in the case, in return for which, the lawyer was not to oppose Rivard's application for bail. Clearly, Rivard intended to skip bail. But what shocked me most was that the bribe offer had been conveyed to the Montreal lawyer by an aide to a cabinet minister in the Pearson government.

When the magnitude of the wrongful conduct began to dawn on me, I decided that it was too much for me to tackle alone, and I felt that I should ask someone with investigative skills to help me establish the truth of the allegations.

The first person I approached was radio reporter Ed Murphy. I was no particular friend of Murphy. I had heard of him and listened to some of his work for Broadcast News. He used to record telephone conversations, unbeknownst to the person, by removing the telephone cover plate from the wall outlet and affixing a pair of alligator clips to the wires there and attaching his tape recorder. (This was prior to any privacy legislation; there was essentially no law which made it an offence for persons to do this. I once asked Ed whether he thought that was proper conduct for a journalist, or anyone else for that matter, and he informed me that it was quite a common practice in the press gallery. I tucked away that bit of information for use in my future telephone conversations with journalists.)

Ed and I made one trip to Montreal together, during which I formed the opinion that he was a person who would not keep to himself any material that we discovered together. We had made an agreement that, if there was a story, it would be broken simultaneously in the House and on his broadcast, but I felt sure that he would not respect this agreement. So I told him that I had lost confidence in him and that I was seeking assistance elsewhere.

I made careful enquiries about the reputations and abilities of journalists in the gallery and finally singled out Paul Akehurst, another broadcast journalist, who seemed very sincere and honest. I was not disappointed in my choice. The remainder of the investigation was conducted by Paul and myself on the basis of an agreement that we would release the results simultaneously. Paul had a story he could have released several days before I raised it in the House of Commons, but he honoured our agreement, and, of course, he received credit for the story, which was his proper due. My professional relationship with that member of the journalistic community was most gratifying, and in accord with what I had come to regard as the highest standard of journalistic ethics.

Paul and I began our work in Montreal, where we worked sometimes together and sometimes separately. Where I might have attracted attention, for example in the court registry, Paul did the work, searching the records for proceedings against Lucien Rivard. I did the other work, telephoning people and setting up an interview with the Crown counsel involved, Pierre Lamontagne.

By this time, we had learned that Rivard was wanted in Canada as well as facing charges of smuggling heroin into the United States and of conspiring to smuggle heroin from Mexico to Texas. His fellow conspirators included a number of Mafia operatives. The police on both sides of the border had caught up with Rivard, who was still languishing in Bordeaux Jail, waiting for bail to be granted so that he could skip. We had also found out that the bribe attempt had been made through Raymond Denis, the administrative assistant to René Tremblay, minister of citizenship and immigration. Guy Rouleau, parliamentary secretary to Prime Minister Pearson, was also involved in these matters. (I did not raise this fact in the House at the outset, for reasons that will become clear.) Pierre Lamontagne had refused the bribe and opposed bail. An extradition order was issued on September 25, 1964. On October 10, a writ of habeas corpus was applied for, but the application had not yet been heard.

My interview with Lamontagne was crucial, since without his confirmation of the facts Paul Akehurst and I had pieced together, the matter could never have been exposed, except as mere rumour. Lamontagne, who impressed me as a fearless, independent, highly ethical young Crown counsel, freely discussed the allegations that I laid before him and, much to my surprise, confirmed the truth of them without hesitation. He told me that he had reported the bribe attempt to the authorities and that the matter had been under investigation by the RCMP for some time. I was surprised at his candour because he was an active Liberal who had undoubtedly received his appointment as Crown counsel as a result of Liberal patronage. However, my faith in the legal profession was fortified by his responses, clearly based on ethical considerations rather than the need to protect his political benefactors.

Once I had this confirmation, I explored the other details with him; where he felt he could respond without violating confidentiality he did so, confirming the information Paul and I had gathered. I told Lamontagne that I found it appalling that criminal influence could infiltrate so deeply into ministerial offices in Ottawa. He agreed. I told him that this was not a matter that ought to be pursued with a view to mere partisan advantage, and that I was going to speak personally to the minister of justice, Guy Favreau, and ask him to act on the information. Only if I concluded that the minister would not act would I raise the matter in the House of Commons. Lamontagne thought that was the most reasonable course to follow.

It was on a note of mutual understanding that Pierre Lamontagne and I parted that day, and I rejoined Paul Akehurst in the waiting room of Lamontagne's law office. I came away with the conviction that I should not take political advantage of these circumstances but give the minister of justice and his officials ample opportunity to take whatever remedial steps had to be taken to purge those who had offended. I decided I would only go public with my disclosures if the justice ministry did not respond to my findings.

On my return to Ottawa after that meeting, I immediately made an appointment to see Guy Favreau. I also made an appointment to see John Diefenbaker, who was confined to his bed at Stornoway, the official residence of the opposition leader, as a result of spraining his back during a walk.

When I spoke to Favreau, I gave him all the details in my possession and told him that I would not raise the matter in the House if he was prepared to institute the necessary remedial action himself. I also learned that Pierre Lamontagne had called the minister's office and had conveyed to Favreau the nature and content of our conversation together, including the nature of his responses to me.

Paul Akehurst and I went out to Stornoway in the late afternoon of Sunday, November 12, 1964. I went upstairs to see Diefenbaker while Paul waited downstairs. I told Diefenbaker at the outset that I had Paul Akehurst with me and that Paul had worked with me on the project. Diefenbaker was not at all pleased at this. I told him much, but not all, of the allegations concerning the bribe offer and who was involved. I had very carefully assessed how much I would disclose to Diefenbaker because of my determination not to have the matter handled in a partisan way. In essence, I hog-tied the story so that no one could raise it without filling in the gaps, and only Paul and I could do that.

As I unfolded the story, Diefenbaker, who was lying in bed, propped up by pillows, became very excited, and actually began to salivate. He told me he would raise the matter in the House of Commons himself. With a degree of firmness that surprised me, I said, "No." I was going to expose this myself, if the minister of justice did not first take the appropriate steps. At this point I was subjected to considerable arm-twisting, but I remained adamant, and I did not give him enough information to go ahead on his own.

Diefenbaker had to be content—or at least resigned—to this state of affairs. He said that the most appropriate moment to raise the matter in the House, if that was the course to be pursued, would be during the debate over the estimates of the Department of Justice, and he arranged a meeting of his parliamentary advisers to discuss tactics.

The interview with Diefenbaker lasted about an hour, after which I rejoined Paul Akehurst. I was frank with him about the leader's displeasure over his presence at Stornoway and told him what the plan was. Paul would have to sit on the story for a week. In the meantime, I reassured him that I intended to adhere to our agreement about simultaneous release.

The meeting the next day was my first exposure to the parliamentary group that advised the party leader; there was a consensus that the proper place to pursue the matter was, indeed, over the justice estimates, on Monday, November 23.

The minister of justice did nothing. He had learned of the bribe attempt in August and had received a preliminary report from the RCMP in September. That report had clearly indicated the role played by Guy Rouleau, the prime minister's parliamentary secretary, and the involvement of Raymond Denis, an aide in the office of the immigration minister. Two officials in his own office were also implicated, not in a criminal way, since they did not know of the bribe attempt, but because they had lobbied Pierre Lamontagne to agree to allowing bail. In the circumstances, the minister should have consulted the law officers of the Crown on the advisability of laying criminal charges. Instead, he decided on his own that no such charges should be laid. He had been clearly warned that he would have to take positive action to rectify matters and he did nothing. He informed the prime minister, but the response of the government to this vital issue was simply to stonewall and hope for the best.

On Monday, November 23, Tommy Douglas asked the first question based on some sketchy information Ed Murphy had given him, but it was clear that he had only part of the story. He did not know, for example, about the involvement of Guy Rouleau. I bided my time, as arranged, waiting for the justice minister to make a statement when his estimates were introduced later that afternoon. Even after Douglas's question, and my clear warning to him more than a week before, Favreau chose not to deal with this matter except in the most peripheral way, and he confined himself to generalizations about the Department of Justice estimates.

Accordingly, I spelled out, during questioning of the minister on his estimates, some of the key elements of the case, and demanded to know why, in the circumstances, he had not referred the matter to the law officers of the Crown. At the same time, Paul Akehurst was breaking the story over his radio station in Hamilton, Ontario.

Even though I held back some of my information, the exposure was electrifying. It was clear to everyone in the House that criminal influence had reached into the highest counsels of the land, and the government could come up with no better response than to accuse me of lying and of using smear tactics. For the journalists, it was a major news story, and I suppose it was even more of a surprise to them to learn that one of their own had been working with me on the case.

During the tumultuous debate that followed, the government ministers appeared to be unable to see anything wrong in the matter. Favreau accused me directly of lying, and when he was forced to withdraw, challenged me to repeat my statements outside the House, which I was perfectly prepared to do. He also contended that no criminal prosecution had been undertaken because there was no chance of a conviction. (History was to prove him wrong on that, too.) Jack Pickersgill, the minister of transport and the acknowledged tactical leader of the Liberal forces, called out "More smears!" as I provided the details that the minister of justice seemed determined to withhold. The leaders of the Conservative party— Diefenbaker, Davie Fulton, and Doug Harkness—joined in the questioning, as did Tommy Douglas on behalf of the NDP.

The next day, Guy Rouleau rose in the House as soon as it met to report that he had resigned as parliamentary secretary to the prime minister. A moment later, Favreau rose to announce that a judicial inquiry would be held into the Rivard affair.

By this time, the media were having a field day with the story, and the atmosphere in the House was more charged than ever. Davie Fulton and Doug Harkness pursued a line of questioning to determine when the prime minister had first been informed of the bribery allegations. Pearson responded that the first he had heard of these matters was a day or two before I brought them into the House of

Commons, when he received a phone call from Guy Favreau. That was untrue. Favreau had told him about the bribery attempt and the involvement of his own parliamentary secretary as early as September 2. For more than two months, nothing had been done, no inquiries had been made, even though the prime minister and his justice minister were aware of the RCMP inquiry. Pearson also claimed he had first learned of Guy Rouleau's involvement only after I brought the affair into the House.

Later, when Guy Favreau saw himself being destroyed by the imputation that he had kept this crucial matter from his prime minister, he demanded that Pearson set the record straight. Pearson refused to do so, much to Favreau's distress, until after the House of Commons rose for the Christmas break. Then he wrote a letter to Chief Justice Noel Dorion of Quebec, who was conducting the judicial inquiry, in which he made it seem that he had "forgotten" a casual reference the justice minister had made to him on September 2. It was, all in all, an astonishing and mendacious performance.

Day after day, information had to be pried out of the ministry. There came to be a pattern to the performance. I would ask a question to which I already knew the answer. Guy Favreau, or Jack Pickersgill, or one of the other ministers would accuse me of lying, or of employing McCarthy tactics, or of cowardice. This would be followed by confirmation of the facts that had been so vigorously denied. Not surprisingly, the nation's business came to a halt as this drama was played out.

In due course, Chief Justice Dorion found that while there was no criminal intention on the part of the minister of justice, he fell short of exercising his ministerial discretion appropriately when he had knowledge of the bribery attempt. Guy Favreau resigned as minister of justice forthwith. As for Raymond Denis, Chief Justice Dorion found that there was prima facie evidence for the laying of a charge of obstructing justice against him, and he was eventually convicted and sentenced to serve two years less a day.

When the Dorion Inquiry was established, I took steps to obtain counsel and requested financial assistance from the party, which was generously granted. Dick Bell, who had been minister of citizenship and immigration in the Diefenbaker cabinet, acted for me: a fine individual as well as an extremely competent professional counsel. During my cross-examination, counsel acting for the RCMP repeatedly tried to extract from me the source of my original information, and it was obvious in the courtroom that Chief Justice Dorion was growing ever more impatient with my refusal to answer the question. I kept refusing because I believe that citizens have a right to approach members of Parliament in confidence, and that if they cannot rely on the confidentiality of private discussions with their MP, the ability of that MP to discharge his or her parliamentary duties is seriously impaired. Finally, His Lordship called an adjournment and summoned counsel to his chambers. When Dick Bell came back, he told me that I would have to answer the question or I would be held in contempt and could be sent to jail. I told Dick I was not going to answer the question, and if that meant going to prison, then so be it. My answer was taken back to His Lordship. When the hearings resumed, the matter had been dropped entirely.

One of the comic-tragic aspects of this case occurred when Lucien Rivard escaped from Bordeaux Jail. He had asked to water the jail's skating rink, although the temperature at the time was well above freezing, and he and another prisoner simply dropped the water hoses over the wall and climbed down to freedom. They were recaptured a few months later. Rivard was eventually sentenced to twenty years in prison on the narcotics offences.

His case was over, but the reverberations of the Rivard Affair continue to this day.

Chapter Eleven

Fallout

Mr. Douglas: When a minister of justice tries members in other parts of the House in a trial before a press conference, and then refuses in the House to get up and substantiate what he said, it becomes very apparent that what the government is trying to do is tell the people of Canada that while they may be bad, the people in the Conservative Party are no better. This is a queer way to run a country.

Hansard, March 11, 1966

There were three major consequences, along with some minor ones, of the Rivard Affair disclosures that began in the House of Commons on November 23, 1964. One was the effect on myself and my family; the second, the effect on innocent bystanders who were caught up in what can only be described as retaliatory vengeance by the government and by the prime minister; and the third is the effect upon the environment of the House of Commons itself, for changes occurred as a result of these incidents that are still bearing bitter fruit today.

My inquiries in Montreal had involved phone calls to people who were strangers to me but whom I subsequently learned were principal figures in the Canadian underworld. I remember trying to call a Willie Obront. I had hoped to obtain an interview with him, because I had been told that he could tell me about Rivard. I never did get through to Obront, but spoke instead to one of his minions, who sounded like a hood and probably was. This same Willie Obront was one of the principals called before the Cliche Inquiry into organized crime in Quebec and found to be deeply involved with the Canadian Mafia.

In the course of my inquiries I had gathered an amazing amount of data having to do, not with the attempted bribery of Pierre

144

Lamontagne, but with some questionable bankruptcies in the lumber business, questionable transactions by ministers with furniture companies, and questionable conduct by Liberal party supporters. In all, I have two filing-cabinet drawers full of papers dealing with these matters, including organization charts complete with pictures of individuals in the Canadian underworld.

That I was fairly well informed on such potentially embarrassing matters came to the attention of the government. My co-workers told me that a source within the Prime Minister's Office had passed along the information that Pearson himself had called for any files the government had on me. I learned that two of the files supplied to the prime minister concerned matters that touched me deeply and directly; one dealt with representations I had made on behalf of two employees of the Indian Affairs branch of the Department of Citizenship and Immigration; the other was my personal income tax file.

The first file might have shown the prime minister, if he did not already know, something about the kind of government he ran. The employees involved were Bill Grant, who was the resident director of the Yukon branch of Indian Affairs, and his chief assistant in Whitehorse, Joe Armishaw. The two had used money approved in the estimates for providing welfare for native people in Yukon to build new housing for native people instead. Grant and Armishaw had determined that their first priority had to be decent housing for native people to replace the tents and sod-roof huts they lived in. Nothing else would do as much for their health and morale. A noble idea, but their actions were technically an offence under the Financial Administration Act, which stipulates that money passed by Parliament for one purpose cannot be used for any other.

Grant and Armishaw were criminally charged, and when this became known in Whitehorse and throughout Yukon, people were aghast that these two public employees could be treated so shabbily. As MP, I had representations from dozens of respected citizens asking me to intervene; I even had a letter from Bishop Coudert, the Roman Catholic apostolic vicar of Yukon.

I therefore called on the minister of justice, some time before the Rivard affair broke, and made representations on behalf of Bishop Coudert. I relayed the concerns raised in Yukon and added that I agreed with the bishop's assessment that there was no justification for proceeding against the two men criminally for trying to improve the lot of natives in their jurisdiction.

Grant and Armishaw were eventually tried; the trial judge said, "If I were in Grant's shoes I only wish I would have the courage to do as he did," and acquitted them. The Crown (which in this jurisdiction operated as an agent of the federal Ministry of Justice) appealed the acquittal and the appeal court registered a conviction but imposed a minimum fine. The public service careers of both men were ended; they joined the private sector.

The delivery of this information to Pearson resulted in an attempt to link me with a charge of having made improper representations to the minister of justice to interfere with the proper work of the courts. I could not believe either the pettiness or the method employed in this attempt at revenge. This incident opened my eyes to the extent of the vengefulness and ruthlessness that politicians in office will use against those who oppose or offend them.

The use of my income tax file provided more evidence along this line. George Van Roggen and I had decided as our law practice progressed that it would be a good policy to have the firm purchase houses and have those houses leased back to staff—including George and myself—for a figure that would amount to subsidized rent. This was quite a common practice in northern posts, and indeed it was followed then and is followed today by the federal government itself in their isolated post allowances, through which Ottawa pays a portion of the rent, fuel, and utilities of federal employees working north of 60. The same policy was commonly followed in the private sector as an incentive for employees to accept northern postings. Even so, before we followed this course, we discussed the matter thoroughly with the district taxation officer. Although he clearly had no authority to make decisions of this nature, and said so, he stated that he could see nothing wrong with the arrangement, which he knew to be common in the North.

At the same time we asked his opinion as to whether the partnership could own an airplane for partnership business conducted over the 207,000 square miles of Yukon as well as elsewhere that our business happened to take us. Naturally, the non-business use of the aircraft would be accounted for, but our purpose was to obtain a tax write-off on its depreciation cost attributable to business use.

The district taxation officer again said he saw nothing wrong in such an arrangement, which was followed widely in Canada.

Accordingly, the firm purchased an aircraft, and we were allowed to operate in this way for five years—until the Rivard matter was raised in the House of Commons. At that point, the Department of National Revenue descended with full force upon me and my very disillusioned Liberal partner. Our taxes were substantially reassessed, with interest penalties. The extent of the reassessment was in the neighbourhood of $60,000 in my case, a huge sum to handle on a salary of $12,000. George was not in a much better position.

We both took the position that we were justified, that we had acted in good faith, and that we had done nothing that had not been cleared with departmental officials. The matter went to the Income Tax Appeal Board, and we succeeded in reducing the amount by two thirds.

It did not stop there. Later I received a further reassessment of $29,000. Of course, I was still pursuing the government on scandals that followed the Rivard Affair. This time I wrote to the minister of national revenue, Jean-Pierre Coté, a very fine gentleman whom I had met. I explained the circumstances of my confrontation with the officials of his department and told him that in my opinion what was happening was sheer harassment. If I were to be forced to pay additional taxes which, in my view, I did not owe, I would have to leave the House of Commons and work exclusively at my law practice to raise the money. In effect the government would be preventing me from discharging my duties as a member of Parliament. I was fully prepared to raise the issue as a question of privilege in the House. The minister, to his credit, intervened, and the reassessment was withdrawn, presumably because the government reached the same conclusions as I had done, namely, that the second reassessment was unjustified.

Another result of the Rivard Affair was my loss of respect for the national media. I had already reached a deep disillusionment about the political system; the Rivard case and subsequent events launched me along the same road as regards most journalists.

In the first week or so following the allegations of bribery in the House of Commons, the media without exception throughout the country were complimentary about my actions. Then, suddenly,

the treatment was reversed. Eventually my role came to be characterized as muckraking, scandalmongering, and dirty pool. The
impression given was that I had done something that a gentleman
member of the House of Commons would never do. It was as if I
had been the one who had committed an offence, not those involved
in the bribery attempt.

Naturally, one of the matters the journalists kept probing was
the source of my information. At one point, I was backed against
the wall by a journalist for Broadcast News, Paul Taylor (who was
later elected to the Ontario legislature as a Liberal MPP for a brief
time). He asked me a number of questions, which I answered, and
then asked me about my source. I replied that I was not in a position
to answer the question. He repeated it; I repeated my reply. He
came back to it again and again until eventually I simply remained
silent. He turned off his tape recorder after a few moments of such
silence and went away. I heard the subsequent broadcast, which
ended with Taylor telling his listeners that he had asked me about
my source, "and this is what he said." He then played the hiss of
the silent tape, as if I had never given him an explanation of my
position. I considered that a despicable thing to do. I never gave
an interview to Paul Taylor again.

I have met scores of fine journalists, yet that and similar incidents
taught me to be always on my guard. My caution has led many in
the media who have never known me (or tried to do so) to the
opinion that I am unapproachable and will not speak to them. Those
who know me know that I normally enjoy speaking with them.

A further result of the Rivard Affair was that other MPs, including John Diefenbaker and a number of his former cabinet members,
were subjected to a concerted, deliberate effort to besmirch their
characters and reputations. That came about gradually, because the
Rivard Affair led to a series of revelations (not all of them, by any
means, introduced by me), the collective effect of which was to
portray the Pearson government, quite correctly, as sleazy in the
extreme.

Diefenbaker himself raised the issue of Hal Banks, an American
union thug with a lengthy criminal record in the United States, who
had been brought to Canada by the Liberal government to take
over the Seafarers' International Union and who initiated a wave
of terror with his gang of goons. The Americans wanted him
returned to face criminal charges, but the Canadian government

My father with my brother Gordon,
Regina, 1924

My mother, Thorhild, 1937

My father (in the bow tie), Gordon (middle), and myself (at left) with
Danish friends, standing beside the Buick Durant, c. 1929.

My brother Leslie and myself in our cub
scout uniforms, Edmonton, 1932

Myself (middle) with two friends,
Edmonton, 1940

Myself (bottom row, far right) with the crew of our Lancaster, 101 RAF Squadron, Ludford Magna, 1944

On leave in Kew Gardens, London, 1944

The brand-new MP, with John Diefenbaker and Alvin Hamilton, just before I was marched into the House of Commons for the first time, Ottawa, 1957

Myself, P.J., John Diefenbaker, and Olive Diefenbaker, on the occasion of the first visit of a prime minister north of 60, Yukon, 1958

My son Lee, aged seventeen, Ottawa, 1965

My daughter Roxanne, my son Rick, and myself at our house in Whitehorse, 1972

Myself with Bob Stanfield, Faro, Yukon, 1972

Joe Clark and myself, standing on the float of the Cessna, Quiet Lake, Yukon, 1976

Chatting with miners at the Whitehorse Copper Mine, 1974

The opening of the Dempster Highway, Yukon, 1979: Diefenbaker had died two days earlier, while working on the speech he was to have given on this occasion

With my brother Leslie in my office, Ottawa, 1983

Shelley and myself, chatting with constituents during the 1984 campaign, Mayo, Yukon

Myself with Shelley in front
of the board showing the
election returns,
Whitehorse, 1984

Signing the roll of members of the House of Commons, Ottawa, 1984

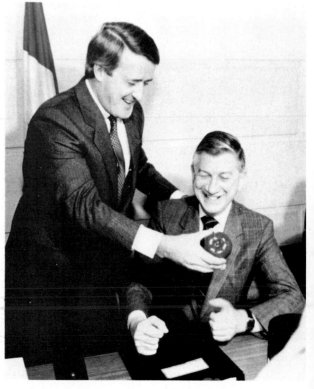

Getting the apple from Brian Mulroney in caucus, Ottawa, 1984

Talking to Perrin Beatty in the government lobby of the House of Commons, Ottawa, 1984

Myself and Ray Hnatyshyn in a caucus meeting, Ottawa, 1985

Being sworn in as minister of national defence; beside me, Ray Hnatyshyn is waiting to be sworn in as president of the Privy Council, Ottawa, 1985

U.S. Defence Secretary Caspar Weinberger and myself at the Quebec summit meeting, 1985

Transferring from HMCS *Terra Nova* to HMCS *Yukon* by jackstay, Pacific Command, 1985

A presentation to mark our first CF-18 Squadron in Europe, Lahr, Germany, 1985

Flying the CF-18, Lahr, Germany, 1985

Shelley and myself leaving Whitehorse after opening the new Whitehorse air terminal building, 1985

Presenting the report of the Task Force on Program Review in the House of Commons, 1986

With George Bush during his visit to Canada, 1986

resolutely refused, blocking every attempt to bring him to justice. An Ontario police commission into organized crime turned up the case, along with that of Onofrio "Nono" Minaudo, another known criminal. The police commission wrote to the federal minister of immigration to ask why these criminals had been admitted and why, once admitted, they had not been deported—and received no reply. This caused another political furor.

I had also passed on some of the information gathered in the Rivard research to MP Donald MacInnis, a former coal miner from Glace Bay, Nova Scotia. On November 30, a week after the Rivard case broke, MacInnis placed a question on the Order Paper. It concerned certain activities of Maurice Lamontagne, secretary of state, and René Tremblay, minister of immigration, and their relationship with Mac and Adolph Sefkind, brothers who had managed a furniture business in Montreal until suddenly, early in 1964, they fled to New York, leaving behind a string of bankrupt companies and some $2 million in debts. Among their creditors were the two Liberal cabinet ministers. Lamontagne had bought $6,800 worth of furniture from Futurama Galleries, a Sefkind firm, during 1962 and 1963. He had made no payments whatever between the time of his original purchase and the time when the Bank of Montreal, Sefkind's main creditor, sent him a bill after the bankruptcy in 1964. Tremblay had bought $3,600 worth of furniture from Futurama in November 1963. He had made no down payment, but the furniture was being sent to him in installments. He had still not received the final installment when the firm went bankrupt, and as soon as he received a bill from the Bank of Montreal, he paid it in full.

Tremblay's case was quite straightforward, but Lamontagne had received furniture on conditions that seemed unusual, to say the very least; he had set up what could justly be called the pay-me-if-you-see-me method of acquiring home furnishings. The fact that Quebec was then being racked by a series of bankruptcies involving criminal fraud, even though they were not related to the Sefkind bankruptcy, added to the affair.

The furniture scandals, as they came to be known, were far less significant than the others, but probably hurt the Liberals just as much. Not everyone shields criminals, nor offers bribes, but everyone buys furniture; the case hit home and forced the resignations of both Lamontagne and Tremblay (although the latter had really done nothing wrong; such was the government's ethical myopia that it could not even distinguish between the two).

Then there was the affair of Yvon Dupuis. Dupuis, who had been made a minister without portfolio by Pearson as a reward for his unrelenting attacks on the Social Credit party in Quebec, had been approached by a syndicate formed to operate a race-track in his riding, St-Jean, Quebec. A member of this syndicate, Roch Deslauriers, later claimed he had given "a present of $10,000" to Dupuis to smooth the way for the obtaining of a race-track licence from the Quebec revenue department. The licence was not forthcoming, but the $10,000 disappeared. Eventually, the RCMP were alerted, and began an investigation.

Eric Kierans, the Quebec minister of revenue, found out about the case and reported it to Ottawa, expecting action to follow. Nothing happened. Kierans even visited Ottawa to confront the minister of justice, Guy Favreau. Still nothing happened, so Kierans wrote a blunt letter to Favreau, which concluded, "On his own admission, Hon. Yvon Dupuis received $10,000 for purposes that are impossible to justify. We must assume, for lack of evidence to the contrary, that he kept this money."

Dupuis was at long last confronted by Pearson and maintained that he had passed the $10,000 to a revenue official in a dark corridor in a hotel. He said he did not know who the official was. Pearson dithered—his usual response to crisis, until it became clear that the story was going to surface. On January 22, 1965, he fired Dupuis. (Dupuis was later convicted of influence peddling, but the conviction was overturned on appeal years later.) The case was another clear example of the moral disintegration of the Liberal cabinet.

The final straw was the case of George Victor Spencer, a Vancouver mail clerk accused in July 1965 of spying for the Soviet Union. The case bobbed up during the 1965 election campaign as one involving unnamed government employees and the Soviet Embassy, though Spencer's name was never mentioned. Finally, a Vancouver newspaper printed a story naming Spencer as a spy. That was followed by an astonishing performance on television by Lucien Cardin (who had taken over the justice portfolio from Favreau), in which he said that, even though Spencer had not been convicted of, or even charged with, any offence, he had been fired from his job and would be kept under RCMP surveillance for the rest of his life.

However the affair was regarded—as the case of a man punished without charge, as a case of an admitted spy remaining at liberty, or simply as a case of bungling—it revealed the government in a very bad light. We continued to pound the justice minister with questions, week after week. We demanded a public inquiry into all the circumstances, which Cardin resolutely refused. Pearson said he would "give consideration" to such an inquiry, but later announced that, having considered it, he would not allow such an inquiry.

The case finally blew up with a fuse that had been lit, although I did not know it until much later, the week after I first raised the Rivard matter in the House. Prime Minister Pearson had summoned George McClellan, the commissioner of the RCMP, to his office and had asked him if he had "any information indicating any impropriety or anything of a scandalous nature involving any MP of any party over the last ten years." The "hounds of vengeance" were being unleashed. Gone was any notion that a government ought not to rummage in the cupboards of its predecessor. We were to face a ten-year search for dirt, any dirt, with which the Liberals could fight back.

McClellan mentioned a case involving one Gerda Munsinger. She was an East German citizen who had married an American but had been refused entry to the United States because she had been classified as a security risk for unspecified activities in East Germany. She had come to Canada and settled in Montreal, where she worked as a prostitute and where, during the Diefenbaker regime, she had formed a liaison with Pierre Sévigny, the associate minister of defence. There were some other aspects to the affair, including a report that the RCMP had installed a video camera in the chandelier of a Montreal hotel room to record some of the bedroom activities, and an assignation reported with, and denied by, Transport Minister George Hees. But the major concern was whether the associate minister of defence had placed himself in a position whereby Canadian security had been at risk.

The RCMP had reported on this affair at the time, to Justice Minister Davie Fulton, who had reported to Diefenbaker, and Sévigny had been ordered to terminate the association forthwith. He was not removed from his post, and no charges were laid. The matter was not made public.

When McClellan told this story, Pearson asked him to send over the file, which he did. Guy Favreau and his successor, Justice Minister Lucien Cardin, both wanted to use the case to attack us, but Pearson forbade that. He did not, however, send the file back to the RCMP. It was lodged in safekeeping in the Privy Council Office. And then, more than a year later, during the Spencer case in early 1966, the file was hauled out.

The first inkling I had that this was about to occur was through a rumour that Cardin was going to resign. To explain what happened next, it is necessary to clear up yet another matter that has continued to haunt me through the years, because of an entirely false interpretation placed on events by the media. This is the famous affair of the Liberal caucus leaks, what came to be called, quite erroneously, the Eavesdropping Affair. The facts are these.

In 1963, extensive renovations were begun on the West Block, in accordance with a plan developed when David Walker was minister of public works in the Diefenbaker government. These renovations took years to complete and involved the construction of a tunnel from the Centre Block to the West Block and the modernization of that building, including the installation of translation equipment in the caucus and committee rooms on the third floor. The sound equipment was installed late in 1965.

In each of these rooms there was a translation booth, with a panel controlling all the headsets and microphones. During committee meetings, the sound was transmitted to a recording studio, where accurate transcripts could be made. In the Conservative caucus room, each chair was equipped with an earpiece so we could listen to a translation or an amplification of what was being said by speakers during caucus. I normally used the earpiece for amplification, since I did not want to miss anything.

One day, I was startled to hear unfamiliar voices speaking through the earpiece. It was a caucus meeting, all right, but not ours. I looked around, and I could see that other members were hearing the same thing. We quickly concluded that we were listening to the proceedings in the Liberal caucus room. Evidently there had been some mix-up in the wiring system.

Now, we had ninety-seven members of Parliament in the Conservative caucus, in addition to a number of senators, any of whom could and most of whom did thereafter plug into the Liberal caucus by listening through their earpieces. We never discussed whether this should be reported to the House officials. I suppose the attitude of our party leaders was that it is not our responsibility to ensure security in the Liberal caucus room; let them look after themselves.

And so from late 1965 until well into 1966, we had a pipeline into the Liberal caucus. John Diefenbaker did not attend caucus at that time, but he knew what was going on. Those who were responsible for planning our Question Period questions used the information, although they were careful not to reveal where they were getting it. Many embarrassing questions were framed on the basis of this information, which was used, I repeat, by dozens of our caucus members over this time. Often I would look across from my position in the fourth row of the opposition benches and see the looks of consternation on the faces of cabinet ministers who could not understand how information only recently released within their caucus was being used to frame questions fired at a particular minister. For a time, the cabinet believed that someone was peddling their secrets to us, so accurate was our information. It was not until the next summer break that they tore the room apart and discovered what had happened. When we came back for the fall session and tuned in, we heard only our own caucus meetings. The leak had been plugged.

I am at some pains to describe these events before going on with the Munsinger story because it is important to be accurate, if for no other reason than to illustrate how distorted is some of the reporting on politics in Canada. Twenty years later, in January 1986, when I was deputy prime minister in the Mulroney government, I was confronted by a *Toronto Star* journalist, David Vienneau, outside the Commons chamber. He told me that unless I agreed to meet with him, he was going to break a story that would be very embarrassing to me. I knew of nothing that could be embarrassing to me except my personal affairs, and I calculated that Vienneau would not be stooping so low as to raise those matters in the *Toronto Star*.

In a 1978 interview with journalist Peter Stursberg, who had written two books on John Diefenbaker, I said that we had had a method whereby we knew every single thing that happened in the Liberal caucus. Stursberg did not use the material but turned it over to the national archivist, telling him that he had gathered it for a commission paid for by the archives to record the events of the Diefenbaker era. Vienneau had obtained this old material. Later, the archivist wrote to me and asked for my permission to release the material. I replied that I would not provide ex post facto permission!

When the Vienneau article came out, it was designed to give the impression that I and I alone had eavesdropped on the Liberal caucus. The reader would be justified in concluding that I had achieved this by somehow planting an electronic device in their caucus room. There was nothing to indicate the truth of the matter. Once a wrong impression is created in a national newspaper it is impossible to reverse, but the facts are as stated here. Any conscientious journalist, including Vienneau, who wanted to print the truth had only to address his questions to any of the scores of Conservatives who were there at the time.

I waited in vain for any of my colleagues from that time to step forward and say, ''That's not what happened at all.'' The only one who commented was Alvin Hamilton, who, when the Vienneau story appeared, was asked about it. He said, ''Of course it happened, but it was no big deal.''

Ironically enough, I had given the information about our electronic access to an author whose article was published in *Saturday Night* magazine in May 1985. If Vienneau did not know about that, he ought to have done. There was nothing at all new in his report, but when it was splashed on page one of the *Toronto Star*, passed off as a fresh news item, it created a sensation.

In the end, I apologized in the House of Commons for my role in the ''eavesdropping'' and said nothing of all the others who had done precisely the same thing.

This diversion has been necessary to explain how it was that we knew, when the Liberal caucus met on the morning of March 2, 1966, that something big was about to happen. There had previously been a confrontation between Justice Minister Cardin and Pearson, on the issue of releasing the Munsinger material, and Cardin had threatened to resign. Pearson gave way, and gave his permission to bring the matter into the House.

That led to an extraordinary and belligerent Liberal caucus meeting on the morning of March 2, which we overheard in our caucus room. I was one of a number of Conservatives who were agog at what we heard. The Liberals were in a fighting mood; they had been savaged for weeks over their scandals, and they were desperately seeking a line of offence that would not only ease their pain but also provide the morale boost that an attack on the opposition would bring.

The Munsinger affair was to be the answer, but it was not directly mentioned. Instead, there were fighting speeches by Pearson and Cardin and Léo Cadieux, the associate minister of defence. Pearson's was a rally-round-the-leadership speech, not terribly inspiring, but in their desperate mood the Liberals cheered it vigorously. Cardin's speech was vicious and personal, as he urged the Liberals to fight and castigated the sleazy scandalmongers in the Conservative party who had dared to raise matters like Hal Banks and Lucien Rivard and George Victor Spencer. But the most notable speech, as far as I was concerned, was that of Léo Cadieux, someone I had always thought of as a mild-mannered, Victorian gentleman, who suddenly made the most vitriolic personal attack on Diefenbaker and myself that I have ever heard. He set for the Liberal party and caucus the objective of ridding Parliament at the soonest possible moment of Diefenbaker and Nielsen, not just because we were the nemesis of their government and party but because we were unhealthy cancers on the democratic fabric and institutions of the country.

The Liberals were primed, and Cardin had been given the go-ahead. It remained only for the bomb to go off. It did, two days later, when the Spencer spy case came up again and Diefenbaker was pressing the government for an inquiry, which Pearson and Cardin had both adamantly refused.

Cardin launched a vicious attack on Diefenbaker, which included the line—as recorded by Hansard—"I want the Right Honorable gentleman to tell the House about his participation in the Monseigneur case when he was Prime Minister of this country." (Much was later made of the misspelling of Munsinger, and it was taken to indicate that Cardin had not seen the file. The slip is more likely the rare fault of a Hansard reporter.)

Over the next few days, more tidbits were fed out. Cardin repeatedly said that he could not discuss the matter because of national security, but he compared it to the Profumo scandal in Britain. On March 10, he called a full-scale press conference to report that the matter had never been referred to the law officers of the Crown. He stated, quite erroneously, that a "security leak" had occurred and, equally wrongly, that Gerda Munsinger was dead. (She was later discovered in Munich by *Toronto Star* reporter Bob Reguly.)

He also said that two or more Diefenbaker cabinet ministers had been involved with the prostitute, though he refused to name them.

On March 11, Prime Minister Pearson established the Spence Commission. It was not what we had been demanding, an inquiry into the George Victor Spencer affair, but an inquest by Justice George Wishart Spence (a well-known Liberal before his elevation to the bench) into Cardin's allegations that Diefenbaker had not handled the Munsinger case properly in 1961 and that there had been a security leak. It was aimed directly at the issues first raised in the House on March 4 and during Cardin's press conference. George Victor Spencer disappeared from the scene, for all practical purposes.

The Spence Commission was entirely different from the Dorion Inquiry, which had dealt with my charge that criminal offences had occurred and resulted in a finding that they had indeed occurred. Spence was to discover whether a former prime minister had "mishandled" a case—a matter of political judgment. (How a judge came to be an expert in these matters remains a mystery to me.) In any event, if Diefenbaker had made a mistake by not removing Sévigny from his post, that was a matter for voters to deal with, not judges. The Spence Commission was a modern Star Chamber court; it set a precedent—the very precedent that Pearson had first so vigorously eschewed—under which any new government could go rummaging among the effects of a predecessor to seek embarrassing incidents for exploitation any time it was under attack.

There was never a charge for a court to deal with, and Cardin, the accuser, never appeared. Prime Minister Pearson, who had had the report of the Munsinger case before him for fifteen months, was never called, nor was Gerda Munsinger, although she was interviewed extensively by the media. The rules of evidence were suspended, and material that was never placed in evidence at the inquiry was released to the public in what Mr. Justice Spence referred to as a "handy document." It had the handy effect of damaging people who had not been present when the material was under consideration. In this way, for example, a totally fabricated story that Diefenbaker had once met this woman was circulated.

I and others inveighed against the terms of reference of the inquiry, to no avail. The fundamental objection was perhaps best put by Tommy Douglas, the NDP leader, who pointed to where this had all begun, with Pearson calling for any damaging files in the possession of the RCMP. He said, "The moment we begin to destroy this basic principle of democracy, the moment we allow a prime minister, no matter who he may be or what party he heads, to begin collecting RCMP files for his own use, at his own discretion, we have taken the first step toward establishing a police state in this country."

Because the Munsinger revelations followed closely those of the Rivard affair, there is a widespread belief even among those who should know better that I was responsible for both. Young people in the parliamentary press gallery, twenty or so years later, still link my name with the Munsinger Affair before they think of Lester Pearson or Lucien Cardin, who were the real publicizers of the top-secret Munsinger file in the House of Commons. Among the minor ironies of this incident is the fact that Pearson, in the name of national security, allowed the release of secret documents. He justified his action by the need to bring these matters to light as soon as possible even though he had sat on the file for fifteen months. My only connection to it was that I had exposed the Rivard Affair that led the Liberals to seek such vengeance.

In due course, Mr. Justice Spence produced his report. There was no evidence that Gerda Munsinger had been a security risk in Canada, or indeed, that she had ever been one at all. The RCMP evidence was that she had been kept under constant surveillance and was not spying. His Lordship found, however, that the prime minister was derelict because he had failed to order further investigation "with a view to determining whether any security breach had occurred already or whether a situation which constituted a security risk existed."

If this was a failure—and a case can be made for that argument—it was a matter of political judgment; Mr. Justice Spence undertook to substitute his political judgment for that of the former prime minister. He said it was "difficult to understand" how Sévigny was retained in government. That is my view too, but it has nothing to do with a criminal charge; it was simply a comment by a judge who should never have been dealing with the matter in the first place.

The Spence Inquiry did Diefenbaker great damage. The public was left with the impression that a grave security risk had been created by his "mishandling" (Cardin's word) of the case. Five years after Gerda Munsinger, who may or may not have been a security risk somewhere, at some time, had left the country, it was found that Pierre Sévigny (who had since retired from public life), although there was no evidence that he had violated his privy councillor's oath or betrayed or exposed any state secrets, had been placed in a position in which he might have done so had she in fact been a spy and not just a prostitute. Therefore, Diefenbaker ought to have acted other than he did. In his book *The Chief*, Thomas Van Dusen wrote, "After the Spence Commission report, the result was a foregone conclusion. Diefenbaker would have to go."

Certainly that was a widely held feeling at the time, and it was a matter of some bitterness to me that this was the result of what I had begun with the exposure of criminal activities of certain Liberals.

Perhaps the most long-lasting and damaging fallout of the Rivard Affair was the manner in which it changed for the worse the conduct, the atmosphere, the very meaning of the institution of Parliament itself. Previous scandals had been discussed on the floor, from the days of the building of the CPR through the Beauharnois scandals and others. We had the case of the horses discovered on the payroll of the Department of National Defence and the building of a house financed by the government for an employee of that government, and dozens of other instances, large and small, that caused repercussions in the Green Chamber, but for some reason the disclosure of the Rivard case was different. It was the start of a long chain of events that culminated, under the Liberal opposition led by John Turner, in the emergence of the Rat Pack, composed of John Nunziata, Sheila Copps, Don Boudria, Brian Tobin, et al. They have carried the atmosphere of the days of the Rivard disclosures forward in a far more vicious manner than existed even in those bitter months of the scandal-ridden Pearson government.

In my view, the changes have destroyed the civility of the House of Commons; they have made the institution an object of ridicule by a large number of Canadians who watch it on television; and they have made Canadians ashamed when House proceedings are brought to the attention of people in other countries. The Commons has never before been held in such low esteem, even by the members who sit there. Certainly most Canadians have a low regard both for the manner in which proceedings are conducted there, and for the intelligence of its occupants. Anyone who cares at all for the institution of Parliament as the guardian of our fragile freedoms must feel a sense of concern. Pessimists will give up, optimists will hope that something can be done to restore the place to what it once was, a civilized debating forum where violent clashes of opinion were commonplace but gave rise to eventual consensus rather than the continual waging of personal vendettas.

Parliament has been so weakened by this process that the very freedoms it was designed to protect are in jeopardy, in the sense that, as Parliament becomes weaker, the executive becomes stronger, as does the bureaucracy. This situation prepares the way for the anarchy of, or results in the growth of, bureaucratic power at the expense of the voters and their elected representatives.

A sign, to me, that Parliament as an institution was under attack came when I discovered that it was not only the media who had taken a 180-degree turn in their regard for me as the author of the Rivard disclosures; there were several members in my own caucus who felt the same way. While I received support from those who felt that one of the duties of Parliament was to root out criminal activities wherever they are found, and especially when they threaten the office of the prime minister itself, many of my colleagues quickly indicated that if I had been a gentleman, I would not have raised the matter in the House, no matter how heinous the crime.

That came as quite a shock to me. Of course I had not consulted anyone, let alone caucus colleagues, as to whether I was doing the right thing. It seemed to me that my actions would naturally be approved by anyone who had any respect for the application of the laws of our country. When the minister of justice declined to act on the complaint laid before him, it seemed to me that the only proper thing to do was to expose these events on the floor of the House, and this would lead to their correction and not to a chain of vengeful attacks on individual members of the opposition. If the House was the forum it was intended to be, I thought, it would be strengthened, not weakened, by this proper use of its facilities. It astounded me that not all Conservative members saw it that way. Perhaps they were wiser than I.

One MP came over to me after the initial exposure in the House and said, "Erik, you did a good job. You went just far enough and not too far." That had been my intention all along—to confine myself to the statement of facts and eschew anything in the way of smear or innuendo. The member who said that to me was a new back-bencher, John Turner.

Chapter Twelve
The Death of P.J.

Therefore do not worry about tomorrow, for tomorrow will worry about itself. Each day has enough trouble of its own.

Matthew 6:34

When I first ran for election, I did not believe that I would be remaining in office as a member of Parliament for more than one term and we therefore maintained our home in Whitehorse. Seven campaigns and ten years later, we made the decision to move to Ottawa and finally purchased our own home in 1968. As subsequent events were to prove, that was unfortunate timing. It was, however, a question of trying to keep the family together. Then my activities as an opposition MP intensified. One of the consequences of the Rivard disclosures was a stream of abusive telephone calls, most of them anonymous; some of them were placed to my office, some to the Commons security staff, and some, unfortunately, to my home, where they were invariably taken by P.J.

Some of these were threatening calls. Those that were made to my home were threats not only against my life but against the lives of my family. Naturally, P.J. worried about the safety of our children. She was a nervous and excitable person at the best of times, and did not need the added tensions generated by such calls. Over time the calls, together with the publicity attendant upon the Rivard affair as it unfolded in the House of Commons, caused serious health problems for her.

These developments contributed to the deterioration of our marriage. P.J. constantly urged me to abandon politics and return to the comparative peace and tranquillity of my law practice. She did not wish, however, to return to Whitehorse; she preferred the life of a larger city.

I discussed the advantages and disadvantages of this course very thoroughly with P.J., and in the end we agreed that I should at least serve out the current term, which was due to end in 1965. However, as events unfolded I became more deeply embroiled in the debates raging in the House of Commons, and increasing reliance was being placed upon me to lead those debates. It seemed that every day brought another scandal or another development that had to be followed up. The 1965 election, which saw Pearson returned with yet another minority government, came and went with nothing resolved. I was easily returned as member of Parliament for Yukon, and I plunged back into the Commons fray. My resolution to leave active politics was pushed back once more, and P.J. grew increasingly unhappy.

After that election, it was clear that Pearson would soon step down. But when the leadership passed to Pierre Elliott Trudeau, I was on the horns of a dilemma once again. My opposition to that man, to his philosophy, to almost everything he stood for, was so intense that resistance to his influence became an obsession with me. I felt that I simply could not withdraw while this man was in charge of the government and the country, and I did not. As a result, between 1963 and 1969, matters worsened in our marriage. There is no doubt whatsoever that the major contributing factor to this deterioration was my absorption in activities in the House of Commons for the Conservative opposition under John Diefenbaker and, after September 1967, under Robert Stanfield. Matters reached the point at which I sought refuge from unpleasant tensions at home by working longer and longer hours at my office.

P.J. and I had discussed separation and divorce, but in the end we felt that the interests of the children would best be served by our staying together.

I added yet another fatal wound to the relationship by my own infidelity. I made things even worse by revealing my transgression to my wife, which only added to her burden of stress and tension. My own peace of mind was considerably scarred, and I was assailed by mixed feelings of frustration and remorse.

I made certain decisions during this period that I might not otherwise have made, because of the moral self-condemnation I felt for my own conduct. What might today be called the Gary Hart syndrome assailed me in the months leading up to the 1967 Conservative leadership convention. I was approached to be a leadership candidate, but I declined. I was assured that there would be ample financing available, but I felt that my own immoral conduct rendered me unfit to offer myself as a candidate.

My wife became more and more aggressive and difficult to live with, not only for me but also for our growing children. She sought refuge from her own pain, caused largely by my heavy work responsibilities and by my inattentiveness to her, by increasing her consumption of alcohol significantly. She also obtained tranquillizers from doctors and consumed both simultaneously. She spent much of her final months under the influence of alcohol or tranquillizers or both.

She was seeing a psychiatrist regularly, but given the circumstances, it is not surprising that there was no discernible improvement in her health. A number of times she threatened to kill herself and indeed it sometimes seemed that she was slowly trying to do just that with alcohol and drugs. There were times when I found her asleep and so unresponsive that I called a doctor. On one occasion, she had to have her stomach pumped free of drugs.

In April 1969, I had been in Whitehorse carrying on my practice. I returned to Ottawa, and on the night of April 18 I was working in my West Block office. P.J. sent our two younger children, Rick, 14, and Roxanne, 13, to my office by taxi. (Our third child, Lee, 20, was in Whitehorse.) When I spoke to P.J. on the telephone, she told me that I could care for the children that night. She was in a belligerent mood and sounded as though she were under the influence of alcohol or drugs.

I said, "Well, fine, but we will not come home. We will be spending the night at a hotel."

Rick, Roxanne, and I booked into the Chateau Laurier. They were quite excited at spending the night there. The next morning, I sent them home by taxi early enough to prepare for school and went to my office to work. It was not long before I received a telephone call from Rick, who told me that they had found their mother in the garage, on the floor, and that she appeared to be dead. I immediately went home by taxi.

What had apparently happened was that P.J., probably very much under the influence of alcohol and tranquillizers, had gone to the car, intending either to come downtown to find us or to subject herself to carbon monoxide poisoning. However, she had obviously changed her mind, because she had opened the car door to get out. But she had waited a little too long and the combination of alcohol, drugs, and carbon monoxide overtook her. She fell and hit her head on the concrete floor. Since carbon monoxide seeks the lowest level, it would not have been long before such a position proved fatal.

We remained in Ottawa until the two children finished their school term and then returned to Yukon in June of 1969. There we joined my son Lee, who throughout these events had been living in our apartment in Whitehorse and working at various jobs. I spent the next two or three years caring for two growing teenagers and seeing them through their final high school years, so that most of my time was spent in Yukon rather than Ottawa. Fortunately, the frantic pace of parliamentary work had eased enough to make this possible.

All in all, when I consider the repercussions, I have often wondered whether I did the right thing in opening the Pandora's box of the Rivard matter in the first place. After that first luncheon with Lowell Murray, I could have let the matter drop. When the minister of justice failed to act, not only after the police investigation but after I caused the issue to be brought to his attention again, was it right for me to say, "Well, no one else is doing anything, so I should raise this matter in the House"? To what extent should such a matter be pursued publicly? Where is the line to be drawn between the need for public disclosure and the need to avoid the difficulties and tragedy such disclosures cause? There is no question that offenders against the Criminal Code, against the law of the land, should be brought to justice, but I ask myself today, "At whose expense?"

At the time, I knew there was nothing to be gained by going to the police—they had already given the minister of justice their report. There was no point in laying the facts before the minister—that had already been done. There was no point in going to the prime minister—the minister of justice had spoken to him. Where does one go as a citizen to insist that justice be done? In 1964, I had no doubts on this score—to the House of Commons. But in following that course I exacted a fearful price not only from myself but from many others.

During the unhappy years with P.J., I had formed a relationship with a young woman. I knew better, but I was too lonely to heed common sense. This young woman had already had one abortion during that relationship, and, after my wife's death, she became pregnant again. She informed me that the child was mine and that this time she intended to have it.

She also intended to have me. Her words to me were, "Nobody else seems to want you, so I may as well have you." (In my relationships with women after P.J.'s death, I have always frankly informed them that there could be no question of marriage, for it was not my intention to remarry, and that was the fact. Indeed, it was not until more than fourteen years after the death of P.J. that I again gave serious thought to marriage.) I had told the young woman that I did not intend to remarry, but she insisted that she was going to have the child anyway. That confrontation terminated our relationship. After the child was born I was confronted with her lawyer's demands for support payments.

I was willing to pay reasonable support, and that is still the case. I did not and do not take any refuge in the possibility that the child might not be mine. But her demands were not within my means at the time. I was served by the sheriff with court documents at my office in Whitehorse, and several attempts were made by process servers in Ottawa to gain access to my parliamentary offices. All of this was naturally quite embarrassing, but it could have been much worse if I had been any more prominent in party leadership circles.

I finally appeared in family court, where an original order had been made in my absence. The result of my appearance was to have the amount of support reduced by half. Those financial demands follow me to this day and have inhibited almost every single decision that I have had to make with respect to my life in public office, as well as my current work in the public service.

I conclude this part of my narrative by offering some advice to those who aspire to elected public office. The morals and personal conduct of those in public office must always be above reproach. It is only the unblemished who are worthy of public trust, but even more importantly, it is only they who can act within the dictates of a totally free and clear conscience, devoid of hypocrisy.

I set down these painful recollections both for whatever moral and political instruction they may contain and to allow the reader, and those who were kind enough to offer me their confidence, to understand why I acted as I did when I was approached to run for the leadership of the party.

Chapter Thirteen
Swallow the Leader

*There is nothing sillier than people in a party turning
against the leader of the party. I think they were all
crazy, they were out of their minds. There is no way
of accounting for disloyalty. I used to say to them
when I was talking to them, "What is the matter
with you? You hadn't a hope in the world of ever
being anything but a backbencher in opposition all
your life, but because of Mr. Diefenbaker you are a
cabinet minister, and now you want to be prime
minister." That was the real problem, they all
wanted to be prime minister.*

Allister Grossart, 1972

It is an understatement to say that Diefenbaker was never held in
universal esteem within the Conservative party. He was defeated
in his first two bids for the party leadership, and although he
emerged victorious on December 14, 1956, his election left some
members disgruntled and embittered. Léon Balcer of Quebec and
James M. Macdonnell, who had been the opposition finance critic
under Diefenbaker's predecessor, George Drew, were two of those
he appointed to his first cabinet who never ceased to work against
him. He also appointed Davie Fulton and Donald Fleming, the two
men who ran against him in 1956, to his first cabinet. Both turned
against him when the going got tough, although Fleming did so to
a considerably lesser degree than Fulton.

Of course, when he won a minority government in 1957, to form
the first Conservative administration since 1935, everyone was
behind him, and when he produced the overwhelming landslide of
1958, you would have searched in vain to find any enemies of Diefenbaker within party ranks. He was the fair-haired leader, and
could do no wrong; support was universal. This was to change only

165

too soon, and watching that change was one of the major contributing factors to my disillusionment with the political system. I had taken it for granted after entering politics that loyalty to the party and its leader was automatic. It did not make any difference to me, short of highly immoral or criminal conduct, what that leader did or who he was; my loyalty to him and to the party was not open to question. So it came as something of a surprise to me that when things did start to go wrong, not only backbenchers but also members of Diefenbaker's cabinet lost any reticence they might have had in expressing their dissatisfaction.

Not in public, mind you—at least not at first. Instead there was the sniping at dinner in the Commons restaurant, or in conversations in the halls outside the Commons. There was a lot of "corridor courage," but not much inclination to challenge the leader openly until much later.

I suppose the rot started to set in when the big defence issues arose—the Bomarc, the Arrow, the Bay of Pigs invasion of Cuba by President Kennedy (when Diefenbaker was slow to express approval and flatly refused to disengage Canada diplomatically and economically from Cuba, despite Kennedy's increasingly irritated urging). Obviously there were two very distinct views in cabinet on these matters, one a good deal more sympathetic to the United States than the other. Doug Harkness, who became minister of national defence—a very highly principled man—resigned rather than prostitute his principles. He could not accept the Bomarc decision, and stated his views openly and without flinching. Others were not so dedicated to matters of principle as they were to the prerogatives of office, so they continued in cabinet while carrying on their resistance from within. While the rot was spreading within cabinet, sides were being taken within the higher echelons of the party outside the House.

The anti-Diefenbaker forces received substantial assistance and impetus when Wallace McCutcheon was made a senator and, later, brought into cabinet. Diefenbaker was not fully aware of the detailed organization of the forces that were being marshalled against his leadership, although he knew that some people opposed him. In fact, McCutcheon was working against him even in those early days. In his memoirs, the Chief was to describe the appointment of this Bay Street giant as "the most serious mistake I could have made."

Not quite. There was also his appointment of Dalton Camp as

the party's national organizer. When Allister Grossart, who had formerly held the post, was appointed to the Senate in September 1962, Camp, a member of the national executive, took over most of his functions. He was not a full-time employee and did not receive a salary, so he invented a new title: chairman of the national organizing committee.

Camp was from the start a close ally of McCutcheon. The senator knew exactly where Camp stood with respect to the movement to shunt Diefenbaker aside. (McCutcheon thought the way to go about that was to have the Chief made chief justice of the Supreme Court of Canada, which would have led to the astounding spectacle of the prime minister appointing himself to the bench.) I had a friend in McCutcheon's office, and naturally his loyalties were in the same areas as the senator's. I had a good knowledge of the way the anti-Diefenbaker movement grew during the final months of his first term. When we went to the polls in 1962 and returned as a minority government, the gloves really came off. The newspapers began to blossom with stories of defections, or potential defections, until it became clear that something would have to be done.

Diefenbaker's solution was to turn the party's annual meeting, in January 1963, into a vote of confidence, which, after a rousing speech, he won handily. He also helped to push through a resolution on defence policy that managed to straddle the issue of nuclear arms and defied both logic and understanding. (The crucial clause read: "This meeting recommends to the Government of Canada that such steps as necessary be taken, and that such negotiations with the United States as are required be concluded that recognize fully and completely Canada's sovereignty so as to make readily available for the Canadian installations and equipment that form part of the NATO and NORAD forces such nuclear warheads as are required for the defence installations, provided that the use of NORAD armaments be under the joint control of Canada and the United States, in the event that a system of nuclear disarmament with proper inspection controls is not adopted by the major powers by December 1963." Warheads if necessary, but not necessarily warheads.)

On January 12, the Liberal party's firmly anti-nuclear position was reversed by the unilateral decision of Lester Pearson, who, in a speech in Scarborough, Ontario, embraced a nuclear policy for Canada and exacerbated the split within our party on the issue. The tortured resolution we endorsed four days later was an attempt to paper over that crack, but it did not work.

The thunderous cheers of the Tory delegates had hardly faded from our ears when, on February 5, 1963, the fragile alliance with the Social Credit party that had kept us in office shattered. Robert Thompson, leader of that party, reneged on a promise to support the government on a vote of confidence, and we lost it, 142-111. We were off to the polls again.

This led to the two-day caucus I have already described that brought George Hees back to a position of "enthusiastic loyalty" for a period of somewhat less than twenty-four hours, after which he resigned and decided not to offer himself for re-election to Parliament.

On April 8, the Pearson Liberals won 129 seats to our 95—not enough for a majority but enough to form a government. Pearson met the House on May 16 to begin what was to be his Sixty Days of Decision, but which might have been more aptly named Sixty Days of Derision. The first Walter Gordon budget was hastily introduced on June 13, amended on June 19, and then withdrawn for a thorough revision, which was tabled July 8. With the aid, usually, of seventeen NDP members, the Liberals clung to power through crisis after crisis, while the Social Credit party split (the Quebec wing became the Ralliement des Créditistes, under Réal Caouette). The cabinet was shuffled, and, in May 1964, Pearson announced that Canada would have a new flag, thus setting off one of the most bitter debates in the history of this nation.

You might think that all this turmoil would have served to rally the Conservatives behind their embattled leader, but it did not; scarcely a day went by that he was not subject to defections, disloyalty, and the sniping of those who owed him, in theory, either their support or their resignations.

The scandals that began with the Rivard revelations and continued for months thereafter helped briefly; people could not help but conclude, as the Pearson government looked worse and worse, that, "Well, by God, Diefenbaker wasn't so bad after all, when you compare his government with this bunch!" However, that short rebirth of popularity was not sufficient to offset the pressure that had built up within the caucus and the party hierarchy.

When Pearson went to the country once more, on November 8, 1965, in hopes of winning a majority at last, the result was another stalemate. The Liberals came back with 131 seats, a gain of two; we also gained two seats, to come back with 97. Once again, Diefenbaker was blamed for our inability to defeat a crew whose incompetence and moral bankruptcy we had made manifest.

The internal bickering grew worse, exacerbated by changes within the party structure. In the 1964 party convention, Camp had been elected to succeed Egan Chambers as national president, and Dick Thrasher, the national director, who might have blocked some of his manoeuvring, resigned to run in the 1965 election. As a result, Flora MacDonald, who had begun working at PC headquarters as Grossart's secretary, was now running the office while Camp ran the party. Diefenbaker's enemies effectively controlled the party machinery. In early 1966, the Chief appointed a new national director, James Johnston, and as soon as Johnston discovered what was going on, he fired MacDonald, an act that Camp later called "a declaration of war."

Matters came to a head at the 1966 party convention in Ottawa, which opened on November 14, after the release of the Spence Commission report. A vote of confidence in the leader was forced by the anti-Diefenbaker forces, and although the Chief won that, Dalton Camp was able to push through a motion calling for a reassessment of the leadership issue at the next meeting. The resolution indicated that another meeting must be held by January 1, 1968. He also narrowly defeated Arthur Maloney, a Diefenbaker loyalist, in the voting for national party president. I have never been able to understand how Camp could re-offer himself for this post when he had made his dislike of and disloyalty towards the man who led the party so obvious.

Some of the background manoeuvring at the party convention, which led to the leadership convention in 1967, is worth recounting.

On November 13, 1966, the eve of the convention, the national executive officers met as a preliminary attempt to bring about a leadership convention. There were two ways to arrange such a convention. One was by a vote of national party officers and the other by a vote of the party assembled in convention. The former was tried first, and since Camp was the national president, there was no difficulty in putting the question on the agenda of that private meeting of party officers.

The constitution of the party stipulates that the national officers must be drawn from the representatives of the constituencies throughout the country. At that time, there were 125 such officers, so it would be possible to call a leadership convention on the basis of 63 votes. Camp and his group thought that presented no difficulty.

The November 13 meeting was held on the fourth floor of the Holt-Renfrew building in downtown Ottawa. Three floors of this building—everything above the fur business on the ground floor—were occupied by the national headquarters of the party. It is an old building, and the fire escape is an external one, of the steel-step type. The top of the fire escape led into one of the windows of the boardroom where our meeting was taking place. More than a dozen journalists crept up that fire escape and took up positions where they could eavesdrop on the proceedings. They were discovered and asked to leave, and they slowly and reluctantly climbed down the fire escape.

All the northern representatives were on hand for this crucial meeting—six from each of the Northwest Territories and Yukon, so we had twelve votes out of the total of 125. That number turned out to be critical.

Davie Fulton spoke and was followed by several other well-known anti-Diefenbaker ministers, all of them very critical of the man who had put them in cabinet. Diefenbaker listened with a stony face as one by one his enemies marched to the podium and enumerated his sins, real and imagined. The meeting lasted well over two hours. I had prepared for the occasion, and I spoke for about fifteen minutes. I spoke of loyalty, and of unity, and of political cannibalism. I spoke for young people who were distressed at the cavalier manner in which the virtues of loyalty and dedication were being ignored by senior party members. I spoke of the likelihood of an accelerated alienation of our own party supporters throughout the country, who were now sympathetic to the Progressive Conservative political philosophy and repelled by the Liberal record of corruption and incompetence, but who would share our own disillusionment if there was to be a decision by the national officers to execute the leader of our party.

The vote at that meeting was carried in Diefenbaker's favour, and the motion to hold a leadership convention was rejected, but the margin of victory was less than ten votes. The votes of the northern officers, who were solidly for the Chief, represented the margin of victory with a little to spare.

When the count was made known, I could see the chagrin on Fulton's face, and, though he was usually impassive, I could see the same reaction on Léon Balcer's face. Dalton Camp was fuming. Of course, those people resolved to redouble their efforts at the open meeting to begin the next day.

Our national meeting was held in the ballroom of the Chateau Laurier Hotel. It was to open with an address by Diefenbaker, and meticulous preparations had been made to receive him. When he entered the hall to address his party, he found that the front ten rows were solidly occupied by those whom I think I can be forgiven for calling Camp followers. Each one had received a memo instructing him or her how to behave. They were not to rise when the leader entered, they were to cheer Camp's name, and they were to sit on their hands when Diefenbaker spoke. They carried out their instructions to the letter, and though their behaviour brought a stern rebuke from Arthur Maloney in his speech the next day ("When the leader of my party enters a room," he said, "I stand"), the result was to portray the party as hopelessly divided and more concerned with self-destruction than election.

The next day, with Dalton Camp looking like the cat that swallowed the canary—the canary being Diefenbaker—the party passed the resolution to call a leadership convention before January 1, 1968. The entire sequence of events had been avoidable. Perhaps now is the time to put on the record a story that has never been told about those crucial days.

It was just prior to that convention that I began to participate in the planning and strategy sessions of Diefenbaker's inner circle, along with Gordon Churchill, Michael Starr, Angus MacLean, and Monty Monteith. The Chief called this group together for a meeting at Stornoway to discuss what should be done in the best interest of the party. All of us knew that there would be an acrimonious, divisive debate as to whether there should be a leadership convention, and it was to settle that issue that we met one day in October 1966. When Diefenbaker phoned me to let me know about the weekend meeting, he asked me if I thought there should be anyone else invited to join the usual advisory group. I naively suggested

Eldon Woolliams, the MP for Bow River, Alberta. Everything that I had heard up to this point—and you often heard Eldon, who was nicknamed "The Boomer" because of his deep, resonant voice—suggested his loyalty to the party and its leader. After I suggested his name, Diefenbaker paused, and I had come to know him sufficiently well by this time to know that this pause represented some doubt, and then he went on to say, "Fine, all right, you ask him."

Eldon was quite surprised at the invitation, but I thought, considering the number of times I had heard him voice expressions of loyalty, he would be a fine addition to our inner circle.

The meeting at Stornoway lasted a couple of hours. It was opened by Diefenbaker saying that he felt that by remaining as leader of the party, he was simply aiding and abetting the forces of disunity. He said he knew that the influential members of the party hierarchy and of the caucus would continue their efforts to force a leadership change, and this continuing activity would sap the vitals of the party when we should be concentrating our efforts on rebuilding and on winning the next election. All in all, it was his view that it would be best for the party and the country if he were to step aside so that a leadership convention could be held and the rebuilding begun. When he finished speaking, he went around the circle of advisers and asked each of us for our opinion.

The majority agreed that Diefenbaker had read the party right, as he usually did. A few held out—I was one, and Gordon Churchill another—but the Chief had already gone to the trouble of drafting a resignation which, with the concurrence of the advisers present, he planned to read the following Monday in the House of Commons. In the end, we all agreed on the wording and the timing of the resignation.

The sitting of the House in those days started at 2:30 p.m. and I was at work in my office as usual by nine o'clock on the Monday morning. I was going through my morning mail when Dick Southam, the member from Moose Jaw, burst into my office in tears. He said, "Erik, is it true?"

"Is what true?"

"Is it true that the Chief is going to resign today?"

I asked, "Who on earth gave you that idea?"

"Well, Eldon Woolliams just called into my office seeking my support for himself as party leader at a leadership convention. He's calling on members up and down the hallway, doing the same thing."

"But we have a leader," I said.

"But Eldon says the Chief's going to resign."

I told him that he ought not to worry about that. "Perhaps you'd better ask Eldon to confirm his facts."

I calmed Dick down as best I could, and when he left my office I called the Chief and told him what had happened.

Diefenbaker expressed no surprise and did not tell me how stupid I had been to suggest that Eldon take part in the first place. Nonetheless, I apologized, and he took it very gracefully. He went on to tell me what he intended to do, which was nothing. He then and there discarded the written resignation.

Thus the indiscretion of one member propelled us into the decision for a leadership convention. We thereby lost the opportunity to resolve an extremely difficult problem for the party without the bloodletting that would so wound us all.

The leadership issue had come up on an earlier occasion when I went to Stornoway to discuss a number of matters with Diefenbaker. After our business was concluded, he left to visit the washroom before luncheon, and his wife, Olive, and I began to discuss the efforts of the anti-Diefenbaker forces and who on earth could ever replace the Chief. Olive suddenly said, "Why don't you run, Erik?"

This took me completely by surprise: I had given the matter no thought. When Diefenbaker returned and we sat down to lunch, Olive opened the conversation by saying, "I was just telling Erik that he should be seeking the leadership of the party," and the Chief said, "Well, of course he should. That's a good idea."

I replied that there was no question of that; I could see no reason to change leaders and every reason to remain as we were. I analysed that luncheon event more than once after leaving and came to the conclusion that that was the Chief's way of "flying a kite" to determine my interest. It might have been initiated by Olive without prompting, but I do not believe so.

What the incident does do is confirm that the Chief had decided to step down. But he was a fighter, and when the Woolliams incident occurred, it convinced him that he would be replaced by someone whose activities would be inimical to the best interests of the party and the nation. That is what made him resolve to stay and fight. He has been treated by history as if he were an idiot, who could not see that he was doomed to defeat; of course he saw that, but since he could not see a satisfactory replacement on the horizon—the names being bandied about were those of Fulton and Fleming and Hees and now, heaven help us, Eldon Woolliams—he stayed and fought. He could not bear to be replaced by one of the men he considered a traitor.

When the 1966 annual meeting voted for a leadership convention, I was approached to allow my name to stand. I replied that since we had a leader, I regarded it as quite wrong to entertain any such notions. Taking this position allowed me to avoid the difficulty of confessing that I would not seek the position because of the embarrassment my personal life might possibly bring to the party. I was later approached again, after Alvin Hamilton, Davie Fulton, Donald Fleming, and a number of others had declared for the leadership, but my answer had to be the same.

I knew, however, that the Chief accepted the fact that he was not going to continue in office, even though he would allow his own name to stand once again, so I went to see him when Michael Starr asked me to manage his own leadership campaign. At first I rejected the idea on the grounds, so oft repeated, that we had a leader, but Starr assured me that he had discussed the matter with the Chief and had received his approval to run. I phoned Diefenbaker to ask him about this, and he told me, "Mike's free to do as he pleases," which was certainly not an enthusiastic endorsement. Just the same, it seemed to me that the Chief had, in effect, thrown his hands up in despair at otherwise loyal people going off in all directions. So I told him that Starr had asked me to manage his campaign and that if he had no objection, I would do it. He said he had none.

I told Starr (as I had told the Chief) that I did not believe he had a hope in hades of winning but that I certainly would not convey that impression to others. Mike still wanted me, though, despite my pessimism.

Starr's campaign was not the best organized or financed one in the world. There simply were not the funds or the manpower to do much. When the convention opened at the Royal York Hotel in Toronto, we quickly saw what we were up against. George Hees had a band to precede him everywhere he went, and so did some of the others. They would parade through the hotel with the brass blaring and the baton-twirling majorettes attracting attention. We had nothing with which to compete. However, I had seen this fellow with a tame chimpanzee on a chain, and I decided to hire him and his ape as our "attention-getter." Mike Starr's arrival anywhere at the convention was heralded by the chimpanzee capering along ahead of him. We certainly attracted attention, which is all that sort of thing is supposed to do. The difficulty was that when the time came to vote, the delegates were not looking for Mike Starr's name on the ballot, they were looking for the name of the ape!

Mike asked me how many votes I thought he would get on the first ballot. I said, "Not more than forty-five," which is precisely what he tallied. When that failed to improve on the next ballot, he was knocked off. He took his loss in very good form, and Robert Stanfield went on to win the leadership on the fourth ballot, over Duff Roblin.

Diefenbaker made an excellent speech that appealed for one Canada, but the old fire, though it flickered once or twice, was not there. He was exhausted and disillusioned. It was the best speech of all that were delivered at the convention, but it was not enough.

I could not help comparing the oratory of Diefenbaker in 1967 with the speech he had made, and I had been swayed by, in 1956, when I came to Ottawa to vote for Davie Fulton and ended up voting for Diefenbaker. It is my conviction that if Diefenbaker had summoned the same fire as he had in 1956, he would once again have shown his heels to his enemies. Fortunately for the party and the country, that did not happen, and I am satisfied that the Chief breathed a huge sigh of relief in the privacy of Stornoway when he returned home after the convention to begin the process of handing over to Bob Stanfield.

I know that Olive did.

Chapter Fourteen
Stanfield and Trudeau

*Moral leadership emerges from, and always returns
to, the fundamental wants and needs, aspirations and
values of the followers.*

James MacGregor Burns

*Men are so simple of mind, and so much dominated
by their immediate needs, that a deceitful man will
always find plenty who are ready to be deceived.*

Machiavelli

One of the first things Bob Stanfield did after being elected leader
on September 9, 1967, was visit every member of the Conservative
caucus in the member's office. He did that in an unhurried and
relaxed fashion, even though he undoubtedly had much work to
complete in his own office. What he was doing in those personal
visits was healing the wounds and consolidating the elements of
unity within the parliamentary caucus. I have never seen another
leader do this, and I thought at the time that it was an outstanding
example of the quality of leadership that was so necessary in a fractious caucus. Stanfield's entire leadership period was to be accompanied by other similar gestures. Unfortunately, the kind of decency
that led Stanfield into that gesture led him into a major parliamentary
blunder.

In early 1968, the Liberals were in considerable disarray. Pearson, unable to gain a majority, had announced his resignation,
and a leadership convention was to be held in Ottawa in April. In
January, Eric Kierans, Robert Winters, Paul Hellyer, Allan
MacEachen, John Turner, Mitchell Sharp, and Joe Greene in turn
announced their intentions to seek the leadership, and in February,
Pierre Elliott Trudeau, then minister of justice, joined the fray. (In

making his announcement, he lied about his age, saying he was two years younger than he really was.)

At Stanfield's request, I had agreed to coordinate the work of our members on the nineteen standing committees of the House and in turn to coordinate that work with the Commons calendar. We developed an overall strategy of exploiting whatever weaknesses we would find in the government's program to defeat those measures that we thought ought not to become law or to improve upon measures that had some merit.

We were in a minority position, with 97 seats to the Liberals' 131. As long as the government enjoyed the support of the NDP, they did not have to worry, but NDP support depended upon the consistency of that party in attending the House. If the NDP numbers fell short, and if the Liberals were sparsely represented, we had an opportunity to defeat the government. If the government could be defeated on a "money measure," parliamentary tradition and convention would leave them no option but to call an election.

The Liberals, at the insistence of Finance Minister Mitchell Sharp, had produced a budget to which we took strong exception. On February 19, the budget resolutions were working their way through the Commons. I had anticipated that the government might get careless and that we might have a chance to defeat them. I and other planners therefore carefully timed our debate to ensure that a vote occurred soon after the supper hour on Monday evening, when members are often missing from Ottawa and when, we knew, a number of Liberal cabinet ministers were out scouring the country for votes for their upcoming leadership convention. When the vote was called, sure enough, the numbers of both the Liberals and their NDP supporters were short, and the outcome of the vote on the money measure was a victory for the opposition, the government being two votes short.

Robert Winters, who was acting prime minister because Lester Pearson was vacationing in Jamaica, communicated with Pearson, while the remainder of the evening sitting was taken up by Liberal members on points of order. We had won the vote at 8:10 p.m. and ought to have adjourned forthwith. Instead, we sat until 10:00 p.m., with the government still balking at resigning.

I could understand why the Liberals would give the prime minister time to return from Jamaica and appear in the House to submit the resignation of his government, but I assumed that there was no question about the resignation itself. Every precedent told me that an election had to follow.

Pearson rushed back from Jamaica and immediately arranged to have Louis Rasminsky, governor of the Bank of Canada, call on Stanfield to tell him that the world faced a monetary crisis, which would be made worse somehow if the Canadian government were to be defeated on its budget. This was another of the many instances in which Pearson, who was reputed to be "too nice to be in politics," played the most astounding political tricks and got away with them. It was highly improper to send a civil servant on a political mission, but Rasminsky did as he was told. Stanfield could hardly refuse to see him. He bought the line that the Canadian dollar would somehow be affected, and on that basis agreed to a twenty-four-hour adjournment to allow Pearson to prepare to meet the House of Commons.

Pearson used the twenty-four hours to round up his troops, to secure the support of the Ralliement des Créditistes, who were terrified of another election, and to go on television to tell the country that his government's defeat was "a hazard of minority government" and not a true defeat. On Wednesday the government introduced a motion framed by Allan MacEachen that read, "This House does not regard its vote on 19 February in connection with third reading on Bill C-193, which it carried on all its previous stages, as a vote of non-confidence in the government."

In the Conservative caucus that morning, there were many who argued that we ought to refuse to re-enter the House, to allow any motion to come to a vote, to attend committees, or indeed do anything else until we forced the government to call an election. However, Stanfield had bound the party to go back into session, and we really had no choice but to live up to his word. Gordon Churchill, our house leader, was so irritated that he left the caucus to sit as an independent. On February 28, the government motion won easily, 140 to 199, with the support of the Ralliement des Créditistes. Most of the NDP, knowing that the Liberals could win this vote without their help, voted against the government with hypocritical bravado.

Notwithstanding the fact that I had been the principal architect of the government's defeat, which could not have taken place without the full cooperation of all of our members, Stanfield did not consult me at all after the vote. Had he done so, I would have strongly advised him against the adjournment and against cooperating in any way with a government that, once defeated, suddenly decided to change one of the most fundamental rules of a parliamentary democracy. Stanfield, always the perfect gentleman, displayed what was, from my point of view, a most appalling political naïvete, allowing himself to become the victim of shabby political trickery.

(Incidentally, during the debate in which the government miraculously restored its own virginity, Justice Minister Pierre Trudeau argued quite strongly that there was no tradition or convention that would require a government to resign if defeated on a money measure. I never knew whether this was sheer ignorance or deliberate falsehood, but it was an argument that black was white.)

When it was all over, I had formed the conclusion that there was not really much use in going on with the task of trying to defeat the government. Even so, I did agree to stand for the election we could now see would be held as soon as it suited the Liberals. My reason was simplicity itself. I had determined that I must do whatever I could to defeat Pierre Elliott Trudeau, whom I regarded then, and regard now, as one of the greatest electoral disasters ever to overtake the Canadian people.

When Trudeau took over a minority Liberal government in April 1968, he was riding a wave of adulation in the media; he was not one to waste such an opportunity, nor did he. He was sworn in as prime minister on April 20, and three days later he called an election for June 25.

He won, handily.

That election, so far as the Yukon riding was concerned, was the closest I have ever come to being defeated throughout the eleven election campaigns in my career. My opponent, Chris Findlay, was the resident geologist, a federal government employee, who took leave without pay to seek election and who probably made the best-calibre candidate that the Liberal party or the NDP had ever put forward in any of the campaigns in which I participated. His biggest difficulty was that he was such a fine gentleman that he failed to get the working person's vote in Yukon. Nonetheless, he came within sixty-two ballots of defeating us in Yukon in that 1968 election.

Believing that they would pull a rabbit out of the hat the way we had done with the 1957 election, the Liberals brought proceedings to try to show at least sixty-two irregularities in the voting in Yukon. Had they succeeded, the election would have been rendered null and void. However, the proceedings were not long under way before the Liberals discovered that there had been none of the jiggery-pokery that had marked the 1957 election, and they had no case. The attempt was abandoned.

Following the election of 1968, Stanfield toured the Pacific Northwest, including Yukon and the state of Alaska. Because of the increasing likelihood that an oil or gas pipeline would be built to tap the resources of the Beaufort Sea, Stanfield wanted to inform himself as fully as possible about the Alyeska Pipeline, which seemed likely to be the model for our own northern pipeline. The tour was very much a success, in part because of Bob Stanfield's cool and unflappable nature and his magnificent, though wry, sense of humour, which allowed him to enjoy what might have seemed an ordeal to many. When he arrived in Whitehorse, he had spent hours and hours on a DC-6B, the ancient, propeller-driven aircraft that was still being used by Canadian Pacific Airlines to service Yukon. On the way from Edmonton, the plane had made stops at Grand Prairie, Fort St. John, Fort Nelson, and Watson Lake. As he came down the aircraft steps in Whitehorse, Stanfield said, "My God, I feel as if I've been flying around the world."

Stanfield and his party came away from the tour with a new appreciation of Canada's North and of the people who live there. He accepted my invitation to spend some time at Quiet Lake, northeast of Whitehorse, my favourite spot in Yukon. The day he visited was brilliant and hot, and he took the plunge into the icy, glacier-fed waters of the lake five times, without any change of expression and without any acknowledgment of the perishing cold that embraces any swimmer in those waters. One of the young journalists travelling with the Stanfield party, a man whose well-developed torso attested to his dedication as a body-builder, was so encouraged by Stanfield's performance that he donned bathing trunks and plunged in too. He gasped loudly, his face registered shock, and he came out of the lake almost as fast as he had gone in, never again to challenge those frigid waters. After a few minutes, Stanfield rose from his chair and went swimming again, as placidly as if he were bathing in a heated pool.

That was my introduction to the imperturbability of Bob Stanfield; I was to observe and admire his many fine qualities on several other occasions.

Canadians were in for an almost uninterrupted sixteen years of Liberal government, led by a man who was going to alter the face of our country. As soon as Trudeau was elected leader of the Liberal party and thus became, automatically, prime minister of Canada, I began an intensive study of everything that he had written over the years. I came to the conclusion that he had the philosophical convictions of a Marxist-Leninist at the most, and at the very least was an extreme left-wing socialist. I have not had any occasion to alter that assessment of Trudeau the politician-philosopher. Almost everything he did while in office appeared to me to have the objective of taking Canada down that philosophical road to socialism, whether the policy surfaced in the form of such far-reaching economic measures as the National Energy Policy or whether it was the establishment of core funding for natives.

He was also the man who invoked the War Measures Act in the October Crisis of 1970. My colleagues and I voted with the government on that occasion, but it is a vote I am ashamed of now. We ought to have seen that we were being misled by the prime minister and by such cabinet ministers as John Turner about the nature of the ''apprehended insurrection'' in Quebec, but my loyalty overcame my instinct and I went along with a caucus decision to vote contrary to the maintenance of the civil and individual liberties that I have fought for all my life. Habeas corpus was suspended and the rule of law was treated with contempt. Canadians were arrested without charge and made offenders by retroactive legislation that made it a crime ever to have joined the Front de Libération du Québec, which was legal one day and retroactively illegal the next. My strong repugnance for separatism undoubtedly affected my decision, but it was the wrong decision. Ironically, one of the moments when I was proudest of Robert Stanfield, after he had left the leadership of the party, was when he told the nation that he had erred in backing the government on that occasion. We all had. Trudeau's action reflected the instincts of a man who believes that political power ought to be vested in the state, not the individual, and his social policies displayed the same outlook.

The welfare state flourished in the Trudeau years as it had never before, and Canada moved into the ranks of the world's leading socialist nations. This has resulted in the virtual destruction of the Canadian virtues of independence, self-reliance, initiative, resource-fulness, the work ethic, and all of the attributes of character that, in my view, make a nation strong. The seeds of today's monstrous deficits were sown during these years.

The year 1968, when the Trudeau government was first elected, was the beginning of the Great Rip-off of the Canadian Taxpayer, who has had to pay for all these socialistic programs. These were to come under my closer examination during my time in the Mul-roney cabinet.

The "Trudeauization" of Canada had been under way for about a year when my whole approach to the future was abruptly altered by the death of P.J. in April 1969. I naturally thought long and deeply about personal priorities for the future. There could be no question that the primary priority had to be my two teenaged children.

In June 1969, after Rick and Roxanne had completed school, we returned to Whitehorse, where I was determined that we would re-establish our home. That fall, we moved out of an apartment into a newly constructed house. Lee was working on various con-struction jobs in and out of Whitehorse, so he was home only occa-sionally. Rick and Roxanne finished high school in Whitehorse.

During this period my absences from the House of Commons were understandably quite lengthy, since the major portion of my time was taken up with caring for my two youngest children. It was during this time too, that I discovered the art of cooking, and the techniques of housekeeping, since it was virtually impossible to obtain the services of a housekeeper. I did most of these tasks myself, with the assistance of the children. In the main, cooking was my bailiwick, and I became so accomplished at it that my weight went from 165 soaking wet to 195. When I found myself gasping for breath and having difficulty bending over to pump the bilges of the floats of my aircraft, I knew that I had to do something about my weight problem. I embarked upon a program of nourishment that eliminated most carbohydrates, and I soon lost the unwanted weight.

In the meantime, the two children were re-established in a warm, loving home environment where they freely enjoyed the company of their friends, whom they invited over at any time. The remainder of the school terms leading to high school graduation were normal in all respects including the worries and problems that accompany the maturing of any teenager.

One of the principal reasons for my decision to re-establish a home in Whitehorse was that, once I chose to make the raising of my children my first priority, I came to a conviction that I never afterwards changed. It seems simple, but for a politician it was not. I realized that getting re-elected was not the most important thing in my life. Until I reached that conclusion in 1969, I, in common with 99 per cent of all politicians who have succumbed at one time or another to the "power of the vote," had done certain things that I would not otherwise have done.

Let me give one homely example. It was my habit as a politician always to submit to the blandishments of panhandlers on the street, albeit reluctantly. What if the person recognized me? What if someone else saw me brushing off some poor unfortunate who was just trying to get enough money together to get plastered again? Better to submit to the genteel blackmail of the extended palm than to follow my own instinct, which was to tell the panhandler to try some other method of making money, such as work. Sometimes when I was asked for money, "just to buy a bowl of soup, sir," I made arrangements for the individual to go to a restaurant to have a meal at my expense; the offer was always traded for cash, which found its way into the cash register of the closest bar.

I stopped every form of hypocrisy, from such tiny matters as the way I dealt with panhandlers to the expression of my own opinions on matters of public policy. Like most politicians, I had formed the habit of responding to questions in a manner that was likely to be pleasing to one particular audience or another. I gave my own views, but edited to make them acceptable to voters who might not share my opinions on such matters as capital punishment, or the welfare state, or native rights. When I received impossible requests from constituents, as every MP does, I always replied with the soft answer that turneth away wrath (and keepeth votes). That changed in the months following P.J.'s death, and, to my amazement, my support increased in the riding. It seemed that the ruder I was to panhandlers and the franker I was about impossible requests from constituents, the more I endeared myself to them, a result that was reflected in the polls at each successive federal election.

So, to those young and not-so-young persons who aspire to a

political career, I offer another piece of advice: do not prostitute your beliefs or principles for a potential vote. Be yourself, be honest, be forthright, be blunt, but always be tactful when you are the bearer of bad news.

Roxanne went on from high school to a year's study in private school in Switzerland before enrolling at Acadia University in Nova Scotia. Her postgraduate studies were in criminology at Simon Fraser University in British Columbia. Before completing her postgraduate studies, she joined the RCMP in 1979 and served mainly in Alberta before marrying another member of the force and moving to Ottawa in 1986, where she lives today with her husband and their baby son, Erik.

Rick graduated from high school at the same time as Roxanne and then attended Northern Alberta Institute of Technology, where he graduated as an accomplished heavy-duty mechanic. He returned to Whitehorse, gained considerable flying experience, and went on to become the manager of an automobile complex. He is married to the daughter of my friend Rolf Hougen; they too have a son, born while this book was being written and within three weeks of my other grandson.

Upon the departure of the two youngsters for postsecondary education, I was left alone in a very large house. I therefore sold it and have since lived in rented accommodation either in Whitehorse or in Ottawa. Once the children were away, I plunged back into politics again, but never, until the very end, with the self-destructive intensity that had marked my early years.

I was happy and proud to be working with a leader like Bob Stanfield, and in 1972 I was so sure that he had done a good job during that year's election that, when he called me in Whitehorse while the returns were still coming in, I addressed him as "Mr. Prime Minister."

"Well, Erik," he said, laconically, "everything's not in yet, we'd better wait for a while. But in any event, I want you to cover off the solicitor general if you're prepared to take on the responsibility." The wording was precise and illuminating: I was being offered the post if we formed a government, and the shadow cabinet post if we did not. Stanfield was too shrewd to leap to any conclusions, but at the same time he wanted to waste no time getting organized for the return to Ottawa after the election. I gave him the same assurance that I gave to all the leaders of the party, namely, that I would undertake whatever responsibility he as leader thought would be in the best interests of the country and the party. As it turned out, we lost that election by two seats, so I became the critic for the solicitor general's department, in a very strong opposition during two years of minority Liberal government that prostituted itself entirely to the NDP.

When I gave Stanfield the assurance that I would accept the new responsibility, I had, in effect, committed myself to politics permanently. I was no longer the pilot and lawyer who went into politics for a time; I was, and would remain, a politician. The move to Whitehorse with my children had been another attempt to distance myself from politics, but as I looked ahead to another period of Trudeau rule, I knew that I could not leave while that man was in charge. By the time we got him out I would be well into middle age. (As it turned out, I was fifty-four when we first defeated Trudeau, and sixty before we got him out of the Ottawa woodwork permanently.) Certainly I tried to resign on later occasions, but in my heart of hearts I should have known that I had reached the Point of No Return.

Ironically, the 1972 election that led to that decision on my part saw the voters of York-Simcoe in Ontario send a new MP to Ottawa, Sinclair McKnight Stevens, who would change my mind for me fifteen years later. Later, in Stanfield's office, I met Sinc Stevens. I do not now recall the reason for Stanfield calling the two of us together; I suppose it probably came about because of some disagreement about the coordination of subcommittee work with the work in the House of Commons, for which I was responsible.

What remains clear in my memory is the violence of Stevens's disagreement with a political strategy I had recommended to Stanfield. He became visibly angry and showed the kind of temper no successful politician can afford. I made a mental note of that deficiency and was later to learn that he would never conquer it, to his sorrow, and that of others. Of course, I had no inkling of what lay ahead when I returned to Ottawa to take up the challenge Stanfield had placed before me.

Although I now had much more time for parliamentary work, it was necessary for me to continue with the law practice, because my House of Commons income was still insufficient to enable me to discharge all of my financial commitments, which still included a substantial debt. At the same time, I once more took on the job of coordinating the work of the official opposition in the standing committees, which were becoming ever more important as the House of Commons gradually ceded the decision-making process to the executive and the bureaucracy.

In the shadow cabinet post of solicitor general, another important task fell to me, and that was the review of the penitentiary system in Canada by a subcommittee especially set up for that purpose. This subcommittee was established as part of the Standing Committee on Justice and Legal Affairs. The penitentiary system had been the subject of mounting criticism as a result of unprecedented violence, rioting, and hostage-taking in various prisons, which led to the conclusion that there was something fundamentally wrong with the system itself.

Our subcommittee visited most federal institutions, some provincial jails, and some of the prisons in the United States. After almost a year of work, we concluded with a list of sixty-five recommendations, most of which were adopted by the government. Of the rejected recommendations, the most important, and the one that in my view formed the heart of the report, dealt with the question of the incorrigibles whose activities had caused most of the violence and rioting.

We tried to deal with criminals of the stamp of Clifford Olson, those whose crimes have been such that there is no reasonable hope or expectation of rehabilitation, either in a medical or a social sense, or criminals who simply refuse to follow prison rules and become the instigators of violence within the system. We recognized very quickly that this kind of prison inmate was going to be a problem in our report. We arrived at a proposal whereby those individuals who had persistently resisted discipline, work, socialization, and any efforts at rehabilitation and those who were assessed as being impossible to rehabilitate in a medical or social sense were to be incarcerated not with the rest of the prison population but segregated in a limited number of special correctional units. Such institutions would have all of the programs and services of any other maximum security institution, including the medical and therapeutic facilities, but they would exist as separate facilities within the system. A man like Clifford Olson, a serial killer of children, must now be kept in protective isolation in a maximum security institution, at enormous expense, since, if he were to mix with the general prison population, he would not be allowed to live long.

That recommendation received the unanimous approval not only of our subcommittee but of the Standing Committee on Justice, when it went forward to the House of Commons. NDP, Liberals, and Conservatives were all in agreement, but the proposal was rejected by the Trudeau government.

Mark MacGuigan, who was chairman of the standing committee, later became minister of justice under Trudeau and now sits on the federal court bench. He had four years as minister of justice to act on his conviction that something had to be done about these human time-bombs in our penal system. Indeed, I reminded him several times while he was minister of justice of the chance he had to act on our joint recommendation, but he never did, and the problem remains.

Despite that disappointment, I found the penitentiary study to be a satisfying project because of the scope of our accomplishment, since the unanimity that all of us had to work to achieve found expression in the implementation of the major portion of the report by the government.

To me, that subcommittee's efforts represented the manner in which a parliamentary system should work in such matters. The ideal, of course, would have been for the House of Commons to have adopted the entire report. However, ideals, as I had learned many years earlier, are not achievable in politics, if indeed they are anywhere.

Probably the most important of the internal reforms that Bob Stanfield brought about within the parliamentary caucus was to establish regular meetings of his shadow cabinet. We not only had a shadow group that consisted of a critic for every minister of the Crown, we had an organization that existed in the cabinet sense. We met as a policy group to rehash all the decisions that were made by the government in light of established Conservative programs, as if we were a cabinet ourselves. The outcome of those debates was then taken to caucus, where the subject was debated by all party members. This was an extremely useful process, making all members feel that they were making a meaningful contribution, which indeed they were. That process was followed by Joe Clark and for a time—but only for a time—by Brian Mulroney during his time in opposition. It seemed such a natural and logical thing to do that when Stanfield introduced it, I wondered why it had not been done before.

So sophisticated did that management approach become that there is no question in my mind that if we had won the 1972 election, the shadow cabinet would have been eminently capable of moving their discussions quickly and easily to the official cabinet table. We were not so much an opposition under Stanfield as we were a government-in-waiting.

Having served the party under four leaders, Diefenbaker, Stanfield, Clark, and Mulroney, I can say that the years of Stanfield's leadership saw the highest level of unity in the party caucus. Naturally, there were elements who wanted to see the leadership change when we lost the 1972 election, but because that vote had been so close, the overwhelming consensus was that we should remain united in support of Bob Stanfield to face the next general election, which, under a minority government, might come about at any time.

And indeed, in 1974 we had another election, which was won by the Liberals, in my view, by deceit. That was the election in which the Conservative party supported wage and price controls, and Trudeau used them as a club to beat us over the head. He went around the country shouting, "Zap! You're frozen!" and ridiculed us into defeat. Then, shortly after his majority victory in that election, Trudeau imposed wage and price controls. I had been opposed to the controls at first, but had accepted them when the party consensus accepted them. It was bitter indeed to find ourselves ridiculed for a policy that our opponents had eventually adopted, but by this time I was past being surprised by anything in the world of politics.

After the 1974 election, I told Stanfield that I would not stand for election to Parliament in the next vote. Thus, when he decided to resign and paved the way for a leadership convention in 1976, I understood how he felt, although I believed then as now that he made the wrong decision.

The Trudeau government, after that first blush of victory in 1974, was plunged into a series of scandals involving cabinet minister after cabinet minister. There was the judges' affair, in which cabinet members were found to have called judges, clearly with a view to interfering with the normal processes of the law; the skyshops affair, which involved alleged improprieties in the awarding of airport concessions; and the Francis Fox affair, in which the solicitor general tried to cover up a love affair by forging the name of his lover's husband on a hospital form in order to obtain an abortion for the lover; and such monumental financial disasters as the building of Mirabel Airport, the only airport in the world to use, correctly, a white elephant as its official symbol.

The people of Canada were fed up to the teeth with the Trudeau Liberals before long, but the chance to defeat them resoundingly was lost when Stanfield stepped down and made way for the new leader of the Conservatives, Charles Joseph Clark.

Chapter Fifteen

Joe Clark

In fact, it may not be an exaggeration to suggest that a national leader has rarely, if ever, assumed office with lower expectations concerning his ability to govern.

Tory Pollster Allan Gregg, June 13, 1979

It was during the Stanfield years that, with his approval, I set up an organization of caucus resource persons to use as a kind of flying squad in the House of Commons, particularly during Question Period. When subjects arose that required vigorous, concentrated, and thorough exploitation, we hurled this group into the breach. We never named the group, for fear of ridicule. We did not want to attract a nickname like the Liberals' infamous Truth Squad of the Pearson years, or what later became the even more infamous Rat Pack of the Turner years. (We did have one named group, though its name was seldom used aloud and has never before appeared in print; this was our Angel Squad: Jake Epp, Benno Friesen, and Perrin Beatty. They were all young, handsome, clean-cut, and straightforward—their halos were almost visible. They would question ministers whose television appearance and reputations suggested something not entirely wholesome, such as John Munro and André Ouellet. The television camera quickly exposed and emphasized the contrast between the appearance of the Angel Squad and the appearance of the members of the Liberal front bench.)

Our unnamed group comprised three central, permanent questioners who were skilled at the process in the House, with provision for two other specialist positions that were filled from time to time by various members who were knowledgeable in the particular subject matter under discussion. It was the political equivalent of football's special team squad. The permanent members on this team

190

were Jake Epp, Perrin Beatty, and myself. When I discussed the composition of this group with Stanfield, he asked me if I had considered the MP from High River, Alberta, Joe Clark. The manner in which he asked the question conveyed to me his wish that Joe Clark be there. That, and further observations, convinced me that Stanfield regarded Clark as a leading contender for the leadership of the party. I naturally put Clark on the list of the inner group, but frankly, I thought Stanfield's regard for his abilities was misplaced.

Initially, I did not have a high regard for Joe Clark. I must confess to a well-established bias in this respect since I resented him for his prominence in the activities to undermine John Diefenbaker. When he first came into Parliament in 1972, I thought he was, from the outset, overly aggressive to the point of being objectionable; I was not alone in this view. He had a tendency to assume, on his own initiative, positions of authority and leadership in matters that I thought he should properly have left to others.

On one occasion, the members of one of our caucus committees held a strategy meeting at which we decided upon the apportionment of responsibilities among the various members of one of the standing committees. I undertook to perform some tasks, and others were assigned to other members. Immediately following that meeting, I received a lengthy letter from Joe, who was not in charge of that committee (or anything else at that point), setting forth in great detail those responsibilities I had undertaken and indicating that he expected to hear from me soon. It was the sort of avuncular letter a friendly elder statesman might write to one of the freshman members. Such was my resentment at that approach that I did not respond to, or even acknowledge that I had ever received, Joe's letter.

Just the same, at Stanfield's suggestion I started to use Joe more and more in the strategies and tactics that we had developed for our position in the House of Commons. I was pleasantly surprised with the results. Joe was invariably our most effective questioner: he was always well prepared and inevitably had the government on the receiving end of some of the most effective, and often scathing, criticism of its policies and activities. His extensive vocabulary and mental agility provided him with a powerful talent for articulation both offensively and defensively. He was never at a loss for a riposte. The more I saw of him in action, the more impressed I was. This was not the feeling of others in the caucus, who seemed to become more resentful of Joe as his impressive performance increased.

Eventually, I found myself concluding that Stanfield had read him better than I had, that Joe had a very fine intellect, with a great skill for assessing political situations and designing strategies and tactics to meet them. I still did not see him, however, as a party leader or future prime minister, because of his difficulty in getting himself taken seriously by the Canadian public. His appearance worked against him in an age of television, and the media spoke of his physical deficiencies far more often than they extolled his intellectual qualities. Led by the cartoonists, the media dwelt on his receding chin, his large head with its floppy ears, and usually depicted him as some kind of beagle. Throughout his rise, the media, instead of reporting a measured balance of successes and failures, invariably dwelt on Joe Clark's stumbles. If Bob Stanfield thought he represented someone who should be included in any list of his potential successors, I, for one, thought the odds were stacked against him.

Stanfield's determination to leave led us to the leadership convention of 1976. The unique feature of that convention—for the Conservative party—was that it was called as a result of a voluntary act of Stanfield's, who announced that he was relinquishing the leadership but would stay on in Parliament to serve out his term. It was thus on a relatively peaceful basis—compared to 1967—that we entered the contest.

Once again I was approached by a delegation of western party officials, along with representatives from Atlantic Canada and one prominent politician from Ontario, who urged me to put my name forward for the leadership. Once again I declined.

I supported Claude Wagner all the way through that convention, because I believed that he was the kind of prominent, well-respected Quebecker who would be well regarded throughout Canada and had the greatest potential for bringing about unity within the country and within the party. At the time, I was unaware of the arrangements that had been made to induce Wagner to leave the bench and seek election to Parliament and to the leadership of the party. If I had known of these matters at that time, I would not have offered him my support.

Wagner almost made it, but naturally, that is not good enough in any race, and to the surprise of many, not least of all myself, when the dust settled Joe Clark was the new Conservative Leader. "Joe Who?" the *Toronto Sun* called him, signalling the very problem I had foreseen.

After the 1974 election, I had reached the end of my 1972 commitment to Bob Stanfield that I would go one more election. I was determined that I would not be making any further commitments. I would serve out that term to 1978 or 1979, and that would be it. Indeed, I solicited interest in the constituency to determine whether one or more acceptable candidates could be identified who would stand for the nomination. I had made such efforts previously without significant results.

I was successful in identifying someone who would have made, in my opinion, an excellent candidate for the next federal election, Tim Koepke. Tim is a land surveyor and engineer. He was a highly valued employee of Underhill and Underhill, an engineering firm whose principal work in Yukon was land surveys. That work took Tim to all parts of Yukon. He had met many people and had employed local labour in various communities. He was well known, young, with an attractive wife and two young children—in all, a very electable individual. He was quite serious about taking on the challenge, and his wife, Jan, supported him in this. During one of his visits to Ottawa, I invited him to a social function—I believe it was the birthday of Joe's daughter, Catherine—being held in the leader's boardroom on the fourth floor of Centre Block. After meeting Tim and Jan, Joe informed me in private that he was impressed and was generally encouraging about asking Tim to seek the nomination of the Yukon Progressive Conservative Association.

In the meantime, Tim had spoken with the partners in Underhill and Underhill, since he was rising rapidly within the company and was about to receive a proposal that would have made him a full participating partner. Neither Tim nor the principals of his firm saw any impediment to Tim following that course, since the election was still likely two or three years away.

With the passage of time and my activities in the House of Commons, I came to appreciate more fully Joe Clark's capabilities as a very talented and well informed debater, whose oratorical skills were of a high standard indeed: as good or better than any member serving in the House at that time. Clark likewise had an increasing appreciation of the degree to which he could rely upon me to carry out any assignments or responsibilities that he requested of me.

As a result, as we approached the countdown to the 1979 federal election, Joe asked me to allow my name to stand for re-election, even though I had told him that I would not be running again. He put the request in such a way that I felt obliged to accept. In the entire history of Yukon's representation in the House of Commons since 1903, no Yukon MP had ever been a cabinet member (although George Black had served as Speaker of the House). Joe Clark left no doubt in my mind whatsoever that he wanted me to be part of any government that he formed after the election.

He did not make a direct statement to that effect, which simply is not done by prime-ministers-in-waiting, but when he responded to media questions he left little doubt in the mind of the questioner that I would be part of his government.

Before I responded, I talked to Tim Koepke at the earliest opportunity, since he was prepared to run and had committed himself. Tim at once saw the benefits to Yukon and agreed that I would be doing the only proper thing to run once again. As it turned out, the election of May 1979 brought a minority government that lasted just under eight months.

The Clark years, as compared to the Stanfield years, were to revive the fractious worst in the Conservative caucus. Where Stanfield had managed to bring about a degree of peace and comparative tranquillity, and an unheard-of level of unity after the tumultuous Diefenbaker years, we were back to a raucous caucus during the Clark years.

The conduct of the Liberal government at that time was so bad, and the majority of Canadians were searching so eagerly for respite from a prime minister perceived by many to be a despot, that few people noticed the damage that was being done by our own internal bickering. I am convinced that if Clark had been able to establish the kind of presence in caucus that Stanfield had brought to bear, 1979 would have seen the election of a majority Conservative government.

The problems in caucus were not entirely Joe's fault. The caucus reflected the mood that was being created in the public mind by the vicious and ignorant approach of most of the media, who simply would not give Joe the chance to be judged on his own merits but made up their minds that he was incompetent and adjusted the facts to fit this view.

I suppose the best example is the so-called lost luggage episode during Joe's world tour, not long after he assumed the party leadership. There was, indeed, some delay in getting some of the tour luggage forwarded—as indeed there had been in Trudeau's day, on occasion. But in Trudeau's case, the press was silent on the subject. For Joe, the lost luggage became a metaphor for incompetence.

In the same way, when one reporter wrote that Joe Clark had almost backed into a bayonet while reviewing Canadian troops in the Middle East, that became magnified into a vision of Clark stumbling around, avoiding calamity by a hair's breadth, like a character in a Mack Sennett film. There are thousands of Canadians who believe to this day that Clark impaled himself on that occasion, when what actually happened—and has happened hundreds of times—is that he came within a few inches of a weapon. The media could well have spoken of the accomplishments of Clark's international visits, but chose instead to belittle him. When Trudeau went abroad, the media's treatment was invariably positive; he was portrayed as an international statesman and a Canadian jewel in the world's crown. Joe Clark was made to look like a political comedian who did not deserve our confidence. That attitude remained in the mind of the public, and when we won the minority government in May 1979, it was very grudgingly given, even though Canadians were crying out for a change. In the atmosphere that led up to that election, the cry "anything but Trudeau" gradually became transformed into "anything but Clark," and the majority that might have given him a chance to carry out his program was denied.

Once in office, Clark found that, instead of receding, the media contempt for him redoubled, and no occasion was ever lost to picture whatever we did as either mistaken, desperate, or bungled.

True to his word, Clark made me minister of public works, as well as vice-president of the Treasury Board and a member of the cabinet committee on security and intelligence. This last was an unusual appointment, since the minister of public works did not normally serve on that committee, but because of my background and familiarity with the subject, and the reliance that Joe placed on my advice in these matters, he wanted me on that cabinet committee.

The Clark government, for the eight months it existed, was, despite some of the good work that was done, a government waiting to be defeated. No minority government has any security, and with the attitude being displayed by the media, which fed on and in turn exacerbated the discontent in caucus, it was only a matter of time before we lost a vote in the House and had to go to the country once again. Frankly, I looked forward to that; I believed, quite wrongly, that the Liberals had blundered when they engineered our defeat on December 12, 1979, with the aid of the NDP.

Trudeau had announced on November 21 that he was resigning as party leader, and the party's national executive called a leadership convention to open March 28, 1980, in Winnipeg. On December 10, John Turner, who had quit first the Trudeau cabinet and then politics in disgust, announced that he would be seeking the leadership. The December Gallup poll showed the Liberals ahead, no doubt a result of the media's dim view of Joe Clark, but earlier polls had shown us holding the bare margin of victory that had propelled us into government. In the circumstances, it seemed highly unlikely that the Liberals would defeat our budget, but they leapt on the proposal to increase the excise tax on gasoline by eighteen cents a gallon (which in fact was considerably lower than Finance Minister John Crosbie had been urged to impose). The NDP had already announced their intention to vote against the budget, and when the Liberals decided to do the same, we were defeated.

The Liberal leadership convention was called off. Trudeau "unresigned" and, reinstalled as leader, led the Liberals into the election that followed.

I had expected that the leaderless Liberals would go down to defeat before Trudeau announced his miraculous resurrection and return to the party's helm. When he did, I was sure that the Canadian public would deal him the rebuke he so justly deserved. I clearly underestimated the damage that had been done by the media's Chinese water torture of day-by-day reporting that Clark was ineffective, his caucus divided, his party in disarray, and his tie crooked. Trudeau ran a typical Trudeau campaign, attacking us and making the most of the proposed increase in gasoline prices. (Again, he promptly reversed tactics when he regained office. Gasoline prices did not go up eighteen cents a gallon under Trudeau—they went up over a dollar a gallon!)

We won our Yukon riding by a respectable margin, and I

returned to Ottawa to clean up some tag ends that had to be cared for as out-going minister of public works before turning the ministry over to the Liberals. I also attended the final meeting of the Clark cabinet in the cabinet room of the Langevin Building. It was a meeting fraught with tension and emotion. Joe Clark explained to his ministers how sorry he was that we were not continuing in office and shouldered the entire responsibility for having lost the election. Then he broke down and wept. I assume that most people there felt as I did—that we wanted to protect this man, who after all had led us to victory in 1979 and, even though it was a minority victory, had provided us with our first taste of office since 1963. Jim McGrath, Clark's minister of fisheries, broke the uncomfortable silence in the cabinet room by starting to sing, "For He's a Jolly Good Fellow," which we all sang with gusto, and at the end of the chorus, Joe had himself under control and carried on that final meeting with dignity.

As soon as Trudeau's cabinet was sworn in on March 3, 1980, I left for a rest in Hawaii, where I have some very good friends. Unbeknownst to me, Joe Clark and Maureen McTeer, his wife, were on Maui with their daughter, Catherine. Joe tracked me down and phoned to say he wanted to see me. My friends had a twin-engined Cessna 310, so we flew from Hawaii over to Maui to pick up Joe, Maureen, and Catherine and bring them back to the Big Island, where we spent the day before flying them back to Maui.

I had a good idea what Joe wanted to speak to me about. It was not merely to conduct a post-mortem on the election campaign, although we certainly did that. He wanted to talk about the new Parliament and party morale. I was amazed at the degree to which Joe had rebounded from the humiliation of our defeat. Gone entirely was the depression of the last cabinet meeting and in its place was confidence and good cheer.

When we returned to the House, I of course informed him that I would serve out the term and assist in whatever capacity he believed would best serve the country, the party, and himself as leader. I told him that he had my unswerving loyalty as all party leaders have had, and that I would do whatever I could to bring about his victory in the next federal election.

I did not see Joe again until late that summer. Parliament convened with the new Trudeau cabinet, which was pretty well the same as the old Trudeau cabinet. After the summer adjournment,

I returned to Ottawa for the fall session. Joe sent word that he wanted to see me in his new office in the South Block, where the opposition leaders have their offices. He asked me to assume the responsibilities of opposition house leader. I said I would do this only if I had the wholehearted support of Walter Baker, then serving in that capacity. Joe assured me that he had discussed the matter with Baker, and he was satisfied that Walter had the same attitude as myself, namely, that he wanted to serve the party and its leader in the manner that would, in the leader's judgment, be in the best interests of both. Indeed, Joe had arranged a follow-up meeting with Walter immediately thereafter, during which we talked about the strategies that we should be adopting in the coming months of opposition.

Walter Baker had been house leader for a number of years before the 1979 election and was government house leader during the Clark government. Since coming into Parliament in 1972, he had endeared himself to all members of the Conservative caucus. He was every inch a gentleman, always eager to be helpful—a fine, upstanding, honest, forthright politician, a very rare bird indeed in modern Parliaments. I had a great respect and admiration for Walter, who was to die of lung cancer not long afterwards, but where his approach as opposition house leader had been one of peaceful co-existence in the House, my approach was quite different—much more blunt and confrontational. In my view, the opposition had an objective, and that objective was to get rid of the Trudeau government, which the vast majority of Canadians wanted dethroned, and to replace it with a Conservative government. We could not achieve our objective by continuing to allow Trudeau to run roughshod over everything and everyone in the House. His idea of compromise was capitulation. I was determined to end that despotic approach in the House.

Life became, I am sure, far more difficult for the Liberal government from the time of my appointment. The Liberal house leader, Yvon Pinard, was a fine parliamentarian with a good deal of spine. He was certainly no pushover, but his rigidity became a failing, because when he could have and should have ceded ground, he refused, to his own cost. It was not difficult either to prod Ian Deans, the NDP house leader, into losing his temper or to create a situation in which he would lose control of himself without provocation. Once, during a house leaders' discussion in Pinard's office, Deans became very red in the face and could not suppress his anger at a proposal I had made. He offered to roll up his sleeves then and there and engage in fisticuffs to settle a point. I said that I was of the view that the House of Commons was a debating forum, not a boxing ring—which did not contribute at all to defusing his anger. However, he finally realized he was making a fool of himself and, with a visible effort, brought himself under control. Pinard was aghast at the notion that his office might be the scene of a brawl.

I was able to deal with the other house leaders effectively enough; but I also had to deal, in quite a different way, with my own colleagues. I survived World War II by knowing the difference between my enemies and my friends and by fighting the former but not the latter. Unfortunately, that rule is not understood by all Conservatives.

Whatever strategy was to be adopted in the House had to have not only the endorsement of the leader but the support of caucus, or it would not work. That meant a good deal of consultation, even some coaxing, in fact quite the opposite approach to the confrontational tactics used on our opponents. Without the cooperation of caucus, the most effective (and spectacular) event that took place under my house leadership could never have taken place; that was the famous incident of the division bells in March 1982.

We had before us in the House of Commons the Liberal government legislation to embody their new National Energy Policy, a policy, I say in passing, as misguided and foolish as any ever thrust through Parliament, as events were to prove. Given the minority situation in the House, the legislation would have been doomed to defeat without pre-approval by the NDP. This is a classic example of the minority government "dog" being wagged by the balance-of-power "tail"! To accomplish their massive changes, the Liberals had put all their proposals—essentially nineteen separate bills—into a single, omnibus bill. The fundamental theory behind putting bills through the Commons is that the members shall have a clear opportunity of voting Yea or Nay on each individual proposal. It can readily be seen that if a government brought in a single measure that dealt with the dual issues of, say, abortion and capital punishment, an MP who wished to vote one way on one of these issues and the other way on the other would be denied the right to do so.

That offence in this case was compounded eighteen times, and no amount of reason would persuade the government that parliamentary custom required that members be free to vote on the nineteen issues separately.

A lengthy procedural argument was laid before the Speaker, Jeanne Sauvé. Several arguments were raised, but all were routinely rejected, and after one of these rejections, in order to focus attention on these events, we moved the adjournment of the House. The normal practice is for the Speaker to instruct that the division bells be turned on by the chief page in the Commons and be left on until the government whip and the opposition whip appear at the Commons door, march down the centre aisle of the chamber, bow to the Speaker, and take their seats. This is the signal that the members are all ready to vote. It is not possible to take the vote until the whips appear. Our tactic in this case was simple; our whip would not appear. And so the bells rang, and they rang, and they rang. For fifteen days.

Yvon Pinard, instead of swallowing his pride and calling me almost immediately, decided to wait us out—a tactic that was bound to fail, since it was their legislation that was being stalled, not ours. It was our view that the best interest of Canada would be served if the legislation never went through, particularly in such a form. It was Pinard's responsibility to steer legislation through with as few difficulties as possible, and not merely to sulk in his office when something unexpected came up.

Every day while the bells continued their maddening din, the Conservative caucus met—sometimes we met more than once a day—to make sure that everyone understood and approved of the tactics. There was, of course, outside pressure on us, and, in the beginning, many angry editorials about our obstructionist tactics appeared in the newspapers. But as time passed and people began to realize both the nature of the legislation and the unprecedented ploy the government was using in wrapping its proposals in this single indigestible bill, the mood began to change, and the accusations of being the enemies of progress changed to recognition of our defence of the rules of Parliament. Had caucus support weakened at any time during those two noisy weeks, the whole strategy would have blown up in our faces. It was a question of who would blink first, Pinard and the Liberal government, or myself and the Conservative caucus.

There were certainly rumblings within caucus as the days

dragged by and MPs began to get phone calls from constituents (which we had warned them was bound to happen). But in the end, we won our point, and a good deal of the credit must go to the resolution Joe Clark showed throughout.

The Speaker was in an unenviable position. As the guardian of the rules of the House, she had to see that these rules were not abused; but she could not interfere with the application of the rules by the opposition when that application was clearly proper. Naturally, she wanted to see the Commons back at work doing its business; it was not her job to decide whether that business was good or bad for the country—that is what Parliament is for. We took the position that the legislation was bad for Canada, and we were entitled to use the tactic of the bells to combat the government's stupidity and intransigence in its omnibus bill. (Indeed, one of the first acts of the Mulroney government was to abolish the National Energy Policy, and there were few who mourned its passing.)

The Speaker called two meetings of the house leaders to try to resolve the matter, and I attended only on condition that the meetings be confidential and that the Speaker alone should speak to the media, without revealing the content of our discussions but only that they had taken place. If we became enmeshed in media games, I knew we would never get the matter resolved, and there was a good chance our strategy would dissolve. Both Yvon Pinard and Ian Deans respected that promise of confidentiality, to their credit, but after the second meeting broke up, still without an agreement, the crush of journalists around the door of the Speaker's chambers was such that one could scarcely move. While the others remained trapped at the door to Sauvé's office, I dropped to my knees and crawled between the legs of the journalists and out the other side. The elevator was about fifteen feet away, and I was into it with the doors closing before most of the journalists knew what had happened.

The bells incident came to an end when Pinard called me to request a meeting of house leaders in his office. Following further meetings with Marc Lalonde and other ministers, the Liberals agreed to break down the omnibus bill into seven separate pieces of legislation—not as many as we had wanted, but at least the government had conceded the main point. For the sake of compromise, we accepted the arrangement, and the damn bells were silent at last. We had won, with a united caucus. A signal victory for Par-

liament itself and, just as important, an indelible lesson for Conservatives on the value and benefits of a united caucus.

Although Joe Clark was not always so fortunate in caucus, he
did win a notable victory in the great constitutional debate of 1980-
82. The Liberal government was determined to patriate the written
part of Canada's constitution, the British North America Act, which
was an act of the British Parliament. At the same time, Prime Minister Trudeau was determined to have a new Charter of Rights (now
known in some circles as the Lawyers' Endowment Act). Most
Conservative MPs, myself included, were dead set against both.
However, Joe Clark backed the government position, and he gradually imposed his will upon a reluctant caucus. Considering the
"wimp" image he has been tagged with, it was a remarkable achievement. I never voiced my reservations about the constitution except
to Joe, and I told him I thought he was taking us in the wrong
direction. A Gallup poll released shortly after the proposals were
announced indicated that a majority of Canadians were opposed,
but my guess is that caucus opposition ran close to 90 per cent.
Joe knew those proportions, but he also had a very deep conviction
about what he believed was right for the country, and consequently
what position ought to be taken by his party, and he was able to
make that view prevail.

An arrangement was set up in caucus whereby various teams,
each expert in one area, would be brought into play as the constitutional changes worked their way through Parliament. The
underlying assumption was that we would not be working to block
the legislation, but we would do whatever we could to improve any
shortcomings we found. The entire effort was coordinated, as far
as content was concerned, by Jake Epp, while I and my advisers
on the house leader's side were responsible for strategy and tactics.

Jake and his assistants did a magnificent job, which became clear
to all Canadians when, for the first time in Canadian history, the
special joint committee of the House and Senate considering the
legislation had its proceedings televised. The committee's work took
more than a year, and several changes were made as a result, some
of them to the visible distress of Pierre Trudeau. The legislation
that did emerge, and of which he was so proud, was to contribute
more to changing the face of Canada than anything he did in his
entire sixteen years as Canadian prime minister.

The impact of the Charter of Rights and Freedoms has only

begun to be felt. Its major effect is to make our judges, as the all-powerful interpreters of its provisions, into makers of law instead of implementors; they have usurped (not by themselves, the job was done for them) many of the functions of Parliament and moved us to a system very like the American one.

This process was taken to its climax with the Meech Lake Accord, negotiated by the Conservative government of Brian Mulroney. Had I been a member of the cabinet when those proposals were going forward, and had I been unable to have them changed, that, and not the Sinc Stevens affair, would have propelled me out of politics, for the Meech Lake Accord flies in the face of everything I have fought for throughout my political life. It dismisses the rights and privileges of Canadians living north of the 60th parallel out of hand by denying them the opportunity ever to form one or more new provinces within the Canadian federation. This was brought about without discussion, consultation, or any form of contact with those involved until it was far too late, and it contradicts the publicly declared policy of the Progressive Conservative Party of Canada as propounded by John Diefenbaker, Robert Stanfield, and Joe Clark, and by formal resolutions adopted by the party itself at successive conventions.

Until the 1982 Trudeau constitution, all that was required for any part of the Northwest Territories (and this applied to the territories as they existed in 1867 until 1982) to become a province was for the House of Commons and the Senate to present a joint address to Her Majesty the Queen requesting such action. This was done in the creation of British Columbia in 1871 and of Prince Edward Island in 1873; Manitoba was carved out of the District of Assiniboine in 1879 in this way, Alberta and Saskatchewan in 1905. (Newfoundland was admitted in 1949 through an amendment to the British legislation.) The Manitoba Act, the Alberta Act, and the Saskatchewan Act were examples of the kind of legislation that was required. If the constitution had remained the same, and if the government of the day decided to agree to create, for example, the Province of Yukon, the matter could have been accomplished by the passage of an act of Parliament. In 1982, Trudeau changed all that with a provision that required the agreement of seven provinces containing at least 50 per cent of the Canadian population. I entered the debate as a member of the opposition at that time and I had some very harsh things to say about that provision as a betrayal of

Canadians living north of 60. I hold those same convictions with equal passion today. The Meech Lake Accord, however, makes the difficult impossible by requiring the unanimous consent of all existing provinces to the creation of a new one. The rules are changed and the other provinces pull the ladder up after them. Prince Edward Island, which represents 0.01 per cent of the land area of Canada, is given the right to blackball an area constituting 40 per cent of the nation.

Quite apart from the constitutional monstrosity born of that approach, it must surely be repulsive to any fair-minded person that the premier of PEI, with a population of 125,000, should be able to veto the hopes and dreams of 75,000 Canadians who live in the northern territories.

In summing up Joe Clark as leader of the Conservative party, I am struck by the many strengths he had, and I can say with fervour that at least he did not dream up the Meech Lake Accord! In my view, he had more attractive qualities as a leader than Brian Mulroney, but the latter has the edge in the charisma department.

At the same time I realize that it would be a disaster for the party if he were to become its leader again; he would lead the party down the slippery slope to defeat, not because he is lacking in prime ministerial qualities, nor for any faults that he has, but because of the perception of the man irreversibly fed to the nation by the media.

Chapter Sixteen

The Media Is the Mess

The newspapers! Sir, they are the most villainous —
licentious—abominable—infernal—Not that I ever
read them . . .

Richard Sheridan

Joe Clark's failure as a leader lay not in himself but in the media. He had, and has, most of the qualities required of a modern prime minister: he is intelligent, honest, well-intentioned, and has the necessary toughness. What he does not have is a pleasing television image; his jerky movements, enlarged head, and diminished chin have doomed him. Although many historians argue that William Lyon Mackenzie King was our most successful politician, our longest-serving prime minister could not have been elected in the television age—he walked like a duck and talked with a shrill quack. I doubt if Franklin Delano Roosevelt could be elected in the United States today; the television camera's unrelenting eye would focus remorselessly on his wheelchair, and whatever sympathy that might elicit would be overwhelmed by the image of his handicap.

Image has always been important in politics—think of Julius Caesar's careful grooming of the Roman citizenry—but it remained for our age to allow a visual impression to overshadow character and to reduce all questions of policy and performance to one almighty query: how does he or she come across on television? Pierre Elliott Trudeau, whom I judged to be a conniving, arrogant, treacherous politician, came across as charming and masterful; Robert Stanfield, an intelligent, witty, trustworthy leader, came across as hesitant and fumbling. And that was that.

When the Progressive Conservative party shifted such loyalty as it possessed from Joe Clark to Brian Mulroney, it was not moving to change leaders so much as to change images; Mulroney has the voice, the carriage, the grooming of a winner, and if he is less

impressive than Clark in assessing a complex situation and for-
mulating a policy response—well, who cares? The gurus who advise
politicians these days have a little trick they are quite proud of when
advising campaign managers: turn off the sound on your television
while watching the potential candidate, they counsel. What he or
she says does not matter; all that matters is whether the image
projected is attractive. Policy, politics, truth, falsehood, likelihood,
lies—all are swept aside, and all that remains to be considered are
the pictures and the mood.

By allowing visual image to dominate, we have in effect abandoned political power to the media, but that power does not appear
to carry with it concomitant responsibility. Consider, for example,
the way much of our political news is brought to us, via the political
"scrum," the fifteen-second clip. A scrum is the jostling mass of
journalists, mostly electronic journalists, we see on our television
sets lying in wait outside the House of Commons, or in the corridor
leading to the cabinet room, or outside the doorway of whatever
cabinet minister they currently have under fire. A face emerges and
a battery of microphones is thrust forward with the noisy insistence
of baby birds jostling their mother for dinner, except that these are
birds of prey. No one, in the midst of such a scrum, can think
clearly, or enunciate policy on a complex matter, but, of course,
that is not what the scrum is about. The purpose of the scrum is
to provide a fifteen- or thirty-second clip to be fed into the next
news report. There are not many subjects in a complex world that
can be dealt with intelligently in fifteen minutes, let alone fifteen
seconds; the scrum provides the television editors with film over
which the parliamentary correspondent can do a voice-over—that
is, substitute his own words for those of the politician, with one
brief spasm of the victim's words to create the impression that what
the viewer is seeing is news. It is not, of course. It is commentary,
but it looks like news, and it becomes news. Listen carefully, some
time, to what the commentator is saying during one of these epi-
sodes; you will nearly always find it loaded with the sort of editorial
comment that would be instantly removed from written news copy,
but which is the very stuff of electronic reporting.

No serious student of politics or journalism believes that the
"scrum" is the proper way to cover politics. Lamenting the development of this approach occupies much of the attention of professors
of journalism in every school in the country, but the politician who

refuses to go along with the scrum is doomed before he begins. He is "dodging the press," he has "something to hide," he may even become, in the worst instances, "old Velcro Lips himself."

It is not my purpose in this chapter to fuel a feud with the media, but rather to set down some of the concerns any thoughtful politician, any thoughtful Canadian, must consider if we are not to abandon politics entirely to the image makers.

The ethical standards of journalists in 1958, when I first came into contact with the parliamentary press gallery, and the standards that prevail today in that same press gallery have, with rare exceptions, altered radically. Perhaps the main reason is the advent of technology, and the increasingly intense competition that the new technology creates between the electronic media and the written media. In the rush to get a story on the air, very little time can be afforded to ensure that the story is true; first it is aired, then it is checked, by which time it has become part of reality; and it is up to the politician who has just been tarnished to try to prove the contrary. Print journalists have, or are supposed to have, more time to ascertain the facts, but as everyone knows who has recent experience of Parliament Hill, the print journalists spend most of their time trailing in the wake of the electronic journalists, because they know that a story takes on life the moment it is aired, and its truth or falsity becomes almost irrelevant.

The media affects the reputation and future of individuals, governments, and political parties in two ways. One is the use by the collective media of the enormous power at its disposal to bring about political change—the defeat of a government and the election of an alternative government, say, or a change in the leadership of a party.

The second is the use of that power to terminate or render ineffective the influence that any member of Parliament might exert on any given issue. The best example is Stanfield, who was left with the important choice of leaving voluntarily or being hounded out by the media. His economic policies were derided and defeated by a hostile media, then embraced when Trudeau proposed them.

The first effect is the most important. It was this power that was turned against Joe Clark, almost from the moment of his election to the leadership. Throughout his 200 days in office, the media, who knew little and cared less about his mastery of the techniques of Parliament or his skill in caucus, concentrated on personal attacks, which are as inevitable a part of parliamentary practice as the Speaker's mace, and constantly made it seem that he was about to be toppled from power at any second. Well, of course he was, and so is every leader of a minority government, yet that was not the only story of the Trudeau or Pearson minority governments. Every complaint of every backbencher—and there is never a shortage of these—sounded like the sundering of the party, until trivial matters became matters of real dispute, and then the media were able to say, "We knew it all along."

Under the Conservative party constitution, the delegates to a general party convention can vote by secret ballot to hold a leadership convention, and in 1981, a third of them did so. Clearly, more than twice as many members were satisfied than were dissatisfied with Clark's leadership, but the newspapers and other commentaries were full of the notion that this was not good enough, and Clark, in response, indicated that he would reopen the issue if he did not do better on a similar vote in 1983. This left all of 1982 for the journalists to devote to speculation, rumour, gossip, and plain ordinary fabrication. Every story produced a reaction in caucus, and the polls, not surprisingly, began to turn more and more against us.

The year of 1982 was used by the forces inside the party who were determined to unseat the leader to prepare for the next convention, in Winnipeg. Among those who worked behind the scenes was Brian Mulroney; indeed, he was so identified with the anti-Clark drive that he felt it necessary to announce publicly, in early December 1982, that he continued to support the party leader. He was not widely believed.

At the general meeting, in January 1983, even though Clark received the backing of 66.9 per cent of the delegates, he was trapped, not only by the media's constant hammering but by his own belief that the figure was not high enough. He chose to consider that vote a defeat. I would not have done so, and I expressed that view to him, to no avail. (I doubt that Brian Mulroney considers 66.9 per cent of the popular vote a defeat.) Joe Clark called a leadership convention for June.

There, buoyed by overwhelmingly favourable media coverage— like myself and many others, he was to find it would not last—Brian Mulroney became the new Conservative leader, on his way to the prime minister's office. It was, from first to last, a matter of media perception, an exercise of power by the mob. This is the most important power the media carry.

These powers were less dangerous in a world in which they were controlled by a set of unspoken but clearly understood ethical standards, including the principle that a damaging story ought to be checked for truth or falsity before it is made part of the public record. With the disappearance of those standards over the past thirty years, there is nothing to restrain this enormous power of the media if it is bent on the destruction or alteration of governments, party leaderships, or individual politicians.

Television was not the sole force behind the erosion of these standards. The decline has been helped along by the advent of a new breed of journalists who have an outlook on life in general, and on their calling as journalists in particular, entirely different from those I met when I first came to Ottawa a generation ago. These journalists are the product of university schools of journalism, rather than the rigours of a newsroom, and, more importantly, they are the product of the age itself. The people in their late twenties and early thirties in the press gallery today were raised essentially in the welfare state of the Pearson-Trudeau era, in which student loans were invented, job-creation programs were designed for the summers, and other very generous programs were created by governments, showered on students, and paid for by taxpayers. In that, they have little in common with the men and women of the 1958 press gallery, who generally had to pump gas, drive taxis, wash windows, or wait on tables to support themselves through school. In those days, journalists became professionals in large measure by dint of their own work, self-initiative, and self-reliance, whereas the young modern-day journalist was assisted all the way along and did not have to worry about where the next square meal was coming from. The two groups, not surprisingly, have vastly different attitudes and expectations and quite different views on the subject of responsibility and indeed about the role of the state and politicians in a well-ordered world.

It is not hard to see the toll taken on the philosophical outlook of journalism students; the evidence is all around us. In the early 1980s, the parliamentary press gallery commissioned a poll of its members to determine where they stood in the political spectrum. An astonishing 80 or 90 per cent were to the left of centre, and

some 40 to 50 per cent were clearly identified as supporters of socialism in its raw form—that is, socialism in its own name, and not
the watered-down version called liberalism. I contend that had such
a poll been undertaken in 1958, only a tiny portion of the gallery
would have had any commitment to the left, and most journalists
would have insisted that they were, as they ought to be, politically
neutral.

Given the results, it is not mere nostalgia that suggests that the
coverage of politics when I first entered the profession was far more
objective and factual than it later became. Then, objectivity was
the expected standard; now, it is spurned. In my observation, the
attitude taken by most responsible journalists in the late 1950s and
early 1960s was that the newspapers printed facts so that their readers could draw their own conclusions, which would inevitably be
coloured by the political beliefs of the reader, not the writer.

Editorials were another matter. Editorials by nature express political opinions and are legitimate and necessary functions of any newspaper. But journalists reporting the news, it seems to me, should
be free of bias. That approach, which at one time existed in far
larger measure, has been amended, especially during the last decade,
so that the so-called factual reports of the new breed are liberally
sprinkled with editorial comment. That comment may be obvious
and obtrusive, or confined to the choice of words, such as describing
one politician as making a "clear-cut statement" while another is
"simplistic," saying that one was "speaking vigorously," another
"ranting desperately." The choice of words can colour the entire
article or radio or television broadcast. Such colour writing, far from
being frowned upon, is encouraged, and it has become commonplace
for editors to find themselves competing with their own reporters
over the writing of opinion pieces.

We live in the era of the media star, in which instant celebrities are
created among people whose assets are not experience or knowledge
or understanding but straight teeth, manageable hair, and an attractive speaking voice. It is these figures whose simple-minded views
set the stage. I have seen some of my colleagues panting to be
interviewed by people whose only attributes, as far as I can see,
are photogenic looks and unquenchable ignorance.

The "star" as journalist has now been translated back from the electronic media into print, so that our newspapers and magazines vibrate with the views of those who have turned their command of the language—even if it is only the language of vitriol—into an entertaining and thus salable product. And, in print as in broadcasting, the ·line between opinion and fact has disappeared; indeed, journalists these days do not even worry about the distinction.

One of the clearest examples of this occurred when I was deputy prime minister. A journalist writing a highly opinionated "factual" column on the op-ed page of the *Ottawa Citizen* used his space to launch a devastating attack on one of Brian Mulroney's cabinet ministers. Then the same man wrote the lead editorial, which came to the same highly critical conclusion. I thought at the time that that was a very foul blow on the part of this journalist, Christopher Young, who enjoys a high degree of respect and good reputation in the journalistic community. I was so annoyed at the way he had abused his power that I described his conduct as "racist" in the House of Commons.

The minister was Suzanne Blais-Grenier, who later resigned from the cabinet and who was certainly no stranger to criticism, yet I was so incensed by this blatant misuse of power by a journalist that my reason was affected. I should never have described Young's conduct as racist, and I apologized for doing so, but that was the first critical term that came to my mind when I was on my feet in the House. I do not believe that such a situation would have arisen in the 1950s and 1960s. Christopher Young was around then, but the rules were quite different.

In the new world of the media star, the journalist focuses his efforts on sensationalism, on bizarre stories that will shock and arouse reaction in the reader. What is more, this is done as a matter of priority, and if the sort of material does not exist on which a sensational story can be based, then facts and truth can be shaded to enable the construction of such a story.

The difficulty with respect to individuals, party leaders, governments, or cabinet ministers who become the subject of such stories is that it is virtually impossible to defend oneself in the face of the whirlwind of controversy that develops. It is like trying to reassemble the feathers of a pillow burst asunder in a gale.

Consider one example from dozens that spring to my mind. While I was minister of national defence, the name of the chief of the defence staff of Canada's armed forces, General Gérard Theriault, was plastered all over the front page of the *Toronto Star* in a story about his use of a Boeing 707 and a Challenger jet, government-owned equipment on the inventory of the armed forces. The story suggested that General Theriault had abused his authority to go junketing around the Pacific at great cost to the taxpayer.

What is not generally understood by Canadians is that members of the air force are required to maintain their flying skills by training flights which, with today's aircraft, reach destinations throughout the world. What General Theriault was doing, as I discovered when I personally supervised a thorough check into the matter, was using these training flights to take himself into areas where he had legitimate armed forces business to transact, and thus saving the taxpayer the cost of a commercial air fare. These flights are an essential operation for any modern peacetime air force, and it is not uncommon for members of the armed forces, legislators, members of the RCMP, and senior civil servants to obtain passage on these flights if they have business at any point en route.

Theriault wanted very much to answer these unsubstantiated charges, but I advised him that he should not do so, because the journalist always had the last word, and that last word would be used not to defend the general's conduct but to find some new criticism to level against him in order to justify the original criticism. Much against his inclination, General Theriault remained silent. In the absence of any reaction from either General Theriault or myself, the front-page story was followed up the next day by a much smaller article, and that was the end of the *Star*'s interest. The matter disappeared from its pages because there was no further material for the journalist to sensationalize or upon which he could base further allegations.

Even though I made meticulously thorough inquiries into every stage of the general's travel and satisfied myself that the story was unsubstantiated in every respect, it left the chief of our defence staff with a tarnished reputation, not only with the general public but more importantly within the armed forces. That, to my mind, was not only a failure on the part of the journalist but a disservice to his country.

When something harmful and completely false is publicized in this way, the journalist who does the damage is able to escape all responsibility. (Most politicians and lawyers will affirm that the remedy of a libel suit is no remedy at all; it leads to years of headache, heartache, and expense, and the facts become even more twisted than before.) This is a problem not only for politicians but for the public in general, because it means that decisions are taken that have nothing to do with anything but the whims of journalists.

This enormous power for inflicting wounds unseated Joe Clark and damaged Robert Stanfield—although Stanfield left before it could destroy him. No one who follows politics will ever forget the front-page picture that appeared during the 1972 election campaign of Stanfield dropping a football. It did not even need a caption to convey the intended message that Stanfield was a fumbler and not the kind of person who ought to be managing the Canadian government. The picture had nothing whatever to do with politics, or with Stanfield as a politician. In fact, Stanfield had been photographed numerous times in that same session catching the football quite adeptly. But the newspapers wanted to use the photograph that showed him fumbling for the impression it conveyed. Stanfield never seemed to resent such treatment; perhaps he was not even aware of the wounds inflicted on him, though I doubt that.

I have always believed that Stanfield's decision to leave when he did was wrong. The same media hostility that had attended Diefenbaker throughout most of his leadership, however, was clearly gathering momentum under Stanfield's leadership. Stanfield's choice was between weathering the storm or resigning while he still retained a semblance of control over his public image. If he chose the former, the party would inevitably suffer, as it had done during the later stages of the Diefenbaker leadership. If his choice was a clean-cut, voluntary resignation, the party would avoid the strife of disunity and be in much better health to go into an election. It was typical of Stanfield to choose the path that he felt would inflict the least harm on the party.

Some might conclude that these assessments of the role played by the media in the downfall of successive Progressive Conservative leaders smack of partisan paranoia. Let me therefore hasten to cite the most recent example of the media remoulding a political leader. Quite apart from his severe internal party problems, John Turner's image was slowly but inexorably eroded by a constantly negative media, so that when the 1988 election was called, no other political leader was held in lower esteem by Canadians. During the first three weeks of the campaign, the media continued to hammer away at him and had clearly written him off as any serious threat to Brian

Mulroney and his government. But around this time there seemed to be a growing concern among some of the more responsible media that something might indeed be amiss in the media's own house. Self-doubts by journalists found more frequent public expression, so that by the time the great two-day leaders' debate rolled around, the media was very much in a penitent mood. The opportunity for recanting came during the English debate, when Turner claimed exclusive rights to Canadian patriotism during an exchange with Mulroney on free trade. The media fired the boosters and Turner went into orbit, much to the alarm of both Mulroney and Broadbent. So thorough was the repentance of the media that they even announced the national results of the debate before the pollsters had completed their work, showing, eventually, a substantial win for Turner.

It was always a source of wonderment to me, and it says something about the collective courage of the parliamentary press gallery, that Trudeau could roundly abuse journalists and receive their praise in return, while Clark, who treated them with civility—never with arrogance, and never with unction—earned nothing but contempt. It led me to the conclusion that the journalists were afraid of Trudeau, afraid that if they confronted him they would be put down, afraid that if they asked questions they would be shown by his sarcastic answers to be stupid. Trudeau could get away with anything, perhaps because he simply did not give a damn what the journalists said about him, and that impressed them. I do not believe him when he says that he never read the newspapers; he must have read the summaries that were prepared daily in his office, to keep current with public opinion, which did concern him. No, his shield was not ignorance but arrogance, and it says something about modern journalism, that the proper defence against it is simple self-centredness.

When I first came to Ottawa, I was civil and respectful with journalists; indeed, I admired several members of the press gallery, even after my experiences with Ed Murphy and Paul Taylor taught me that not all journalists could be trusted.

My first complaint, and it remains at the core of my criticism, was about sloppiness in reporting. I fell a victim of inaccurate reporting during the first Diefenbaker government, when I was a very young member of the House, as a result of a two-and-a-half-inch-long article in an Ottawa newspaper in which I seemed to be attacking the public service of Canada; my remarks to one journalist had been taken completely out of context. Within hours of the paper hitting the streets, I was summoned to Diefenbaker's office. He was quite angry at the words attributed to me, and when I protested that I had never uttered them, he replied that I must have said something to leave the journalist with the wrong impression. Diefenbaker told me that the safe rule to follow is not to speak of such matters if they are going to be misinterpreted. The difficulty, of course, is to know in advance exactly what is going to be misinterpreted and how. I grew to understand that there is no purpose whatsoever in trying to set the record straight once it has been distorted; the journalist's concern will always be to defend the original story. I therefore concluded that the best thing to do was keep quiet, wait for the matter to blow over, and absorb whatever heat had to be absorbed in the meantime.

One of the greatest harms that journalists can inflict is to attack the integrity or credibility of an individual, or to raise questions about the professionalism of someone engaged in a profession such as law, medicine, or engineering. Such damage can never be undone. My own standing as a lawyer certainly came under attack during the Rivard affair, as I went from fair-haired boy and exposer of wrongdoing to the cruel and sadistic prosecutor of the "innocents," the man who hurled unjust allegations around from his position of immunity as an MP. Anyone who was old enough to read the newspapers in 1964 will remember that scandal-ridden time, but very few remember that the principal involved in those allegations, Raymond Denis, went to jail for two years after a full and fair trial and a rejected appeal. What is remembered is that I was a muckraker, not that my actions rooted out serious crime.

I often wonder how many journalists in the press gallery today have even bothered to acquaint themselves with the facts of that time before writing about them in the context of current events; for most, it is obviously simpler merely to drag out the old cliches and to tell the reader that this fellow Nielsen is the same man who was the muckraker and scandalmonger of the 1960s.

Once, not long after the bribery scandals broke, the Chamber of Commerce in Edmonton decided to capitalize on the colourful history of Yukon's Klondike gold rush and commercialize it by celebrating Edmonton's "Klondike Days." We Yukoners, of course, had been using our Klondike gold rush history as a tourist attraction for many years. Edmonton is 1,800 miles from the Klondike River and has about as much to do with the gold rush of 1898 as Winnipeg. I took exception, as member of Parliament for Yukon, to this outright theft of Yukon tradition and history, and I said as much in the House of Commons. Very shortly thereafter, the *Edmonton Journal* published a cartoon depicting me rummaging through garbage tins in a back alley in the city of Edmonton. How the newspaper could make the leap from my criticism of the city's actions to depicting me as some sort of garbage thief was beyond me, until I remembered how closely it tallied with the image of Nielsen the muckraker. Perhaps that was when I realized that I could never win; the media clings to its images, and the facts are not permitted to obtrude.

Surely Canadians have a right to expect, given the enormous unchecked power of the journalists, that they will at least attempt to obtain accurate information on which to base their sweeping statements. What disturbs me as the media become increasingly opinionated and judgmental is the appalling sloppiness of the reporting, even by the most highly respected journalists. It is a fitting symbol of our time that conscientious newspapers now carry, almost every day, a little column apologizing for and correcting the errors made yesterday. Would it not be easier to take more care to get things right in the first place? Canadians are perhaps inured to the errors that seem to be part of the daily reporting game; apparently, they are willing to accept the excuse that there is not time, under the pressures of competition, to determine the accurate facts before releasing the story.

As a politician, I knew that I could never control what was said about me or my party or my leader, nor did I ever want to. All I ever wanted, and seldom got, was the assurance that the information that is so vital to a free society would be conveyed in a fair-minded and impartial way. I regard that failure as a black mark against the modern media, representing great power with little responsibility, and I see that failure as one of the chief dangers to political life in our time.

Chapter Seventeen
Life with Brian

Well, thank God, at last we have got a ministry
without one of those men of genius in it.
A peer, commenting on Lord Addington's
newly formed government, 1801

Whatever the media thought, we in the Progressive Conservative party were quite confident in 1981 and 1982 that we were going to form the next government of Canada, and after we won the battle of the bells, we began to prepare. Joe Clark had always had the conviction that we should be developing and refining policy positions so that we would be ready in every sense to go to the country whenever the next election might be called—although he naturally believed that he would be leading the party when we fought it.

During his time as prime minister, he had appointed Arthur Tremblay, a distinguished and respected Quebecker with a fine intellect, to the Senate, and, in opposition, he turned to Senator Tremblay for leadership in developing policy options for the parliamentary caucus. At Clark's request, I joined Senator Tremblay in this work, and we became co-chairmen of a policy group, whose members included the senior members of the shadow cabinet, such as Don Mazankowski, Michael Wilson, Flora MacDonald, John Crosbie, and Sinclair Stevens, augmented by several members of Joe Clark's staff. The work on policy began in early 1982, while the battle over the leadership was raging offstage, and continued into 1983. Indeed, it had not quite finished by the time Clark called for the leadership convention, but it was fairly complete in April 1983.

Very little that is accurate has been said or written about this policy-development process, because it was swallowed up in the personality battles and the jockeying for leadership, yet it was the key to some of the success that would later be enjoyed by the Mulroney government. The work involved every single member of caucus who cared to make a contribution, along with many of the members of Clark's office. As well, substantial contributions were made by private and academic sources.

Once the main lines of the work were laid down, Senator Tremblay and I were ready to present a report to the leader of the party. The difficulty was in deciding who that was to be; Clark had already called the leadership convention for June and in the meantime had stepped aside as leader of the opposition and hence the caucus as well. (He remained, of course, party leader.) Caucus had elected me leader of the opposition but I could hardly present the report to myself in caucus.

On assuming the leader's mantle, I decided immediately that any member of the shadow cabinet who either displayed or announced an ambition to contest the leadership of the party would be relieved of his or her responsibilities in the shadow cabinet. I retained the shadow cabinet just as Clark had left it, but subsequently Michael Wilson, David Crombie, John Crosbie, and Flora MacDonald left as it became apparent that they would be contesting the leadership. I had the support of caucus in ensuring that all leadership candidates would be placed in exactly the same position as Clark—that is, unable to issue statements or draw attention to themselves because of their respective shadow cabinet roles. Some but not all of them accepted this decision with good grace. Mike Wilson, for instance, professed not to see the unfair advantage gained by continuing to occupy a prominent position in the parliamentary caucus. (He was our finance critic at the time, and when he declared his candidacy, I replaced him with Pat Carney, the first woman in the Conservative caucus to occupy that senior post.)

Since I could not report to myself, and it seemed foolish to report to a caucus many of whose most prominent figures were now busy running for the leadership, Senator Tremblay and I decided to take the process one step further and to refine the policy options into a platform for the next election. We prepared a blueprint according to which our party could govern using financially sound, efficient, and compassionate principles. To do this, we convened regular meetings of some nineteen people, including senior members in the shadow cabinet and principal advisers in the office of the Leader of the Opposition.

By the time the leadership convention was concluded, we were able to present the entire concept—the principles, the proposals, and the means on which we believed the next federal election should be fought and which would be implemented by a Conservative government—to the new leader, Brian Mulroney.

I had never really met Mulroney. I knew that he had, with Joe Clark, been an active member of the Young PCs in the days of Diefenbaker's difficulties with that body. I knew of his candidacy in 1976, when he had lost the leadership race to Joe, and I had briefly greeted him there.

One of Brian's first announcements as leader in 1983 put an end to my final attempt to get out of politics. When the Clark government had been defeated on December 14, 1979, I had had no option but to run for election yet another time, since to have done anything less would have made it appear to all and sundry that I was deserting a sinking ship. I did not agree with the pundits, since I was convinced that the Liberals had blundered in defeating the Clark government on the budget and that the Canadian electorate would see that very quickly and would re-elect a majority Conservative government.

As it turned out, I was wrong, but after the February 1980 election, I felt free once again to plan my future on the basis that I certainly would not be contesting the next federal election. Again I set about identifying suitable candidates and again I was successful in recruiting a young businessman in Whitehorse, Doug Ross, who was married with a young family and who, after considerable thought and discussion with his principals in the insurance firm of Reid Stenhouse, and with the support of his wife, a registered nurse, committed himself to run as a candidate, whenever the election might be called. My ironclad conviction not to run again was demolished at the leadership convention of 1983, in the presence of more than 5,000 delegates, when Brian Mulroney, after his election as leader of the Conservative party, announced to the delegates and to millions of television viewers that he wanted me to continue as house leader of the opposition. There was little I could do, without appearing a traitor, except to carry on.

On June 12, 1983, the day after the leadership convention, a sultry, hot day, I walked in my shirtsleeves down the hill from my East Block office to the Chateau Laurier, carrying a bulging briefcase. Brian had taken a suite of rooms on the fourth floor of the hotel for both business and living, and we met there for about two hours. We were alone, although Pat McAdam, then one of his chief aides, dropped in from time to time, and Mila Mulroney dropped in once to say hello. I remember that we both smoked heavily during that meeting—Brian later quit cold turkey, but I was not able to quit until I left politics—and we piled up a lot of cigarette butts as I took him through the process of policy development that had then been under way for more than a year. I told him how the process worked with caucus, and how far along we were with planning for the next government. I also advised him—and he gave instructions to this effect—that the work should be stepped up so that a smooth transition could be made when we came to office, avoiding the awkward stumbling that had characterized the beginning of the Clark government.

Finally, I gave him a rundown on of some of the more heavyweight members of the previous shadow cabinet, the men and women who would become his closest parliamentary colleagues. Naturally we anticipated that, given a victory at the polls, Brian would have new talent to draw on in forming a government, but it seemed to me essential that he know the strengths and weaknesses of the present team. (I later made these assessments more professional during my work in government planning.) The results, which should prove to be interesting to any students of history, appear as an appendix at the end of this book, a sort of who's who and why of the government-in-waiting. I made some mistakes—I have added corrections at the bottom of some summaries—and some individuals were left out. I could not have foreseen, for example, that Robert Coates, a long-serving but lightweight member, would come to play an important role. However, by and large I am satisfied that a careful reading of these analyses will explain much of what happened in the early years of Mulroney's leadership.

We had several subsequent meetings at the Chateau Laurier in the short time between Mulroney's election as leader and his nomination in the riding of Central Nova, in Nova Scotia, made vacant when Elmer McKay stepped aside. The summer recess came up rapidly, and I returned to Yukon to recharge my batteries for what was bound to be a tumultuous fall session of Parliament.

On August 29, Brian won the Central Nova by-election, and on September 6, when the House re-convened, I stepped down as leader of the opposition in favour of Mulroney. I became instead opposition house leader and deputy national leader of the Progressive Conservative party.

From February 2 to September 6, 1983, I served as leader of the opposition in the House of Commons. Many journalists at the time and subsequently have wrongly referred to me as "interim" or "acting" leader. This inaccurate description has always irritated me as an example of how journalists are too lazy to verify the facts. Clearly they are as ill-informed about the true nature of the function and responsibilities of the leader of the opposition as they are about their description of the position.

A distinction must be made between leader of the opposition—the position in the House of Commons—and leader of the Progressive Conservative party. Although I had been supported by caucus as leader in the House, I was not leader of the party; Joe Clark retained that position and responsibility. When a leadership convention is held, the delegates elect a leader of the Progressive Conservative Party of Canada. (At this time, Pierre Trudeau was the Liberal leader and also prime minister; he was later replaced by John Turner as leader of the Liberal Party of Canada on June 16, 1984. On June 30, Turner was sworn in as prime minister.) The Conservatives, during the leadership race, were in the position of having a national party leader, Joe Clark, and a different leader of the opposition in the House of Commons, myself. After Brian won the convention, he assumed the leadership of the party and after his election in Central Nova, he became the leader of the opposition in the House of Commons. But in the meantime, I held that post.

It would have been theoretically possible and constitutionally correct if I had, for some reason, chosen to refuse to relinquish the responsibilities of leader of the opposition in the House of Commons to Brian as leader of the Progressive Conservative party and had forced the caucus to sort it out. There was no limitation on the responsibilities I was exercising, as long as I had the support of caucus. The media never understood this fact.

The most important work I performed while in this position was the continuation, with Senator Tremblay, of the task of developing our political and fiscal strategy for the next election—the bulging briefcase I presented to Brian at our first meeting. We had also developed a fiscal framework, with detailed costing of our proposals.

This took on a "peek-a-boo" quality when John Crosbie was leaving one of our meetings, and the television cameras fastened on a sheaf of documents he was carrying, showing some of the cost estimates. We had also developed non-expenditure policy priorities for each of the fiscal envelopes involved, to straighten out the order in which things should be done and to cover many matters that did not require spending. Finally, and most importantly, we had developed a detailed blueprint for our approach to the machinery of government when we came to assume office. These recommendations contained some far-reaching proposals, which were further refined by our concentrated work on government planning.

A good deal of nonsense has been written about the planning process that took place in the period leading up to Brian's election as prime minister; perhaps it is worthwhile here to examine briefly the organization and objectives of the government planning process.

In addition to the initiative Joe Clark had taken in appointing Senator Tremblay and me as co-chairmen of the policy-development efforts, he had appointed Finlay MacDonald (now a senator) to undertake the work of government planning—that is, the mechanics of transition during the early days of a new government. Finlay had recruited some very able help for this task, but there was little or no caucus leadership or input in the work, which portended difficulties later if the caucus were presented with a set of plans they had had no part in helping to design. This was remedied when Brian asked me to assume the chairmanship of the committee on government planning, which was already under a fair head of steam under Finlay's direction.

When I took over, I created four sub-chairs. One was to deal with the recruitment and staffing of the many hundreds of positions to be filled within the service of the government and government agencies, boards, and commissions. I left this sub-committee in the hands of Finlay MacDonald.

The second dealt with staffing the political positions—the many roles that had to be filled upon confirmation of a Conservative government, not only in the offices of cabinet ministers but in the Prime Minister's Office and others. This chair was given to Peter White, who remained after the formation of government to assist in the implementation of those staffing plans. (He later became Brian's appointments secretary, returned, briefly, to the private sector, and then back to a key role in the PMO.)

The third group continued the policy work, already well advanced, under the ongoing chairmanship of Arthur Tremblay and me, and the results were reviewed at a meeting at Montebello, Quebec, in April 1984. By the time that ultimate policy meeting took place, we were probably far more prepared for office than had ever been the case in the history of the Conservative party.

The fourth group, dealing with the machinery of government, continued under my direction.

Later, I discovered that another group had been working on a series of proposals for the machinery of government, under the direction of Don Mazankowski. Indeed, that group submitted a report to Brian Mulroney about the same time I submitted, on behalf of the officially appointed group, our report on the same subject. Some members of Mulroney's staff, as I discovered to my chagrin when the matter came to light, were serving on both the official group and the Mazankowski group. The matter had gone too far, by the time I heard of it, to ask Brian to eliminate the overlapping jurisdiction of the two groups, since my own report was all but complete. I simply obtained a copy of the Mazankowski report and analysed it, retaining its beneficial aspects and discarding the remainder. It was, in any case, an echo of the findings and conclusions of the official group. An explanation of this parallel effort was never forthcoming.

That did not allay my concern with respect to a form of leadership with which I found myself in decided disagreement. For a leader to appoint one group and then allow another to perform the same task sub rosa did not strike me as a way to build openness and confidence within the party.

Trudeau had governed by what he called "creative tensions," whereby he would deliberately create, or allow to develop, tensions between ministers, or groups of ministers, or within cabinet or caucus. Any individuals or groups that could be brought into abrasive conflict were deliberately set at each other's throats for the purpose of resolving whatever issue was then at stake. Brian Mulroney, or someone in a position of authority on his behalf, had apparently taken a page out of Trudeau's leadership manual; I was to observe him doing the same thing on several other occasions, but I was never persuaded that it was a good strategy.

Although this technique sometimes brought a temporary solution to a conflict, it always left an emotional residue that might range anywhere from a bruised ego to deep-seated and long-standing resentment on the part of the loser, who saw his or her hard work, done with the best intentions, brushed aside and ignored because another and parallel product had been prepared on the sly. Neither Robert Stanfield nor Joe Clark had ever used the technique, and I found myself far more at home with their straightforward methods than I did with those employed by Diefenbaker and Mulroney. When Diefenbaker used these methods, the ultimate results can only be described as devastating to himself and to his own best interests.

What with one thing and another, I was kept hopping with caucus work from the conclusion of the crisis of the bells in March 1982 through to June 1984. Indeed, in April 1984, such was the burden of my work that I had to ask Brian to relieve me of my responsibilities as opposition house leader so that I could complete my work on government planning by the target date in June. This change and the appointment of Ray Hnatyshyn as opposition house leader was announced by Mulroney in Montebello in April.

It was with a sense of relief that I presented the four completed reports—on policy and the fiscal framework; on staffing; on appointments; and on the machinery of government—right on schedule. I looked forward to being able to relax a little over the summer.

In my discussions with Brian, however, I repeatedly expressed the view that it would be essential for a new Conservative government to plan the first 150 days of its mandate with meticulous care, since it would be within that five-month period that the vital image of the party and the new government would be fixed in the public mind. I proposed that we develop a decision-making process that was coordinated and integrated with the bureaucracy, a process that was firm enough to exercise control but flexible enough to respond to political change and public demand. The lessons of the Clark government had taught us that we had not only to have but to display and project the image of a highly sensitive and aware government, but one which knew precisely where it was going and how it would get there. To bring this about, we would need a transition team to begin at once to design the key elements for a smooth, effective takeover of government and to implement those elements during the formation of a Conservative government.

Brian and I had a working lunch in June, not long after I had presented the final reports on government planning to him. He was pleased with the work, impressed by the recommendations I had made concerning a transition team and, as I half expected, he asked me, first, to run for re-election and second, to head the transition planning and the implementation of that planning after we were elected. He asked for my estimate of how long that transition-planning team would be required to remain functioning once a new government was formed. I replied, "One year."

I arrived at this by the simple process of taking the 150 days we had estimated as vital to the government's beginning and doubling it to ensure the new government was firmly in the saddle, and then rounding that figure out to one year.

Brian thought for a moment and replied, "Two years." He then asked for my commitment to run for re-election and to head the transition team for two years. I agreed, since this was yet one further call to duty from the leader of my party and, I was convinced, the future prime minister, but I reiterated that one year would see the job through.

Shortly after that luncheon meeting I suggested to Brian that there was one other person we ought to recruit immediately to begin work on transition planning. That was Bill Neville, who had done the job for Joe Clark in 1979 and knew some of the pitfalls of transition from personal experience. Brian told me to go ahead and make whatever arrangements were necessary to get Neville. Neville at that time was a vice-president of the Canadian Imperial Bank of Commerce in Toronto. When I phoned him, he told me that he would need the permission of the bank chairman, Russell Harrison, to take a temporary leave of absence to undertake the job in Ottawa. Brian is a former member of the Commerce board, so it seemed reasonable that he should approach his bank chairman. (Some printed reports have suggested, incorrectly, that Neville was brought in at the last minute to clean up the confusion we had created.)

We were in very good shape for an election when the Liberals went through their leadership convention and John Turner emerged as the leader on June 16. He was sworn in as prime minister two weeks later, after an orgy of patronage appointments that were— why be polite about it?—a stench in the nostrils of all Canadians. Though he did enjoy a brief lead in the polls, no seasoned observer ought to have been fooled by it. When he called the election for

September 4, I knew from the outset that we were going to win. We were certainly helped by the Liberals' internal problems—such as the panicky shift from Bill Lee to Senator Keith Davey as national campaign manager—and by Brian's masterful use of the patronage issue in the English-language television debate on July 25. The result was, as everyone knows, the largest parliamentary victory in Canadian history. We were to have another turn in office, and this time we were ready.

In Yukon, I gained the largest majority—4,113 votes—ever obtained by a candidate in the constituency. The next day, at 6:00 a.m., I boarded a chartered jet that had been sent to Whitehorse to take me back to Ottawa to begin the transition. When my wife, Shelley, and I arrived back at the national capital, I discovered to my surprise that Brian wanted me to take on the positions of deputy prime minister and president of the Privy Council, as well as further, unspecified responsibilities he would be announcing after the swearing-in of cabinet on September 17. I of course accepted, although with some misgivings about the workload I was being asked to assume. I had been going flat out for the best part of four years.

Part of the transition planning had anticipated the need for a strategy to allow the prime minister-elect to interview potential cabinet ministers between the election and the swearing-in without setting off a rash of speculation every time he was seen with someone. I suggested that we rent rooms in different hotels and move the prime minister-elect between them for each interview, so that no interviewee would see anyone else coming or going. If we kept the knowledge of the locations confined to a few people, we might escape some, if not all, of the speculation. This was not merely a matter of playing games. In the past, the journalists, lying in wait outside wherever the prime minister happened to be, and comparing notes, had been able to construct pretty accurate versions of the cabinet-in-waiting. These speculations immediately brought pressure not only from the losers in this power lottery but from all the lobbyists. We were determined to design a system in which Brian would be free to make his decisions without these distractions and pressures. The plan went off without a hitch.

I was even able to obtain a decent suit for the ceremony. When I joined the Clark cabinet, after a long-distance phone call to me in Whitehorse, I scrambled to get to Ottawa on time, and there was no chance to buy a suit. I attended in an old business suit, and, when I bent over to pick something up in my office just before the ceremony, the trousers split right up the backside seam—just like a corny movie. My secretary made emergency repairs, but I arrived at Rideau Hall in a far-from-tranquil frame of mind, determined never to bend over, even if the Governor General dropped something! This time, I went in a new suit and full of confidence to join a cabinet of astonishing size—forty members—and somewhat uneven quality.

The day following the swearing-in, a press release was issued from the Prime Minister's Office outlining the additional duties he was asking me to assume. One was the chairmanship of a ministerial task force to review all federal government programs in order to improve their delivery, make them more accessible, and reduce waste and duplication.

The other was a complete review of the ministerial conflict-of-interest guidelines, which we had inherited from the Trudeau administration. The Trudeau guidelines, which were far from adequate, were nevertheless to remain in effect until I had made my report to the prime minister and he had acted on them—or not, as he saw fit.

To the Program Review Task Force, the prime minister had appointed Justice Minister John Crosbie, Finance Minister Michael Wilson, and Treasury Board President Robert de Cotret to sit with me. As chairman, it was up to me to plan our approach to the work. The very first requirement, naturally, was an accurate inventory of all government programs in every department. Although all of these were public, they had never been completely inventoried, and we had to do this before we could determine the extent of the task and devise a method to accomplish it.

I needed a strong right-hand man for this work and recalled how impressed I had been, when I was vice-president of the Treasury Board in 1979, with the work of Peter Meyboom. Meyboom had been in the Canadian public service for years, mainly in the Treasury Board. He has a highly-honed intellect, an excellent ability to analyse problems, and a prodigious capacity for work, which was going to be necessary, since the prime minister wanted us to complete our report in a scant twelve months.

Similar program reviews had been conducted in Great Britain, under Margaret Thatcher, and in the United States, under Ronald Reagan by J. Peter Grace. The difference between them was that the Grace review was conducted entirely by means of contributions from the private sector, with no public financing whatsoever, while the Thatcher review, although it was chaired by a private businessman, was paid for by public funds. The Grace review produced twenty-nine volumes of detail and a wide-ranging set of recommendations, which, if implemented, would have caused certain chaos. Although much of the research was excellent and informative, it did not have much impact. The publicly financed report in Britain did rather better. It was my theory that our approach in Canada should be halfway between that of Britain and the United States— what else?—that is, it would be a joint public- and private-sector effort. My colleagues on the task force agreed. Accordingly, I recruited Peter Meyboom as the number one public-sector adviser, and asked Darcy McKeough, then chief executive officer of Union Gas, to assume the duties of the private-sector adviser. When he agreed, I asked him to help prepare a list of individuals and organizations in the private sector who could provide help and advice. No remuneration would be offered for the work, although the federal government would pay reasonable expenses, including travel. Peter Meyboom launched a similar recruitment drive in the public sector.

I personally approached the leaders of several national organizations, such as the Business Council on National Issues, the Canadian Manufacturers' Association, the Canadian Chamber of Commerce, the Canadian Labour Congress, Fédération des travailleurs du Québec, the Conseil du Patronat, Le Groupement d'Entreprises Québecoises, the Canadian Association of Management Consultants, the Canadian Institute of Chartered Accountants, the Canadian Federation of Independent Business, the Canadian Organization of Small Business, and the Canadian Federation of Labour, all of whom were very generous in their reaction and in the allotment of resources to help us in our work.

From their numbers was formed the private sector advisory committee, which met regularly to review and analyse the work of the several joint public/private sector teams that examined the various departments and programs.

The result was a report of twenty-one volumes, eighteen inches thick, containing masses of information and hundreds of recommendations, the implementation of some of which is estimated to have saved the federal taxpayer more than $500 million in the first year alone. Half of the people involved in this project were private businesspeople who were paid a dollar a year.

Program Review was a unique exercise in Canadian history; never before has such a public and private examination of government programs been undertaken. Because of this, I retained a historian to track the work of Program Review and produce a permanent record. Alas, what was produced was, instead, a comparative study of the British, American, and Canadian exercises, and not a proper history of what we had accomplished at all. The draft history disclosed what we had known all along, that our Program Review was based on quite a different set of assumptions from either the British or the American examples. Their reviews were aimed primarily at cost-cutting, our intent was to make the programs better serve the Canadian public.

Nowhere in our mandate was there a directive to slash costs. The savings that were achieved came about through the discovery of obsolete programs, duplications, and redundancies. This kind of saving was a happy side-effect of our main effort. The influence of Program Review will be felt for decades to come.

We played, at the time, to what the newspapers call "mixed reviews." I was astonished at how often what seemed to be straightforward and common-sense ideas were rejected out of hand, while others were accepted quickly. I insisted—over the fierce objection of some of my colleagues—that the review be made public, even though that was bound to bring instant and noisy reaction from some of those whose oxen were being gored. My argument was that people have a right to know about, and debate, how their money is being spent, and an equal right to know when those spending habits are about to be changed. This meant, inevitably, that we lost some battles, but I would not have it any other way.

For example, our research disclosed that Canadians were paying $29 million annually to subsidize the growing of sugar beets. There seemed to be no reason for the industry to survive in Canada, and the land and people could be more economically employed in other pursuits. We suggested ending the subsidy. You would think we had suggested cutting off the left leg of every farmer in the land. We lost that one. We also lost on recommendations to reduce or eliminate some of our swollen business subsidies, restructure the Indian Affairs branch, and reconsider some of the handouts to funding agencies in the cultural community. On the other hand, most of our recommendations for the Department of Veterans Affairs were quietly implemented: they included such simple things as faster processing of pension cheques. No one objected to our proposal to centralize the management of government property, thereby achieving major savings, or to simplify some of the grotesque regulatory framework within which we live. But these matters do not make headlines, whereas our proposal to scrap Newfoundland's Newfie Bullet did.

Two years later, Jeffrey Simpson, the national columnist of the *Globe and Mail*, commented, "That's where the task force left its legacy—in suggesting better ways of doing things. When it called into question whole programs or existing services, the flak flew and the government ducked." I am not sure I agree entirely; I believe many of our suggestions will come to pass when the political climate is right. No politician can legitimately complain when his suggestions are rejected because they arouse too much public ire; he can only keep cool and try again, in the hope that common sense will ultimately prevail. Program Review, which cost $3.7 million, saved 135 times its cost within a year. Not many government reviews can say the same. It is my belief that this sort of exercise ought to be conducted regularly within any government; it will result not only in savings but in better service to the public.

The work was a good deal more rewarding (and a good deal more beneficial, in the long run) than the task I undertook when I agreed to examine and rewrite the conflict-of-interest guidelines for cabinet ministers. There was no way of knowing it at the time we assumed office, but it was this subject that would bring the new government harsh—and justified—criticism and, in the end, propel me out of politics.

Before taking up the thread of that story, however, I want to deal with one of the key subjects that came up for Program Review, and that is the financing—and, in general, the treatment—of Canada's native population at the hands of the federal government. My concern for and connection with what is often called "Native issues" goes back to the beginning of my career in politics and remains a concern to me even now that I am out of the political arena.

Chapter Eighteen

My Home and Native Land

Nielsen: *What did you call this place before the coming of the White Man?*
Upper Liard Tom: *Ours.*

When there was tremendous excitement brewing in Yukon about the oil pipeline that was going to cross the territory, a series of meetings were held to acquaint the native population with what was going to be done for—or to—them as a result. At one of these meetings, a company spokesman explained how every care would be taken to preserve the natural habitat in its pristine state, with the exception, of course, of this fifty-six-inch-diameter metal pipeline running through the middle of it. One of the elders asked how the caribou herds would follow their traditional migratory routes to and from their calving grounds on the coast of the Beaufort Sea. This of course was not only vital to the survival of these magnificent animals but was of paramount concern to the native people, who gain much of their subsistence from them. The company man said he was glad that question had been asked and explained that the pipeline would, for most of its length, rest on an earth berm, but that earthen ramps would be constructed over the pipeline at intervals to enable the caribou to cross over. The company man went on to say that there would be a sign at each of these crossings to indicate its location.

"That's wonderful," said the elder, "and who is going to teach the caribou how to read?"

I have always been impatient with those who assume that Canada's native people lack intelligence and do not understand the world around them. My own experience has shown me that the native population of Yukon has about the same mixture of savants and fools, thugs and gentlefolk, thieves and scrupulously honest individuals, as does the white population around them, and that they, like anyone else, respond best when they are treated as rational adults and not as wayward children.

The native people do not represent a majority of the Yukon population, as they do in the Northwest Territories; in a total population of 25,000, there are about 5,500 of them, roughly half of them Status Indians, a few Métis, and the rest Non-status. Also unlike the Northwest Territories, there are no Inuit settlements, but rather thirteen Indian bands loosely grouped into the Council of Yukon Indians, and fewer than 100 Inuit. (Of the 68,000 people in the Northwest Territories, roughly 34,500 are natives; of these, 2,600 are Métis, and the rest are about evenly divided between Indians and Inuit; it is an entirely different situation from that of Yukon, although most Canadians see them as one lumped "problem.")

In the early days of my political organizing, and during the campaigns of 1957 and 1958, I visited the native communities many times. Some of these communities were very isolated and out of touch with the rest of the world, except when an aircraft flew in with supplies or visitors. Some of the larger communities between Watson Lake, on the British Columbia border in the southeast, and Old Crow in the northwest are: Upper Liard, eight miles from Watson Lake; Ross River, northwest of Upper Liard; Teslin, 120 miles southeast of Whitehorse on the Alaska Highway; Tagish and Carcross, 45 miles southwest of Whitehorse; Carmacks and Mayo. There are also small native groups at Fort Selkirk and Dawson City.

Upper Liard was one of the most primitive of these communities. Most of its inhabitants moved here from Ross River in 1942, to find work on the construction of the Alaska Highway. I became fast friends with a few of the older people in the community, including an elder named Upper Liard Tom. He told me a story that he said his grandparents had told to him. It concerned the early explorer, Robert Campbell, a Hudson's Bay Company factor who in 1843 built Fort Frances, on Frances Lake, the first trading post in Yukon. As trade expanded, he built Fort Selkirk, at the junction of the Lewes and Pelly rivers, in 1848, but the coastal Chilcat Indians took exception to his intrusion and burned the fort in 1852. Campbell barely escaped with his life. Alone and in the dead of winter, he walked on snowshoes to Lake Winnipeg, 3,000 miles away, a remarkable feat of stamina and endurance. Two years later, in 1854, he returned to the north and was named factor at Fort Liard. Campbell was a heroic explorer to the whites, but to Upper Liard Tom's folks, he was just a man who ran for 3,000 miles.

The story, besides being a gentle poke at me, was a reminder that it was not so long ago that, in peaceable Canada, this was pretty hostile territory. An analogy might be made between those events and the confrontation that took place when the immigrating Europeans were confronted by the native people of the west below the 60th parallel during the eighteenth and nineteenth centuries. To avoid the kind of violence that became so common in the western United States, the government of Canada struck treaties with most of the tribes in the east and some of those in the west, but this process halted abruptly after the signing of Treaty 11 in 1924, which included some of the natives in the Mackenzie Valley of the Northwest Territories. This left many of Canada's native people without treaties, although their land had been occupied by others. I have not been able to find any reason for the abrupt cessation in 1924 of the treaty-negotiating process, unless it was one of the effects of the recession. Not until 1979 was the process reinstituted—and has turned, in my view, into a disaster.

When I first visited Upper Liard, many people were living in sod-roofed huts and some in canvas tents all year round. There was no such thing as adequate housing in any of the native communities I visited in those early campaigns. The most appalling conditions of poverty prevailed, which included unsanitary facilities, illiteracy, unemployment, and alcoholism. Even though their day-to-day existence must have been nothing but misery, my friends living in these communities never seemed to lose their sense of humour; perhaps they looked at their lives from a different perspective, but I simply could not conceive how these Canadians, human beings, could continue to live and raise families in these conditions. I was determined to bring about changes. Little did I suspect that my determination would ultimately contribute to the creation of a native bureaucracy that obtains most of the benefit of government assistance, while the needy beneficiaries, the families in the communities, receive the least.

The natives of Upper Liard followed the political lead of Louis Pospisil, the lone white resident trader there and a staunch Liberal, who usually delivered the votes of the native people to his party. We had little impact there in the early elections; it was not until Louis abandoned the Liberals to support the Progressive Conservatives that we began to win there. This community was segregated from the nearby white community of Watson Lake as part of a deliberate policy of the Department of Northern Affairs to allocate "lands set aside" for natives in areas removed from white communities throughout Yukon. (In South Africa, they called it "tribal homelands.")

Ross River was another such segregated community. This village at the confluence of the Ross and Pelly rivers had a white community on one side and a huddle of native huts on the other. In my first campaign in 1957, I had not visited here, and lost heavily in the poll. I decided during the by-election campaign later that year to pay a call. I flew to Ross River in a Beaver aircraft on skis, and the pilot landed on a strip prepared by the white big-game hunter, Tom Connelly. He turned up to meet me—although he was a Liberal—with the Roman Catholic priest, Father Rigaud. Father Rigaud did not live in the native community, although that was where his church was. He lived on the white side of the river. He arrived at the airstrip with a dog-team and a typical canvas-sided toboggan-sled. My first sight on alighting from the aircraft was of this dog-team, which had become entangled in its harness, and Father Rigaud, wading in among the dogs, in a rage, laying about him with a whip, his boots, and even his fists. I was astonished to see an Oblate missionary displaying such a temper.

I was equally astonished to learn of the conditions under which the local people lived. There were the usual sod-roofed huts and even some families living in tents, at temperatures that could plunge to sixty degrees below zero in winter. The Ross River people, even then, were slow to provide for themselves. Their habit was to wait for someone to provide for them; they were of course, recipients of the old age pension and family allowance, but they did not yet qualify for any other largesse. The income of that community was therefore next to nothing. As they waited to be provided for, they got hungrier and hungrier, until they were so desperate that two of the ablest men would be sent out to hunt. The two would kill a moose and stay with the kill for a day or two, gorging themselves. They would then return to Ross River and inform the rest. The moose would have to be claimed fairly quickly before the wolves got at it, but such was the lethargy—and, by now, the physical weakness—of those in the village that Father Rigaud would have to go out with his dog-team to bring back the moose. The Indian village has now been moved to the same side of the river as the white community, but the main road still separates the two, the land occupied by the natives having been set aside by order-in-council in Ottawa, at the instigation of the Department of Indian Affairs (which had replaced Northern Affairs in 1966). The housing is much improved, but the habits of dependence remain. One of the aims of Program Review in the Mulroney government was to break these bonds by virtually eliminating the Indian Affairs branch of the department and turning the programs and funding over to native groups for self-administration. It was not to be.

I had hoped to encourage the sort of development that has taken place at Teslin. There, the white population was also separate from the natives and boasted luxuries the natives could not afford, such as electricity, a water and sewer system, and much better housing. Just the same, the close-knit native community worked hard to attain some measure of self-sufficiency. Teslin natives speak their ancestral Tlingit language. They are a handsome people, and much more advanced than the people of Upper Liard. They built sturdy wooden homes for themselves and were, for the most part, industrious, their main pursuits being fishing, hunting, and trapping. They did not rely on government handouts to exist; they survived by their own initiative and efforts. Some were entrepreneurs, who made and sold snowshoes and canoes. George Johnston, one of the more aggressive entrepreneurs, established a grocery store on the native side of the community, on the edge of the white side, and attracted custom from both. A museum has now been established in Teslin, dedicated to George Johnston, and containing memorabilia from his personal collection, including photos from the days before the construction of the Alaska Highway, which was built directly through the village.

The Teslin people to this day are fighting a running battle with the bureaucrats in Ottawa. Again by order-in-council, a sizable tract of land was set aside for the exclusive use of the native people, long before the construction of the Alaska Highway. That was the "land base" of the community. The first violation of that "title" came with the building of the highway, which was driven through the land without any consultation with the chief and council; later, another order-in-council carved out the right of way. The next violation was the construction of an airstrip as part of the Northwest Highway system; afterwards an order-in-council was passed to carve out the necessary land and justify the theft. It is hardly surprising that natives think little of the white man's promises.

This is the kind of abuse that I discovered on those early trips. Obviously, the people of Teslin ought to have been compensated for the snatching away of their land without a by-your-leave, but, decades later, the argument still drags on, with no resolution.

At Carcross, much the same sort of thing happened, although it had rather a different outcome. This was also a split community, with the native village on one side of the Nares, a narrow neck of water at the end of Bennett Lake, and the whites on the other side. Carcross is forty-five miles off the Alaska Highway, but it was an important railroad stop on the White Pass and Yukon Railway that ran from Whitehorse to Skagway, Alaska. There is mining activity in the mountains thereabouts; this was the home of Skookum Jim and Tagish Charlie, co-discoverers of gold at Rabbit Creek, later Bonanza Creek, which triggered the Klondike gold rush. As in other communities, the Carcross natives had land set aside for their exclusive use, but the seekers of mineral wealth, without asking permission or providing compensation, went ahead and built a trail, which became a road, through the native land. Later, the federal government did the same thing, when the highway was thrust through to Skagway in the 1970s. By this time, the Carcross natives were part of the Council of Yukon Indians, who were in the middle of negotiating the native land claims with the federal government. They organized resistance, which included a blockade of the road for a time, and were able to bring their claim forcefully to the attention of both the federal and Territorial—sometimes known locally as "Terrified"—governments, with the result that they were paid about a quarter of a million dollars in compensation for the federal land-snatch.

The housing in Carcross has benefited, as have all the communities, from three decades of federal housing assistance that I began fighting for the day I was elected. But appalling problems remain.

For instance, Carmacks (named for George Washington Carmack, the other co-discoverer of Klondike gold) on the Yukon River north of Whitehorse. Today the native community is still on one side of the river and the white on the other. That situation was deliberately created by the federal government shortly after I became an MP. The two communities had been one before the Pearson government separated them. The Roman Catholic church had been lobbying to relocate the natives to the side of the river on which their church stood, and the bureaucrats achieved this by investing housing money only where the church wanted the houses built. This split the community in two.

There were no simple solutions to the larger problems of the native communities. In places like Minto and Pelly, where the housing ranged from primitive to dreadful, the rates of alcoholism, suicide, and homicide were appallingly high, a direct result of the depressing environment. Minto is no longer a native community: it was abandoned when the sole local industry, a sawmill, shut down. At Pelly, the physical conditions have been much improved since I first visited; there are water and sewer facilities, a laundromat and a bathhouse, and much better housing.

But the intellectual poverty still exists, even though there is a school there. Changing the educational standards of a people is a slow, time-consuming process, and it will take another one or two generations to show real progress, notwithstanding the enormous sums of money poured into such communities. (Incidentally, Pelly, which went from a shameful collection of sod-roofed huts to quite an attractive-looking village in large part because of my efforts, consistently voted Liberal. What that community got as a result of my efforts was certainly not rewarded with support at the polls— but that was not the point. I did find it interesting, though.)

It is essential in coming to grips with these communities to eschew the Great White Father approach. One of my favourite Yukon villages is Old Crow, the northernmost community on the Porcupine River, not far from the Beaufort Sea. The Old Crow people are a very handsome race who, when I first visited them in 1957, displayed great industry and individual initiative and, obviously, a great ability to survive, or they would not be there. Their main industries were fishing, hunting, and trapping. The village is much changed from when I first saw it in 1958. Then, there were only a handful of non-native people—the RCMP officer and his wife, the Anglican minister and his wife, a nurse, and later on, a couple of schoolteachers. Now there are quite a number of non-native residents, most of them on government payrolls; there is an airstrip (with a small terminal building dubbed the Old Crow International Airport), the large school of which I have already written, and a nursing station. Housing has very much improved.

The politics have also changed. In my time as MP there were, for many years, only two Liberal families in the community; now there are many Liberal and NDP supporters. The local representative on Yukon Council is NDP. The change represents not merely a generational difference but the influx of a large number of non-native people, many of whom are young radicals of NDP persuasion.

There have been some gains and some losses at Old Crow over the years. On the positive side, the housing, hygiene, and general social environment have improved enormously by reason of the many millions of dollars that have created a new and more wholesome environment. Education has improved a hundredfold, including the preservation of the Lucheaux tongue through language training in the school. On the negative side, the Old Crow people have lost much of their initiative, their independence, the work and survival ethics that served them so well for so long, and they exist now almost entirely on government funding of one sort or another. In my opinion, the government of Canada, with taxpayers' money, has totally corrupted Old Crow. It has taken a generation to accomplish, and the damage is probably irreversible.

The Old Crow story has been repeated in pretty well every native community in Yukon. It is only a question of degree. Although great improvements have been made, a disproportionate share of the millions of dollars spent by the federal government has gone, as always seems to be the case with government largesse, to those who need it the least: in this case, the upper crust of the native bureaucracy and their non-native advisers.

This was not what I expected or fought for when I went to Ottawa. My first speech, in committee, dealt entirely with native affairs, and my second, my maiden speech in the House, expressed my conviction (formed after an examination of the law with respect to the native people of Yukon) that they had an unextinguished aboriginal title to the lands that they had traditionally occupied over the centuries. I had also concluded, as a matter of law, that they had a right to hunt and fish for sustenance at any time.

I was later to be upheld in that view by the Yukon Court of Appeal, in a case involving a native called Tom Smith, who lived at Haines Junction, west of Whitehorse. Before Kluane National

Park was established, there was a game sanctuary in the area, within which it was alleged to be unlawful for any person to hunt or fish. Tom Smith, driving along the Alaska Highway, spotted a cow moose, which he shot, butchered, and took home to feed his family. He made no secret of what he had done, and was charged by the RCMP. Tom was illiterate, spoke only a little English, and, since there was no interpreter in court, did not understand the process by which he was convicted and fined twenty-five dollars for shooting a cow moose out of season and in a restricted area.

I was told about the case by one of his relatives, who explained that twenty-five dollars was a considerable sum for someone in Tom's circumstances. After speaking with him, I launched an appeal based on the argument that since there had been no treaty signed with the Yukon native people, by virtue of the Proclamation of 1863 the game laws did not apply to Yukon Indians. They could, I maintained, hunt or fish for sustenance at any time, except in the case of an endangered species specified as such by federal legislation. The appeal court upheld my argument, reversed the conviction, and returned the fine. The federal justice department rejected my strong suggestion that they ought to appeal the matter to the Supreme Court of Canada, because this point had never been settled by our highest court. Being somewhat less than confident of the outcome, which would be quite devastating if it went against them, the department did not take up the challenge. So that is still the law, and, in my opinion, that is still the right of any native person in Yukon.

I was consistently identified with the question of native rights in Yukon and continued to assert the claim for aboriginal title in the House of Commons and in committees, but my calls for action fell on deaf ears.

Long after, there was a complete reversal; one of those somersaults of which Pierre Elliott Trudeau was capable. In September of 1973, in Vancouver, Prime Minister Trudeau was reported to have stated that there was no such thing as aboriginal title and that there would be no further treaties with any native people of Canada. The rights of half of Canada's aboriginal people were dismissed with a wave of his hand.

Then, in that same month, came the Nishga land claims case in British Columbia, in which that tribe petitioned the Supreme Court for a declaration that "their aboriginal title ... has never been extinguished." The Court split four-to-three on a decision that the title had, in fact, been lost, but Mr. Justice Emmett Hall, in a brilliant dissent, set forth the argument on very much the same lines that I had enunciated years earlier.

Trudeau understood clearly argued law and accepted the minority judgment as the correct one. That process began the negotiations with native groups that have continued ever since, but unfortunately, Trudeau could not help screwing it up.

Trudeau's cabinet approved the concept of "core funding" to help along the process of negotiating land claims and this has proven to be a fiscal disaster. The whole process has now become a sinkhole for funds.

The negotiation of land claims required financing native groups to undertake the necessary research and preparation to give them a fair chance and an effective voice at the bargaining table. I have always supported this idea, but what I did not and do not support was the notion that the money should be handed over without any control and used, in the main, merely to extract more money. Without accountability, millions upon millions of dollars have been poured into a bottomless pit, not to deal with native claims but to provide fat salaries and other perks for native bureaucrats and their non-native advisers. We are not now dealing with matters of justice and principle, but raids on the public treasury, largely because federal aboriginal policy over the last ten to fifteen years has developed in reaction to the demands of carefully briefed and primed native leaders.

Our Program Review research showed that if the present trends continue, by 1992 the total federal sums spent on Indian Affairs in Canada will be more than half the budget of the Department of National Defence. (This estimate is confined to core funding and native program expenditures and does not include the enormous sums that will eventually be paid as settlement sums upon the signing of "final" agreements between the federal government and native organizations.) I do not believe there is the political will in any party in Canada to correct this situation.

My conviction as a fledgling MP was that the question of native title had to be addressed by compensation based on negotiation, quickly, firmly, and fairly. It is now more than fifteen years since the core funding approach was approved; in any reasonable circumstances, the issue of native rights and compensation for aboriginal title should have been concluded within three, or at the very most four, years. No one knows when, if ever, the process will be finished, or how much it will ultimately cost the Canadian taxpayer. The Indian and Inuit people are in no rush, and why should they be? Their communities are being improved, social conditions are being upgraded, all with federal monies, and in the meantime a fat and flourishing native bureaucracy receives enormous salaries. Some of those who started in sod huts have wall-to-wall carpets and two-car garages, and they are not in a hurry to give up the salaries that provide these luxuries.

To get some idea of what I am talking about, consider the situation in Yukon, where an agreement in principle on land claims was finally negotiated in mid-1988, with a final deal to be struck heaven knows when, and for heaven knows how much.

These are the most recent figures available, covering the fiscal year 1984-85:

Payments made to Yukon Indian bands:	$11,781,000
Payments to groups or associations:	$ 6,000,500
Federal programs delivered to natives:	$30,000,913
Total	$47,782,413

The data were provided by Treasury Board officials with the caution that figures dealing with general programs are estimates, and are often pro-rated, so they should not be used to draw inferences about special programs. Just the same, these rough figures give some idea of the extent of the problem.

It should also be pointed out that these are program costs only—no overhead figures are included—so the real total expenditures are considerably higher. Moreover, these numbers do not include the core funding amounts received by Yukon natives to support this activity.

In 1985, the census figures for native people, including Indians and Metis to the fourth degree of consanguinity, came to a total of 4,045 in the territory. If that number is divided into the total federal expenditure in Yukon for 1984-85, the result is an annual payment to each man, woman, and child of Indian ancestry of $11,812.71.

Another way of looking at it would be to use the sum of $11,812.71 to house every Yukon native person in the Hotel Vancouver, where, based on a government rate for double occupancy

($114 a day), native people could be housed all year and an average family of four would have more than $5,500 left over for room service.

It would not be so bad to drop nearly $50,000 on every family of four by way of government support if this money were actually getting through to the families, but anyone who travels in Yukon can see that the average native family is not wallowing in this kind of money; the vast majority of the funds are being swallowed up along the way.

I assume the scale of waste on the national level is about the same as that in Yukon; I have to assume it, because no adequate accounting process exists to allow us to check it.

In 1975–76 federal government expenditures on native programs amounted to $780 million. In 1985–86 these expenditures had increased to $2,860 million, which amounts to an increase of 267 per cent. This amounts to a 76 per cent increase in real dollar terms over a period when the total population of status Indians grew by 27 per cent.

In 1985 the status Indian population in Canada was approximately 360,000 and that of the Inuit was approximately 30,000. There are also approximately 85,000 non-status Indians who may become Indians as the result of Bill C-31, which was passed by the government when David Crombie was still Minister of Indian Affairs. Approximately 100,000 additional Canadians are of Métis origin, according to a government estimate. (The Métis themselves estimate their number to be one million or more.) A fair estimate of the total number of Indian, Inuit, and Métis people in Canada for whom the federal government has a legal or assumed responsibility is between 500,000 and 700,000.

A total native population of 600,000 represents 2.3 per cent of the total Canadian population of 26,164,000. Federal government expenditures on native programs in 1985–86 were approximately 3.5 per cent of total government expenditures. It is important to note that these expenditures do not include sums paid to native people under programs available to all Canadians, such as family allowances, old age security, Canada pensions, and so forth. Of even greater significance, these expenditures do not include the huge sums that are now and will become payable as outstanding native claims are settled. A multi-billion dollar tax burden has already been assumed by Canadian taxpayers as a result of claims settlements with the native people of James Bay, the Inuvialuit, the Dene-Métis, and the Council of Yukon Indians. Those same taxpayers should brace themselves for the additional $12 billion bill that is yet to come, for that sum will be the minimum cost of the settlement of the remaining outstanding claims, assuming that there is no change in the existing claims settlement policy (or lack of it) of the government. In the meantime, the expenditures on programs and other native benefits continue to rise unchecked. (It is worthy of note that the federal budget of April 1989 increased expenditure for Indian affairs.)

Even without polling it may be assumed that the majority of Canadians are sympathetic to the plight of the native peoples. Only the very hard-hearted would not be touched by the hardship, poverty, and tragedy many of them live with. Television has an enormous impact on the shaping of public opinion, and in this case it has helped to arouse public sympathy and support. The other side of this story, however, is the expenditure side. Not surprisingly, since the study of overall expenditure for native peoples is pretty dull material compared with the more sensational stories so readily available, the expenditure story is rarely published or given any attention by the media. Canadians are not, therefore, generally aware of the magnitude of the expenditures on aboriginal programs and benefits and such expenditures are seldom, if ever, looked at from any comparative perspective. Surveys indicate that Canadians are generally in favour of efforts to reduce the deficit. Would such support translate into an irresistible demand for the establishment of control over Indian affairs expenditures if public television (and other media) published the full story of the rapidly escalating costs of aboriginal programs and benefits?

The pattern of escalating Indian Affairs expenditures has not changed and is not likely to change. This will result in a total Indian affairs expenditure in 1992 of an amount equal to or slightly more than the year's projected budget on national defence. From another perspective, Indian Affairs expenditures in 1992 will amount to a sum slightly less than the entire federal budget in 1970. Such an expenditure growth pattern is impossible for the federal treasury to sustain without substantially increased revenues which, of course, would inevitably result in yet greater levels of taxation by the government.

I hope I have written enough, and have enough on my record

as a defender of Canada's original population, to escape the allegation that I am acting like a red-necked racist on this issue. I am simply being realistic, and it is realistic to notice that the billions of dollars now being poured down the drain are neither solving the land claims question nor creating an environment in which native people will attain self-sufficiency. What we have is an accountant's headache and a sociologist's nightmare, a system in which these people are being tied ever more tightly to the government's apron strings, while most of the money just disappears.

During Program Review, I discovered what happens to anyone who tries to investigate and suggest solutions to these problems. The premature and deliberate leaking of the part of the report that dealt with native programs set off a terrific clamour among the lobbyists, led by the Indian Affairs bureaucrats whose jobs we proposed to dispense with. The whole report on this subject was very nearly suppressed because of this political pressure. Fortunately, we did publish, and a substantial number of our proposals have been adopted. Not, however, the central ones having to do with the spending and dismantling of the Indian Affairs bureaucracy. The time bomb we found on native expenditures is still ticking away.

In the end, these matters will be resolved only by the application of political will, when the leader of the government of the country says, in effect, that a given course of action will be followed and adhered to because it is right. That has not been the case in recent years and I regret to say that this assessment applies as much to the Mulroney years as it does to any others. I was to see what this meant to myself, my colleagues, and the country when things began to go wrong not long after we formed our government in September 1984.

Chapter Nineteen
Scandal Time — Again

Send me better men to work with, and I will be a better man.

Sir John A. Macdonald

The two principal reasons that led me to enter politics were the need to develop the magnificent heritage of Yukon and the need to stop the blatant patronage that was occurring among Liberal party supporters in Yukon. I still remember my outrage in 1956, when the Liberal government awarded a contract, for which no public tenders were called, to a local construction firm whose chief distinction was that its head contributed generously to the Liberal party. The contract was worth about $280,000, quite a handsome sum in those days, and it involved the reconstruction of a bridge at a place appropriately called Crooked Creek.

Anyone who takes the trouble to follow my activities will discover that the rage I felt three decades and more ago has never faded; I have spent much of my career condemning patronage, political favoritism, and influence-peddling wherever I found them. So it will be understood at once that when I, along with millions of other Canadians, witnessed the Great Debate between Brian Mulroney and John Turner on July 25, 1984, the climax of the federal election campaign, I was overjoyed to see the leader of my party forcefully inform Turner that he did, indeed, have a choice when it came to patronage appointments.

When Turner became prime minister, he inherited a list of appointments, which included the elevation of no fewer than seventeen Liberal MPs to the Senate, the bench, the diplomatic corps, and various other snug havens. Turner announced these appointments himself, the day the election was called. The highly questionable explanation given was that if Trudeau had made the appointments, so many MPs would have been removed from the

245

House of Commons that the government would have been in danger
of losing its majority; the announcement of appointments was therefore delayed until the House had risen, which made it Turner's
responsibility, since Trudeau had retired. In the middle of the English-language debate, Turner, for reasons best known to himself,
raised the patronage issue, and Mulroney responded with Turner's
lengthy election-day list. When Turner replied that he had "had
no option but to proceed with the appointments," Mulroney's reply
raised a shout of joy across the country: "You had an option, sir.
You could have said, 'I am not going to do it. This is wrong for
Canada.'" More than any other single factor, that clinched the
election for Mulroney.

That was music to my ears, as it was to the ears of anyone who
had crusaded for a fresh approach in a new government. We had
been through some bad moments on this very issue. Not long after
the appointments were announced, Mulroney, in discussing the
most controversial of them all, that of Bryce Mackasey to a diplomatic post, had told a reporter, "There's no whore like an old
whore. If I had been in Bryce's place, I would have been the first
with my nose in the trough." Needless to say, that approach was
not helpful, in political, ethical or moral terms, but now the leader
was indicating that he had learned his lesson; we would, indeed,
run a more respectable administration. That, at least, was my hope
after the Great Debate.

It did not survive long. I was in a position unique in Canada to
see how the theory of respectable politics was translated into the
practice of politics as usual. I suppose it is inevitable that a certain
amount of patronage will remain, but the last flicker of my idealism
was entirely snuffed out when it became clear that we were to behave
in a way that was little better than the conduct followed by the
Liberals before us, and which we had pledged to reform. I had
thought we were going to clean up politics once and for all, but
for some people, it was clear that the intent was simply to clean
up. This was not so much a question of Mulroney encouraging or
countenancing the willful misbehaviour of his followers so much
as an inability or an unwillingness to take the resolute action necessary, first, to correct the situation and second, to send a clear
message to the party and the country that a new standard of ethical
behaviour was now in place. This will be seen in this chapter in
the examples of the Robert Coates resignation, the Marcel Masse

case, and the tuna scandal in particular, and in the next, in the story of Sinclair Stevens's resignation. In each case, the signals that came from the Prime Minister's Office concerned public relations and damage control rather than ethics, and as I pressed forward on what I thought was the proper path, I found myself increasingly isolated and resented. My choice was to conform to directions and decisions that I believed to be wrong or to leave. The Stevens affair eventually forced the choice of leaving.

The responsibilities of a deputy prime minister, as I saw it, were very similar to those of deputy leader of the opposition. One of these was to give my leader the benefit of my advice, views, and judgment on important matters, based on the information available to me. Another, more specific, mandate laid upon me by the prime minister was to oversee "the maintenance of the health of the cabinet"—health in the political sense—as well as of the caucus, the party, and all of its members. Quite a sweeping responsibility, and one I took very seriously. Indeed, I took my appointment to this task to be a signal that Mulroney was himself serious about ethical questions. Members of the cabinet knew I had this task, and some were of great assistance to me in bringing to my attention incidents that might have become much more serious had I not been able to take early action. The Coates case was one that slipped by, and the circumstances leading to the resignation of Bob Coates as minister of national defence provide an example of the difficulties I faced.

I had been surprised when Coates was made defence minister. I had known him for many years, but he was never, in my view, the timber of which major cabinet material is made. I had not given Mulroney an assessment of him, since he was not a member of the shadow cabinet, nor a prominent figure in caucus. He appeared, from the moment he joined the cabinet, to have but a tenuous grip on the defence portfolio.

On November 28, 1984, when the government was barely two months old, Defence Minister Coates and his aides went to Lahr, West Germany, on important public business. After a reception and dinner attended by senior officers of Canada's European Force, Coates and two of his aides slipped out of their VIP suite—leaving behind an armed guard in charge of an empty suite—and borrowed a general's car and driver to visit a nightclub on the other side of

town, Tiffany's, apparently a place with an unsavoury reputation.
When the general's driver reported back to the base that the defence
minister was there without any security, a plain-clothes officer was
dispatched at once. For about forty minutes, however, Coates was
unguarded; he and his aides remained in the nightclub for close to
two hours, leaving at about 2:00 a.m. to take a cab back to the
base.

Although these events did not become public knowledge until
the following February, they were, of course, the subject of considerable disquiet among senior military officers and, before long,
were reported to senior officials in the Privy Council Office. I ought
to have been informed by these officials, but instead learned about
the incident from a cabinet colleague.

Mike Wilson and I were discussing various issues in my office
one day in early February 1985. At the end of that meeting, Mike
told me that stories were circulating about Coates's visit to a nightclub in Lahr, unaccompanied by any security. My immediate
thought—and I soon discovered it had been the immediate thought
of officials in the PCO as well—was that there could well be an
apparent, if not real, compromise of national security, since Coates
was the minister of national defence and his visit was concerned
not only with matters relating to Canadian defence but also to our
allies in NATO.

As soon as I had concluded my discussion with Mike Wilson,
I was sufficiently alarmed to advise the prime minister at once. I
suggested to him that consideration should be given to requesting
Coates's immediate resignation. I am satisfied that the PCO was
advising the prime minister to that same effect. My responsibility
in the matter was discharged when I tendered my strong advice to
the prime minister. It remained for him to decide what action to
take in a matter that might affect the perception of his ministry.

The next I heard of the affair was when I was informed, five
days later and again by Mike Wilson, that the *Ottawa Citizen* had
the story and was about to publish it. I again alerted the prime
minister at once and again suggested that he should consider asking
for Coates's resignation. The next day, February 12, the story
appeared on the front page of the *Citizen*. It was, as I had anticipated,
very damaging to both the minister of national defence and the
government.

Within hours, I was summoned to Mulroney's office, where a

number of his advisers had gathered, including Gordon Osbaldeston, the clerk of the Privy Council; Bernard Roy, Mulroney's principal secretary; Bill Fox, the press secretary; Michel Gratton, his assistant; and Charles McMillan, a policy adviser. Brian asked what action, if any, I thought should be taken. I had already advised him, but in the presence of all assembled I at once repeated that there was no question in my mind that Bob Coates would have to resign and that if he did not do so voluntarily, the prime minister should request his resignation.

Brian had heard these views from me twice before, but his advisers were hearing them for the first time. I reiterated my argument about the potential compromise of national security. I gave as a second, but quite important reason, the fact that the government and the prime minister himself had already been harmed by the story in the public perception. If Coates were allowed to remain in office, the situation would become intolerable. I believe most of those present had already given Brian the same advice. (Although of course Gordon Osbaldeston, as a civil servant, and a meticulously correct one, would not have given his opinion directly; rather, he would have outlined the options available and left the conclusions to be drawn by the prime minister himself.)

That meeting did not last long, and I returned to my office, which was located immediately underneath Mulroney's. Mulroney spoke to Coates soon thereafter, and, within the hour, Bob turned up in my office, wanting to talk about whether he should resign. I was surprised that the matter was even open for discussion. Although he knew he was in serious trouble, he obviously had not been told frankly what he had to do. He appeared blissfully unaware that the likelihood of his vacating office was very real indeed. Hence I concluded that it was left to me to explain to him the extent of the damage he had done and the difficulty in which he had placed the prime minister. I told him bluntly that the only way the damage could be contained was through his immediate resignation. He replied that he would naturally do whatever the prime minister expected or wished him to do. Just then, my telephone rang. (A direct line connected Mulroney's office with mine. Originally it had been a two-way system, but Brian had changed the system shortly after assuming the leadership: he could call me, but I could not call him.)

I told Coates, "That's the prime minister." He blanched, and

I guess that was the psychological effect intended, because when I hung up after exchanging a very few words with Brian, Coates asked me if his resignation was expected. I said yes and suggested he return to his own office to draft a statement for the House that would be delivered after Question Period later that day. It was then about 1:15 p.m., which left a good ninety minutes for Coates to prepare his statement. Others have written of what transpired in Bob's office, and of the calls back and forth to Mulroney's office and the PCO. I was not told anything of this, but was only informed by one of the prime minister's advisers, calling from Bob's office at about two o'clock, that the statement was ready.

Later, in the House, I saw Coates waiting behind the curtain for a moment, visibly distraught and high-strung. He walked to his seat about five minutes before the end of Question Period and then rose to deliver a short, emotional speech in a voice shaking with the tension brought on by the accelerated pace at which he had to come to this difficult decision. He gave as his reason for resigning the fact that he wanted to be free to sue the *Citizen* for libel (which he did, although he later discontinued the suit). By the time he finished speaking, his eyes were brimming with tears, and he quickly turned on his heel and left the chamber.

The prime minister then left his own seat and walked through the lobby and out of the chamber with Coates, to the private members' entrance of the Centre Block, and there Coates entered his ministerial limousine and was swept out of the reach of the stampeding herd of pursuing journalists.

So, who fired Bob Coates? The prime minister made the decision, naturally, but I was the messenger.

As the events leading to the resignation of Coates were unfolding, I did not entertain the slightest thought that I might be his successor. Indeed, it was not until February 25 that the prime minister called me and asked me to assume the defence portfolio on a permanent basis. Joe Clark had been appointed as acting defence minister, and I had not been asked for my views as to the selection of a successor. The prime minister was concerned that the burden might be too onerous for me, but I reassured him that I could manage.

The next one and half years as minister of national defence were the most stimulating, challenging, and rewarding of my entire political career. My emotions on leaving the defence portfolio were the same as those that swept over me when I finally left the Air Force in 1951. I like to seek comfort in the speculation that the members of the forces were as sorry to see me leave as I was to leave. In any event, the account of my stint as minister of defence cannot be fairly described in a book of this nature and size. The story warrants a separate volume of its own, which would outline the many defence policy challenges and future directions planned.

Such a volume would also refute the canard that Gwynne Dyer published in an article in the *Globe and Mail* on April 22, 1988, in which, over a picture of me in an F-18, it is stated "In 1985, Canada tried to withdraw from Europe; its allies weren't amused." That statement is absolutely false, but readers of the article were urged to believe Dyer by way of an introduction to the article describing him as "a London-based Canadian freelance journalist whose column on international affairs appears in 150 papers in thirty countries." Perhaps Dyer takes satisfaction from the fact that the NDP used this distorted statement to oust the Conservative member, Flora MacDonald, from the Kingston riding during the 1988 election campaign.

When Coates delivered his short speech, it was to an audience of government supporters who had, for the most part, been taken completely unawares. There had been no time to discuss the matter in caucus, and when it did come up the next day, several members still did not understand why Bob had had to go. Obviously those members failed to appreciate the very high standards that must be maintained by a minister of the Crown in the conduct of his responsibilities as a minister as well as in the conduct of his personal affairs.

I was surprised at the extent to which this naïvete prevailed, even among some of our experienced members. Since it was part of my responsibility to ensure the continued political health of caucus, I recognized that we had a morale and information problem to deal with. I knew I would be greeted with resentment if I were to make a speech to caucus about the ABCs of political morality, so I decided on the much more time-consuming method of approaching ministers and members individually. In addition, from time to time through the course of several caucuses, the question of standards of behaviour was discussed, and our forum of parliamentary secretaries asked me to appear at their meetings, where the same subject was given an airing.

Somehow, the message never seemed to get through, and resentment, bewilderment, and misunderstanding remained in caucus
throughout the whole string of incidents that followed and ranged
from the globe-trotting capers of Environment Minister Suzanne
Blais-Grenier through the resignations of John Fraser, Marcel
Masse, and Sinclair Stevens. The Fraser case was, in some ways,
the most revealing of these.

John Fraser first came to my attention as a minister about to get
himself into serious trouble in a matter quite unrelated to tuna, but
very definitely related to fish.

I was informed that an Ottawa-based consulting firm, Government Consultants International, headed by Frank Moores, the former premier of Newfoundland, had requested an enormous fee from
some Atlantic fishermen who wanted to obtain an appointment with
Fraser, the fisheries minister. There was to be a continuing fee if
the appointment produced a favourable result, namely the issuance
of a fishing licence to this group.

Not only was this quite wrong, but the government and the
prime minister would be damaged if it came to light, which it eventually did. By this time, however, the dollar figure cited was much
smaller.

The group seeking this entree to the minister had apparently
been trying to get an appointment with Fraser for some time. I
cannot imagine why they had had no success; it is part of a minister's
job to meet with people. In any event, they had encountered such
delays that they approached a consulting firm, which demanded a
fee so outrageous that many might describe it as a fee for the peddling
of influence. Indeed, many regard the consulting (lobbying) business generally in that light.

Again, I informed the prime minister at once, and I believe he
may have taken his own steps to confirm the information I gave
him. I told him that I would discuss the situation with Fraser and
alert him to the danger. When I spoke to John, he expressed absolute
surprise that such a thing could happen. He told me that a meeting
with this group had taken place, and the fishermen were apparently
successful in obtaining their licence, but he had no idea whatever
that someone had paid to obtain an appointment with him. The
matter was subsequently raised in the House of Commons, alleging

a fee of substantially less than my original information had suggested, with some coverage by the media, but there was no need to take any action, since the minister had been manipulated without his knowledge or consent.

About the same time this was going on, John Fraser reversed a decision of his own officials. They had decided that close to a million cans of tuna about to be released by Star Kist of New Brunswick were unfit for human consumption. The company appealed to Fraser, and he set aside the decision of his officials and released the fish. This matter was at first a sleeper, because, although the Prime Minister's Office had been informed that the television program "W-5," was preparing a broadcast on the subject, Ian Anderson, the PMO official involved, did not pass the message along. "W-5," as a result of legal advice, decided not to air the show, but its CBC rival public affairs show, "fifth estate," got onto it, and ran the story several months later, in September 1985.

When that happened, I knew at once that Fraser's action in reversing his officials' decision carried the potential for considerable damage to the government. I was certain that the charge would be made—as it was—that the minister had been careless of the health of the consuming public and that he had given in to political pressures from the producers of the tuna.

I advised the prime minister that Fraser ought to resign at once. Mulroney was loath to request this, although he was deeply disturbed by Fraser's action. I continued to press for the resignation, and the prime minister continued to put it off. He was obviously emotionally torn between his loyalty to a minister and his irritation at Fraser's actions. It was almost a repeat of the agony that he had undergone in the Coates case; he was physically drained by the prospect of having to ask John to resign.

The television show was broadcast on a Tuesday; in the House of Commons, the opposition howled through Wednesday and Thursday. In the House, both Fraser and the prime minister insisted there was nothing wrong with the fish and refused to recall it from supermarket shelves. Then, late Thursday, Fraser asked Health Minister Jake Epp to recall the fish, and that was done at once. The next morning, the prime minister told a press conference that it was "pretty damn obvious" that the fish ought never to have been released, and that he had ordered the recall as soon as he heard about the matter. In a scrum outside the House after Question Period that day, Fraser said that the Prime Minister's Office had known about the case "for weeks" and that he, not Mulroney, had ordered the recall.

The prime minister had been flatly contradicted not once but twice by one of his ministers, and in each case there was some truth to the contradiction. The PMO had indeed known about the case since July—although the prime minister himself had not—and Fraser had requested the recall although it was at Mulroney's behest (for, as Michel Gratton was later to quote him as saying, "When Erik or Bernard tells him something, it's like he was talking to me!"). Fraser would now have to go, not because of his original error of judgment but because he had put the prime minister in a bad light by publicly contradicting him.

Another weekend went by with talk and meetings but no action, and then, on Monday, September 23, I was called to an early afternoon meeting at 24 Sussex Drive. Once again, we went through the scenarios available, and at last the prime minister summoned Fraser. We continued talking about other matters until a manservant announced Fraser's arrival. I went into the living room—I do not believe that Fraser ever knew I was there—and waited until Brian called me back again, by which time Fraser had left. We then went over the timing and manner in which Fraser's resignation would be announced.

I returned downtown to work on the details and the press release. This resignation was to be announced outside the House. Everything was completed by nine o'clock that night and ready for the ten o'clock national news broadcasts. I left the Langevin Block, after completing work on the press materials, with Michel Gratton, and as we said goodnight, he remarked, "This should have happened last Thursday."

I could only agree with him. I did and went home for the night.

Two days after John Fraser's resignation, the prime minister informed me that there was an RCMP investigation under way into alleged breaches of the Election Expenses Act by Marcel Masse, or by those acting on his behalf during the 1984 election. My advice was that Masse should resign at once, until the investigation was complete and decisions were taken as to the laying of charges or otherwise. This time, the advice was taken. The call about Masse came in the morning of September 25, 1985, and, just before noon, I attended a meeting with Masse in Mulroney's office. There, the prime minister asked me to explain to Marcel the basis for requiring his resignation while the RCMP conducted their investigation. He then left the office while Marcel and I sat side by side on a settee and I laid out the position to Marcel. I believe he had heard the explanation before, since he understood at once, and was willing and eager to comply with the prime minister's wishes and my advice. A resignation was prepared and delivered in the House that afternoon. Masse, who was certain that he would be vindicated (he was, and he later returned to cabinet), indulged in no histrionics and behaved with decorum and dignity throughout. I thought that this lesson must have impressed itself on the prime minister, but I was to find out how wrong I was when the Sinc Stevens affair broke.

The prime minister once more delayed the inevitable until the last possible moment. His compassion is admirable, but in the cases of Coates, Fraser, and Stevens, it cost him (and others) dearly. He did not want to hear my advice when the result was going to require painful decisions. I was becoming the constant harbinger of bad news. His reaction (human enough) was to withdraw from me to avoid the unpleasant consequences that would flow from my counsel. One of the most harmful results was the Stevens disaster. The solution from the outset was the quick, clean resignation of Stevens; instead we had a debacle, which, among other things, resulted in the termination of my long political career.

Chapter Twenty

The Sinc Stevens Affair

It is not enough to be technically correct on this question of conflict of interest. You've got to appear to the average person in the country and the average voter that you're not covering up.

Sinclair Stevens, 1974

Sinc Stevens is not the kind of individual that a peace-loving person would want to lock horns with. He is an aggressive and pugnacious fighter for his own point of view, which is more often than not all he sees. This weakness denotes a serious lack of political judgment. I recognized this trait in Stevens very quickly after beginning to work with him.

Stevens had several responsibilities in the cabinet; in addition to being minister of regional economic and industrial expansion, he was responsible for Investment Canada and the Canada Development Investment Corporation (CDIC). CDIC was a holding company for a number of Crown corporations, including Canadair and de Havilland Aircraft, Eldorado Nuclear Limited, Teleglobe Canada, shares in Massey-Ferguson, and the federal government's share of Canada Development Corporation (CDC), a company with extensive resource holdings.

Stevens was also chairman of the cabinet committee on economic development, and in addition was a member of the ministerial task force on privatization, a committee of cabinet then chaired by Robert de Cotret that had been constituted by Prime Minister Mulroney to inventory federal Crown corporations with a view to identifying those that could be offered for sale to the private sector. As a member of that task force, Stevens had often stressed the necessity of obtaining the very best advisers to insure against even the appearance of error or impropriety in the sale of Crown corporations. A laudable precaution indeed.

With the same end in view, Stevens had constituted the board of the CDIC and set up a committee of that board to advise him on divestitures. It was Stevens who identified and appointed the members of that divestiture committee, and the appointments, to say the least, did not appear to meet the rigid standards that Stevens had designed. Furthermore, at Stevens's insistence, Gordon Capital Corporation was retained, at a fee reported by the press as $500,000, to provide divestiture advice on the sale of the government shares of CDC.

Stevens's own holdings had been put into a blind trust by October 1984, in compliance with the existing conflict-of-interest guidelines. The assets in that blind trust included substantial control, which he shared with his wife, Noreen, of a holding company called York Centre Corporation, whose president, Ted Rowe, Stevens had appointed to the board of CDC. Rowe had been Stevens's campaign manager in the 1984 election. York Centre was deeply in debt, having lost close to $300,000 in 1983 and nearly double that in 1984. These losses were a matter of public record, because it was a public company. To raise money to meet the pressing demands of its bankers, York Centre approached a long string of brokerage companies, merchant banks, and pension funds. One of those whose help was sought was Jocelyn Bennett of Gordon Capital.

Therefore, Sinclair Stevens was in negotiation with Bennett and Jimmy Connacher of Gordon Capital to discuss how that company could, for proper reimbursement, work with the government on the matter of the sale of CDC shares while his wife was in negotiation with Gordon to obtain help for York Centre. To add yet another complication, Gordon itself was a major player in those shares: "We are the market-maker in CDC shares," was how Connacher put it later.

When I learned of this, I became concerned that there might be a de facto conflict of interest or at least the appearance of one. York Centre was approaching a long list of firms that would be involved in handling divestitures of the Crown corporations—that is, there would be sales of shares, which these firms would, in some cases, inevitably be handling or buying. There was also the specific problem of Gordon Capital. Jimmy Connacher, the chairman, had a reputation for brashness on Bay Street, but there was divided opinion as to whether that brashness was a breath of fresh air or whether it was something less laudable. One of the many difficulties raised concerned the interrelationships of all these firms and the aggressiveness with which they pursued opportunities.

In 1979, Connacher had played a central role in the takeover of Brascan Ltd., on behalf of Edper, the $100-billion empire of Peter and Edgar Bronfman. Brascan became the central company though which Edper worked. Its chairman was Trevor Eyton. Stevens had approached Eyton to be the full-time chief executive officer of CDIC; Eyton said he could not take on the job and recommended instead Paul Marshall, president and chief executive officer of West-min Resources, a Brascan subsidiary. Marshall was given the job by Stevens. At about the same time, Trevor Eyton gave Stevens a list of the names of others who might serve on the CDIC board, and he went on the board himself in October 1984.

Eyton and Connacher, to put it plainly, were old friends and allies. After the Brascan acquisition, Gordon Capital had helped Brascan acquire Noranda, the mineral giant.

Gordon Capital was at the centre of a number of controversies by early 1985. When it was acting for Unicorp in the hostile takeover of Union Gas, Gordon had advised institutional clients to sell blocks of Union shares at $13 each, because the follow-up offer would not be as attractive. It seemed unusual to have a firm giving advice to clients concerning a deal it was itself helping to pull together. The Ontario Securities Commission, after a long investigation, con-cluded that Gordon Capital did not act improperly, but that an amendment would be necessary to the information being circulated about the takeover, setting out the facts. Gordon Capital's main role in that hostile takeover was to sequester a large block of Union Gas shares owned by Brascan, its client. These details were made public in the *Toronto Star* on September 3, 1984, and in the *Globe and Mail* eleven days later. The fact that Gordon Capital was acting as an adviser to Stevens worried me.

What really set my alarm bells ringing, however, was the role Gordon Capital came to play in the CDC share sale. On August 20, 1985, the price at which the government block of CDC shares would be sold was set. That same day, there was a flurry of activity in the non-government shares of the firm. Gordon handled 127,000 of the 177,000 shares traded, on behalf of a single client, while the price rose from $11.00 to $11.25. In other words, the government's adviser had handled $1.4 million of the $1.8 million worth of shares being traded on the day when the price of the other shares about

to be released for sale was set. There was a bitter battle over the
price of the government's shares. Burns Fry, the investment firm
that would handle the placement, wanted a price of $11.25; Jimmy
Connacher wanted $11.50. Stevens intervened on Connacher's
behalf, and the price was set at $11.50. The shares were sold within
six days, with the largest block, 6.5 million shares, or 10 per cent
of CDC, going to Noranda, the Brascan subsidiary.

The Ontario Securities Commission and the Toronto Stock
Exchange both conducted investigations, and the press quoted a
number of disgruntled investment firms who were not at all happy
with the way things were being handled. The question might well
have been asked at that stage, "Does Gordon Capital's entrepre-
neurial zest and breath-taking style best serve the government's
need to be seen as purer than Caesar's wife?"

Another problem was that of the Bronfman-Brascan spectre. The
divestiture committee of the CDIC board included some of the most
respected names in Canadian business. Part of their advice to the
government was that revisions to the CDC Act, which had established that company, should include relaxation of the rule restricting
the holdings of any individual, firm, or combination to no more
than 3 per cent of CDC. This recommendation was widely appreciated by those who believed it salutary for management actually
to be accountable to somebody. The other side of the coin was that
raising the limit to 10 per cent allowed Brascan to become a major
force in CDC, and that raised problems of image, if nothing else,
because the board of CDIC and especially of the divestiture committee was heavily salted with Bronfman allies.

Paul Marshall, the CDIC chief executive officer, was a director
of Brascan, Noranda, and Brascade (another Bronfman firm), as
well as president of Brascan's resources firm, Westmin Resources.
Trevor Eyton was CEO of Brascan and Brascade, chairman of Royal
Trustco (which owned 2 per cent of CDC), president of Edper, and
a director of London Life, another Brascan firm, and Noranda,
among many other companies. Patrick Keenan, another CDIC director, was on the boards of Brascan, London Life, and Westmin.
Richard Bonnycastle (who was Sinclair Stevens's nominee to the
chairmanship of CDIC when Paul Marshall left) was not a manager
in the Bronfman empire but, through Pagurian, owned a stake in
Hees International, a Bronfman holding company. Connacher of
Gordon Capital participated in the key meetings of the divestiture

committee planning the CDC share sale and affected its advice to Sinc Stevens. I was told at the time that Bronfmans were an important source of capital for Gordon Capital; this, too, was worrisome.

Bits and pieces of this stew bubbled to the surface from time to time, long before the disclosures that would later rock the government. One such occasion was the appearance of Tony Hampson, the chairman of CDC, before the Standing Committee on Finance of the House of Commons, to discuss the amendments necessary to the CDC Act that would allow the sale of the company. Hampson told the committee that the board of CDC had been unanimous in seeking a more restrictive clause on ownership—he suggested 5 per cent instead of the 10 per cent recommended by, and eventually installed by, the government. Bonnycastle promptly contradicted him; some board members wanted a less restrictive clause, he said. Reports on that disagreement raised the question of Brascan's possible interest in CDC, and, again, that set alarm bells ringing for me.

If Brascan and its affiliates were to acquire a major or controlling stake in CDC, it would be unlikely, given the Brascan presence on the CDIC divestiture committee, that the process would be seen to be as even-handed as the cabinet task force on privatization would want.

Obviously, it was necessary to ascertain the intentions of Brascan as quickly as possible. We in the government needed to know the identity of outsiders holding CDC stock and of those who held installment receipts through which more stock could be purchased. (To make the stock cheaper to buy, and thus more available, it had in effect been split in two; you paid half the price down and got an installment receipt, and then paid the rest later. This backfired, because the price fell. People paid $5.75 for the installment receipt, based on the established price of $11.50 on August 20, 1985, but the stock fell below $6.00 quite soon after, so that purchasers would have to put up another $5.75 to purchase stock worth about $6.00 and on which they had already expended $5.75. It was just another of the problems that plagued this sale.) Overriding everything else, in my view, was an urgent need to reconsider the continued services of Gordon Capital.

Another step that could not be taken without the most serious reflection was the amendments to the CDC legislation then before the House standing committee. According to Hampson's presentation to the committee, anything that would be conducive to accountability in management, or good public policy, or a retreat on the degree of ownership allowed might be likened to a sledgehammer being used to swat a non-existent gnat. We had to deal with that, and, now that the story was becoming public, we had a communications problem that the government would have to solve.

It was also apparent that it might be necessary to relieve the CDIC divestiture committee of its pivotal role. By this time, the die was already cast with respect to the CDC, and those decisions were in place. However, Teleglobe, Eldorado Nuclear, and other targets for privatization remained, and these would have to be handled rather better. A natural breakpoint was coming up with the expected departure of Paul Marshall, and it appeared that would be the appropriate time to dismantle CDIC and have the subsidiaries go their separate ways. If that were done, Stevens would retain responsibility for the aircraft firms, de Havilland and Canadair, while Eldorado would come under the jurisdiction of Energy Minister Pat Carney and Teleglobe under Minister of Communications Marcel Masse. The Teleglobe board were due to meet in Ottawa, but it seemed likely they would be so occupied with other questions about the future of telecommunications policy that no action would be taken on the ownership issue. This meant another problem.

In addition to his other difficulties, Sinclair Stevens also suffered from a serious case of impatience. He found it very difficult to tolerate any delays once a decision had been taken, and he seemed to consider any decision to have been taken as soon as he had made up his mind. This impatience would inevitably collide with the very careful and deliberate pace Marcel Masse was determined to follow. It was clear that as far as Teleglobe was concerned, no sale would be concluded for months.

The only other intervening action would be the sale of de Havilland. There was no concern about questions of conflict, and there could be advantages in allowing the CDIC board to handle that one and then retire with a victory.

In November 1985, when I concluded that Stevens was leading us into serious conflict-of-interest problems that would undoubtedly reflect unfavourably on the government and on the prime minister, Mulroney was attending a meeting of the Commonwealth prime ministers in Jamaica. I considered the matter serious and urgent enough then to cause a message to be sent to him, outlining these concerns in detail. I believed I had discharged my responsibility and that the ball was now in his court. I naturally continued to keep myself informed of developments, and was therefore not at all surprised when a story alleging a conflict of interest on the part of Sinc Stevens appeared in the *Globe and Mail*, and I fully expected that the matter would be raised in the House of Commons.

The first in a series of *Globe* stories turned out to be quite wrong, but a second story appearing soon after had rather more substance to it. This story, which appeared on April 29, 1986, suggested that Noreen Stevens had negotiated what was described as an "advantageous loan" of $2.62 million from Anton Czapka, the co-founder of a company called Magna International, which had a close interest in and received benefits from programs of the Department of Regional Industrial Expansion—Sinclair Stevens's department. The advantage of the loan, which was to help ease the financial crisis at York Centre, was that no interest was to be paid during the first year. There was also, of course, the advantage that the loan was made in the first place. The cheque had been passed on May 16, 1985.

The prime minister was advised by officials in the Privy Council Office on April 30, 1986, that both his government and the previous government had agreed that the spouse of a minister may have a professional and business life independent of the minister. Although spouses were excluded from compliance with the conflict-of-interest code, that code prohibits the transfer of assets to a family member for the purpose of circumventing the code. The PCO officials also told him that Stevens had met the code's strict requirements for public declaration and divestment (which meant that he had put his assets in a blind trust), that no assets had been transferred to Mrs. Stevens, and that Stevens was not in breach of the code based on the reported facts. (What this advice did was point to a gaping weakness in the code rather than provide a legitimate defence.) They added that Mrs. Stevens had been an officer of the investment firm on whose behalf she had sought a loan at least since 1979 and therefore was not stepping into a position vacated by her husband. The PCO officials further advised the prime minister that Magna International denied having any business connection with Mrs. Stevens and that the loan was financed through a private individual, Anton

Czapka. The PCO officials informed the prime minister that I had been briefed and was prepared to answer questions in the House of Commons and suggested that if the prime minister cared to speak to the issue, he might choose to inform the House that he had no intention of limiting the rights of spouses to pursue their own business and professional career interests and that spouses were not chattel. Furthermore, if the prime minister cared to say anything, he might also mention that Stevens had complied with the demanding requirements of the code and that he had divested himself of all his interests, and that it was wrong for the opposition to conclude on the publication of an alleged conflict that the minister was about to betray his public trust.

This advice I considered quite at odds with my own assessment of the problems being created by Stevens, the details of which I had had sent to Mulroney, almost six months earlier. While the circumstances outlined in those events had no relationship to the disclosure in the *Globe and Mail* story in April, I was inclined to believe that they suggested there was nothing surprising in that story. Further, it was clear to me that if the facts reported were true, there would certainly be the appearance of a conflict, if not a de facto conflict, with respect to the $2.6-million loan. The appearance of conflict was also covered by the code, something that seemed to escape the attention of the PCO advisers. What also seemed to escape them was that mere legalistic quibbling would not suffice; most Canadians would be inclined to ask a much simpler question— was it wrong? That question could not be met by citing a code that obviously did not accomplish what was required.

Mulroney was preparing to attend an important function in Vancouver, and from there he was going on an extended visit to the Far East. The *Globe* story of April 29 broke on Tuesday, and questions were answered in the House that day by the prime minister, but thereafter he was absent. He stuck to the line laid down by the PCO in every particular.

I did not have the opportunity to discuss the story with the prime minister, nor to provide him directly with my advice. Everything was passed on by go-betweens. This state of affairs existed throughout the entire Stevens affair until it became necessary for Mulroney to speak to me directly about the procedures to be followed to obtain the resignation of a cabinet minister while he was not in the country to receive it.

There was no agreement, as some journalists have said, for me to "carry the can" in the House of Commons, nor did I devise any strategy in concert with the prime minister—again the language of the journalists—to "stonewall." What happened was simply that as deputy prime minister, with the prime minister away on extensive business, it was my responsibility to speak in the House for the government. But then, journalists hot on the trail of blood do not look for simplicity, but rather for sensationalism.

I believe it is important to describe, from my perspective, the details of these events. Tuesday, the day the *Globe* story broke, is the day the cabinet committee on priorities and planning meets in the main cabinet room. When I arrived for that meeting and took my place next to Mulroney, he immediately asked me to get in touch with his principal secretary, Bernard Roy, who was waiting in the small cabinet room just down the hall, and to find out about the substance of the article. I told my chief of staff, Peter Harder, to chase down Sinc right away and bring him to the small cabinet room along with Robert Boyle, the assistant deputy registrar general, the man responsible for the paperwork on the compliance of cabinet members with the conflict-of-interest guidelines. While we awaited their arrival, Bernard and I discussed the *Globe* article.

I told Bernard that if there was any substance to the allegation that a loan had been made in the amount of $2.6 million, or indeed, in any significant amount, quite apart from whether an actual conflict existed, there was at the very least the appearance of a conflict, and therefore Stevens was in breach of the conflict-of-interest guidelines. The only solution was to request Stevens's resignation.

Bernard's response was that the last thing Mulroney needed was the resignation of yet another cabinet minister. I replied that it was an option that had to be kept open, because I was sure it was the course that would eventually have to be pursued.

"Okay," said Bernard, "but in the meantime, let's devise an alternative, after we get to the basis of the allegations."

During the subsequent meeting, Sinc insisted indignantly that he was innocent and that he knew nothing whatsoever of any loan of any amount raised on behalf of any of his interests at any time since being appointed a minister of the Crown. The loan had been arranged by his wife, and he had no knowledge of it whatsoever.

Boyle then produced the files relating to Stevens's compliance with the conflict-of-interest code and indicated that Sinc had complied with the code in October 1984, in that he had set up a blind trust.

As was subsequently disclosed during the Parker Inquiry, however, the blind trust was not the kind of blind trust that was intended to be impervious to influence by the minister, either directly or indirectly, or by a third party. Nevertheless, it was on that slender peg of strict compliance with the provisions of the conflict-of-interest code that the so-called strategy of the government was to hang. That was the position Bernard Roy took, and I accepted it much against my better judgment because I assumed that Bernard was speaking with the authority of the prime minister, and as far as I was concerned, that was that.

Incidentally—and this is one of those now-it-can-be-told stories—Sinc was at first very feisty about his role and wanted to take on all questioners in the House of Commons himself. Government house leader Ray Hnatyshyn, Peter Harder, and I put him through a few minutes of rigorous cross-examination about his conduct and his knowledge, and no more was said about his answering the questions himself. He would deal with matters relating to his own ministry, and he did that, but on all matters dealing with conflict of interest, I intervened and answered for the government.

There were questions in the House that day, which Mulroney parried before he left. Soon, Bernard Roy left to join him, and within a couple of days, all the senior advisers in the PMO and several of the top members of the PCO were off to Vancouver and the Far East. Guess who was left to mind the store? My only communication with Mulroney throughout most of this period was through long-distance telephone conversations with Bernard Roy wherever the travellers might happen to be. I assume that Bernard passed on to Mulroney the views I expressed, and I had no hesitation in accepting that the views expressed by Bernard were those of the prime minister. From time to time, I reminded Bernard of the option of calling for Sinc's resignation.

As the clamour grew day by day and the criticism by the opposition and the media mounted, that option became increasingly attractive. My replies in the House were monotonous variations on the same theme. This was not stonewalling; I had nothing else to say. The reader will understand that, given my own views, which I had held since the previous November, there was no way I was going to shade the truth or lie in the House of Commons. That left me with nothing but a repetition of the same quite true and quite irrelevant statement: Stevens had "complied strictly with the provisions of the conflict-of-interest guidelines."

It was with a certain bitterness that I read, day after day, the accounts of journalists describing me as carrying out the government's strategy in defence of Stevens. What strategy? What defence? Not once did I state or indicate in response to those many, many questions, day after day, that there had been no wrongdoing, that there had been no conflict of interest, or that I regarded the loan as permissible behaviour. Nothing would have given me more pleasure than to say that yes, I believed there was at least an apparent, and probably a de facto conflict with respect to the loan. That would have led to another question about the resignation of the minister, and again, nothing would have made me more comfortable than to be able to say yes, the minister has submitted his resignation. Neither of these statements were available to me simply because Bernard Roy, acting on behalf of the prime minister, had indicated that the strategy would be that Sinc had complied with the conflict-of-interest guidelines. As a strategy, it was laughable; I cannot call it a defence, it was not.

My difficulty throughout that daily grilling in the House was my conviction that there *was* a conflict of interest. The code ought to have covered the behaviour of spouses, but even in the absence of such a provision, Stevens's explanation that he knew nothing of a $2.6-million loan to one of his companies and negotiated by his wife was, frankly, unbelievable. If there had been the slightest doubt in my mind about that, or if there had been any rational defence or any other action available to me, I would have embarked, as is my wont, on an aggressive stance in the House. But there was no defence.

I recognized very early in the development of the Stevens affair that my own credibility would be seriously, if not fatally, harmed, and after a few days of pounding in the House of Commons I resigned myself to the facts (a) that Sinc Stevens was finished as a politician and (b) that I had best make plans for my own departure. Even without the irreparable damage to my credibility, there was no way I could continue to serve in such uncomfortable and unpredictable circumstances. Having to conduct myself contrary to my beliefs and instincts was taking a heavy toll in terms of my health.

This situation prevailed from April 29 to Friday, May 9, when Mulroney spoke to me directly on the telephone. I immediately reminded him of the resignation option. Obviously he had come to that conclusion himself, and so the necessary groundwork was laid for Stevens's resignation. I do not know whether Mulroney had been in touch with Sinc directly; my belief is that Sinc expected to remain in office. There could be no other explanation for the course I was asked to pursue over that weekend.

Some traditional and conventional protocols must be followed when there is a ministerial resignation with the prime minister out of the country. These require certain actions by either the deputy prime minister or the secretary to the cabinet, in this case Paul Tellier. Both Tellier and I were involved in these activities over this weekend. It fell to my lot to communicate with Stevens at his home near Toronto and to request that he come to my office on Sunday morning. I gave instructions for an aircraft to pick him up in Toronto and bring him to Ottawa. When he arrived, I had waiting for him the wording of a resignation that I had hammered out with Bernard Roy on the telephone.

Until then, Stevens apparently had not realized that his resignation was about to be requested. When I talked to him on the telephone about our meeting, we discussed the matter of an inquiry, and it was Sinc's view that any such inquiry should be conducted by an independent Canadian of stature and impeccable reputation, but not necessarily with legal training. I was inclined to agree with that view, although I could see no reason to exclude the selection of a judge to do the job. I did agree with Stevens that the inquiry should not be allowed to turn into a trial by electronic media, as had happened in the case of Susan Nelles, the nurse wrongly accused of murder in a Toronto hospital—that inquiry had produced enormous publicity and no practical result, but had caused great personal distress and expense to Nelles. I passed these views along to Bernard Roy, with the request that they be transmitted to the prime minister in the Far East.

Stevens came alone to my office, as I had requested. He appeared to be taken aback by the nature of the discussions, which did not turn only on the inquiry but on his resignation. There were several later meetings that day, which Noreen Stevens also attended. I could not do much about that, since I had to get the job done on Sunday for Sinc to tender his resignation in the House on Monday, and the last thing I wanted him to do at this point was balk. I told him that it was the prime minister's view that the political health of the government and his colleagues depended upon the submission of his resignation. He wanted to speak to the prime minister, so I arranged the call and the two men spoke privately, with Stevens in an office adjoining my own. I then went on the line and Mulroney told me that Stevens had agreed to resign. Stevens returned to the Chateau Laurier with a draft copy of the resignation to talk things over with his wife. Our subsequent talks dealt mainly with the inquiry to be set up at the time the resignation was announced and with minor changes in the wording of the resignation.

Before the day was out, we had reached an agreement, and on Monday, May 12, the inquiry was announced and Stevens formally tendered his resignation in the House.

I had no doubt whatsoever that my own career was now finished and that I would not be continuing in office after an expected cabinet shuffle on June 30.

With my wife, Shelley, I travelled to Whitehorse on June 29 and then out to the peace of our place at Quiet Lake, where, far from all outside communication, I proceeded to get plastered, for the third time in my life. Such was the aftershock of the weeks that ended with Stevens's resignation and the realization that my own political career, after three decades, was now in tatters.

I knew this not only from my own long experience but from the attitude of some of my caucus colleagues throughout the Stevens affair. Because Mulroney was out of the country, I presided at caucus on May 14, and, towards the end of the meeting, Allan Lawrence, the member for Durham-Northumberland, rose and, without mentioning me by name, directed a scathing attack on the leadership of the party—meaning me—for the fumbling and bumbling of the "strategy" in the House of Commons. Lawrence made it clear that the leadership—me again—had given inadequate advice to Stevens, who, presumably, should never have been made to resign. I was burning with the urge to inform caucus of my feelings and of the advice I had given, but I was constrained by the same restrictions that had curbed me in the House: the loyalty that I owed to the prime minister. In addition, there was still the inquiry to go through, and had I mentioned any word of the true nature of my convictions, there was no doubt whatsoever that those views would find their way into the media and thus into the hands of the opposition. So I could not explain to caucus, nor could I remain where I was.

Al Lawrence's bitter outburst offended some members (it was not the first time he has sounded off in caucus) and I must say, I rather expected a note of apology, or acknowledgment, or something from him as the subsequent Parker Inquiry hammered home, day after day, the details of the Stevens affair, and made it clear why that minister did not belong in cabinet. No such apology ever came.

I knew, after that day in caucus, that my continued usefulness to the government and to the caucus had been destroyed. It was thus in an atmosphere not of my choosing that I left the caucus and, not long after, the House that had been, for more than thirty years, my office, my place of work, the place where many lasting friendships were formed, the place where I knew success and failure, triumph and tragedy, but a place that was, when I came to reflect on it, never my home.

Epilogue:

Lessons

I know what a statesman is. He is a dead politician.
We need more statesmen.

Bob Edwards

One of the advantages, perhaps the only advantage, of the kind of rough-and-tumble career I have had over the past three decades is the ability to look back and see not only the mistakes I have made but those I narrowly avoided. Twenty-twenty hindsight. As I reread this volume, I jotted down notes to remind myself of what I had learned along the way—for, like most people, I did not always take the lessons in at the time—and I wound up with a list that may serve to guide some aspiring politician of the future, and to help the general public know what to look for in politicians. These, then, are Nielsen's Golden Rules of Politics.

1. Never Mistake Charisma for Leadership

Charisma, in a television age, looks like leadership, but it is not the same thing. In any charismatic politician, you can look immediately for three character flaws that will become manifest, to greater or lesser degree. First, the more charismatic the individual, the less substance will be discovered behind the popular façade; second, the more charisma is present, the more arrogance will be present, and, no matter how great the effort to conceal this arrogance, it will become evident in the end; third, and most dangerous of all, the greater the charisma, the greater the paranoia that will attend every unsuccessful venture or objective of the charismatic leader.

The politician who depends on charisma, which my dictionary defines as "a divinely conferred gift of power," or "the special quality that gives an individual influence or authority over large numbers of people," does not like to face up to real problems. He or she will try to avoid any decisions likely to cause pain, because he or she will want to be considered the most desirable companion.

The person who wants to be liked by everyone, all the time, may be able to sway opinion—we have seen this, time and again—but that is not the same thing as real leadership. Leadership demands performance, not personality. Leadership is being prepared to do what is asked of others; it is getting out of others what one is willing to do oneself, rather than leaving the dirty jobs to followers. Leaders are not nice guys. Unless leaders set high objectives nothing is achieved, and that means making demands that will sometimes be resented. The more difficult the objective, the greater is the substance of its achievement by a true leader.

The war years were full of leaders demanding the impossible and getting it, by reason of the compelling nature of the times, which gave impetus even to leaders with flaws. Those flaws were often compensated for by the nature of the crisis. In peacetime, there is no such overriding factor, and the demands on leadership are correspondingly much higher.

British Prime Minister Margaret Thatcher is a good leader; her sights have consistently been set on the horizon and beyond throughout three successive terms. As a result, she has succeeded with her government, first in the mammoth task of removing the socialist imprint imposed by Labour on the country and then in re-establishing the value of entrepreneurship and the work ethic in Great Britain. She still has a long way to go, not because of any lack of leadership objectives, but because the European Community, to which her nation is now tied, is still afflicted by the same ills that flourished during the Labour years in Britain. She has often indicated, for example, that she would like to remove the massive subsidies that are crippling the European economy and, indeed, the world economy. However, she cannot take unilateral action; she can only lend her leadership to the efforts to cure the continental disease, and that is what she is doing.

Strong leadership, rather than merely charismatic leadership, could make a great difference in Canada. In a way, we are in something of the dilemma that Mrs. Thatcher finds herself in; that is, we cannot act unilaterally to correct a problem such as the massive and growing federal deficit. But strong leadership could still act to redirect the resources of the country to those that are truly in need. Strong leadership could and would tackle the problem of universality in the welfare system with much greater resolve than has been the case.

Strong leadership could, as well, do something about the huge unjustified subsidies to dozens of business and non-business organizations throughout the country. If the resources spent in those areas were redirected to provide support for the needy of our country, we would be meeting a fundamental precept of Conservatism in which I believe, namely, that we have an obligation as a state to look after those who are unable to look after themselves, either by incapacity or illness, or an inability to find a job. But we would not be looking after those who can quite well care for themselves.

To take one of a thousand examples I could cite, it is dead wrong to spend half a million dollars of our native funding to build a piano factory in Cracker Creek in Yukon. When that factory—a magnificent cedar structure, now forlorn and empty—was built, there were not half a dozen residents in Cracker Creek. No piano was ever built or tuned behind its splendid picture window, and the man who designed it, a white man, lives in a lovely home behind it, a home built on rich, black soil trucked in for the purpose, and waits for customers who will never come.

It is easy and popular to set such lunatic projects afoot; it is difficult and unpopular to crack down on the crazy waste of money, and that, in brief, is the difference between charisma and leadership.

2. Conserve Your Energies

When a young politician arrives in Ottawa, the opportunities to become involved in various projects are virtually limitless. There are so many problems, always, so many ills that need correcting, that the temptation is to hurl oneself into more than can ever be accomplished. Instead, the neophyte should investigate a number of options before confining himself or herself to one, two, or three activities at most. A politician who takes on too much cannot accomplish anything. Far better to find one or two specialties and stick to them.

3. Know When to Get Out

This sounds easier than it is. What I mean is to know not only when to get out of a particular situation but also when to get out of politics, period. When a situation becomes corrupt—and it seldom happens overnight—you must walk away. Resist the temptation to think, "Oh, I can clean this up." If you go along with corruption, even if it begins with only a slight bending of the rules, you will make yourself ill, in the spiritual and moral sense.

Corruption is a communicable disease; you cannot live with it in others, and you must avoid it in yourself. That means that no matter how tempted you are just to go along with the herd, no matter what perks are offered, you must get out. An honest person should have no truck or trade with crooks, no matter what profits are to be made.

4. Avoid the Degenerative Diseases of Middle Age

These are, of course, the bottle and the nineteen-year-old. Not being able to recognize the symptoms of a mid-life crisis, which every man and every woman encounters, has been the cause of more visible tragedies among politicians than I care to recount. Consider the case of Peter Reilly, a brilliant, hard-working politician who struck Ottawa with almost physical force in the early 1970s and was burned out and dead within a few years. Or, remember Rene Beaudoin, the Speaker during the pipeline debate of 1956, who wound up driving a taxi-cab (not that I object to driving a taxi-cab, I have done it myself, but it is not exactly a step up from Speaker of the House) after he fell prey to the diseases of middle age.

History has a short memory. Whatever you may accomplish in politics can be wiped out in the flicker of an eye.

5. Morality Is Not Negotiable

I mean this in terms of personal morality, political morality, and business morality. It is my observation that a lack of morality is at least as common, perhaps more common, to the business community as it is to politicians, and when the two play off each other, as they often do, it is usually the politician who is hurt, while the businessman escapes. But both are dangerous to the public weal.

I touched on the deadly effect of the lack of business morality when I described some of the events leading up to the Sinc Stevens affair, and, although I cannot say anything direct about bribes being offered and accepted within my purview, I can make direct comments about the immorality of bribes being offered to entice people to run for public office.

I believe that is utterly wrong, not just because I had to borrow $15,000 to begin my own political career, but because the motives of those who accept money to run for public office are suspect from the outset. Surely the only valid reason to seek office ought to be the desire to serve, the desire to accomplish something for one's fellow citizens, not the almighty dollar.

It is just as immoral (and, although it is not generally recognized, just as common) to offer bribes to persuade people not to run, or to step aside. I am not going to be specific, but on more than one occasion a very significant bribe has been offered to clear the way for a leadership hopeful.

In both cases, the very foundations of public life are being eroded by rotten business morality, whereby the individuals who subsequently become responsible for making decisions through "democratically elected representatives" are placed in their positions of power by means of money derived mostly from business.

Money, after all, is the ultimate power. Many are persuaded into politics by dreams of power, but nothing in political power replaces the power of money, for good or ill, and when it is used to corrupt the democratic process itself, the results are never good.

Everything can be corrupted by money, and the more money is involved, the more greed comes to the fore. There are two ways of looking at the greed of political power. One is the constant striving for power by an elected official. The more that person is motivated by greed, the less attention is paid to the means by which the lust for power is satiated. Pull up the ladder, Jack, I'm all right. The other is the use of, and the amassing of, money by the greed-driven business individual. It seems the more a business person accumulates, the greater becomes the lust for more. Surely, somewhere, the amassing of dollars merely for the sake of acquiring more becomes meaningless, especially when these stacks of wealth are measured against some of the pictures we see on television of starving people in Ethiopia—and some in our own backyards.

6. Have a Timetable

My own career indicates how important it is to enter politics with a firm commitment as to the time that will be devoted to public life. The neophyte should make a commitment (of course, it may be cancelled by the electorate) for one or two or more terms, and stick to that if at all possible. One approach might be to consider that block of time as the time the individual will devote to the service of his or her country before moving on to other things. That noble motivation, though it may not be in every politician's heart, should be there. The worst thing for a politician is to drift from one election to another without any definite plan until, in the end, he or she is forced to leave public life.

7. Always Remember Who Sent You to the House

One of the hardest things for an MP to keep in mind is that he or she did not get to the House of Commons by virtue of his or her own admirable qualities alone, but through the work of dozens or hundreds of electors in the constituency. So many forget, once they become inhabitants of the artificial world surrounding the House, who put them there. That kind of amnesia very often leads to ejection at the next election.

8. To Thine Own Self Be True

The other side of Rule 7, of course, is that even if others sent you to Ottawa, you must be willing to act according to your own morality and convictions. This is the lesson I did not learn until 1969. Do not succumb to the sometimes sickening hypocrisy of the House to evade or conceal your own sense of what is right and wrong because of the need to please others. What a refreshing place the Commons would be if its inhabitants always spoke the plain truth, without self-righteousness or hypocrisy. This is not an ideal we will ever achieve, but it is something for which we should always strive.

So great is the lust for retaining office and power that the holders of such power, for the most part, pander to every whim of any person who might help the office-holder retain that position. Around the cabinet table, ministers are constantly on the alert for signs of aggressiveness, dominance, and influence in others around the table. It is similar to the establishment of dominance in a wolf pack. It is natural enough to see it in the wild; to observe it at work in the cabinet room is fascinating. The resistance of office-holders tends to crumble when it encounters what is perceived to be a stronger force. And, in the case of a prime minister, of course, dominance is ever present.

Some cabinet ministers are constantly testing the waters; one of the most influential members of Mulroney's current cabinet always comes on very strong. If his adversary gives way, he gets even more aggressive, but if he meets determined opposition, the lion becomes a pussycat.

Sinc Stevens was one who always attempted to project dominance in cabinet, but his problem was that he would never back down. He was no pussycat; he was more like a bulldog who bites a piece of poisoned meat and will not let go, even if it does him in.

But for most cabinet members, there is a constant game of bluff and counter-bluff, and we have, when new members enter the cabinet, the edifying sight of the young lions, who have been out on the Serengeti for a couple of years gaining strength, coming back to test their strength against the others, determined to take over the pride.

The only sensible way to deal with all this posturing is to know who you are and what you stand for, and stick to it.

9. Distinguish Real Power from the Image of Power

The perception of power can be every bit as corrupting as its reality. When Lord Acton noted that "power tends to corrupt, and absolute power corrupts absolutely," he might have added, "and the perception of power is just as great a danger." The person who seeks public office must, however, be able to determine the difference between perception and reality.

There is no such thing as a member of Parliament having power per se. There is, however, a perception of power, and we have seen a number of cases recently where MPs traded on that perception and wound up in jail for their efforts. There is a popular and powerful myth that someone, because he or she has been elected to Parliament, has become the fountainhead of all good things. In fact, the MP has the advantage of walking in the same halls as those who occupy the seats of power, and that is all. Others may envy the MP as being one of the great, or even near the great, but there is really no more influence vested in any single member than there would be in any individual who can gain access to those who do wield power. While it might take the ordinary citizen a mite longer to gain such access, it can certainly be done, and, in a good many cases, lobbyists are far more influential, and have far more access, than the ordinary MP. That may not be the way the system is supposed to work, but it is the way it does work.

Perhaps the clearest way to distinguish between real and perceived power is to explain what happened to me when I first became a cabinet minister in 1979.

Life was very much the same the morning I woke up after my first portfolio appointment. I dressed the same way, had my coffee the same way, ate breakfast the same way, and did all the routine things the same way, but suddenly there were dozens of people who wanted to be helpful. What could they do for me? How could they help me? Could they get me coffee or drive me to an appointment, or bring me the latest and most complicated briefings on the matters within my responsibility? When, as is my wont, I asked my chauffeur for some advice about whether I could do something (perhaps it would look better if I had written, "my deputy minister," but in fact it was my chauffeur), he replied, "But of course, you can do anything; you're the minister."

Experience was to teach me that he was pretty well right; there are some limits, but not too many, to a minister's power within the area of his own responsibility. When that power is carefully analysed, it does not take too long to reach the conclusion that the potential for corruption is ever present.

10. Benevolence and Riches Are Rare Partners

The working politician comes into contact with wealthy people from time to time, and they can sometimes be generous with their wealth. But there is usually a motive attached to their actions, to which a politician may or may not wish to subscribe. The wealthy are motivated to be generous, usually in full public view, to charities and other good works more from a wish to be highly regarded and remembered in the community than from any true desire to help the community. As the wealthy approach old age, so their generosity grows in proportion to their desire to be remembered well. Self-gratification from public exposure and recognition is the quid pro quo of the wealthy for their generosity.

11. Let the Journalists Do the Walking . . .
If you are thinking of working on your family tree, do not bother to spend your money for the services of an expert. Just enter politics, and the journalists will do the job for you. If they find any skeletons, you will soon hear them rattle.

12. Keep Your Family with You
My own case leads, again, to this final bit of painfully learned wisdom. The married politician may well feel that he or she cannot afford to move his or her family to Ottawa, but I discovered that you cannot afford not to. Do not become a commuting politician; do not tolerate separation from your family. If you do, you will lose them and learn, too late, that the House is not a home.

Some Key Dates

1924
February 24   Erik Nielsen born in Regina

1945
May 3   Marriage to Pamela June Hall, Louth, Lincolnshire

1952
February 6   Arrival in Whitehorse

1953
August 10   Nielsen manages campaign for George Black, sitting
                   Conservative in Yukon; Black loses

1956
September 21   George Drew resigns as leader of Progressive
                   Conservative party because of ill health
December 14   Conservative leadership convention in Ottawa
                   chooses John Diefenbaker as leader

1957
April 11   St. Laurent announces election
June 10   General federal election; Nielsen wins (standings: PC
                   113, Lib. 106, CCF 25, Socred 19, Ind. 2)
June 17   Service vote swings one seat, Nielsen's, to Liberals,
                   by 49 votes; Nielsen protests election; 687 irregulari-
                   ties uncovered
June 22   Diefenbaker cabinet sworn in
October 14   Twenty-Third Parliament opens; Louis St. Laurent
                   resigns
December 16   Nielsen wins by-election in Yukon by 120 votes

279

1958

January 15	Liberal leadership convention in Ottawa; chooses Lester Pearson as leader
January 20	Nielsen seated in Parliament; Pearson makes his debut as opposition leader; Diefenbaker calls election
March 31	Tories win historic majority (standings: PC 208, Lib. 49, CCF 8)

1959

January 16	Parliament reconvenes
February 20	Avro Arrow cancelled
March 13	Governor of Canada President James Coyne disagrees with government monetary policy
April 10	Fleming budget shows fiscal 1959 deficit of $616.8 million expected, calls for wide-ranging tax increases
December 28	Gordon Churchill in speech says the economy is strong; Fleming disagrees

1960

January 14	Parliament meets; Diefenbaker calls for patriation of the British North America Act
January 18	James Coyne's Winnipeg speech attacks government
March 31	Budget predicts $12 million surplus
August 4	Bill of Rights wins unanimous approval of House of Commons
October 11	Major cabinet shuffle
October 20	Federal budget underscores cabinet rift on economic policy
October 21	Hall Commission on Health Care named

1961

January 12–13	BNA Act Conference
March 16–18	Conservative convention in Ottawa
April 17	Bay of Pigs
April 26	Coyne appears before Senate committee
May 30	Coyne's resignation requested; he refuses
July 7	Commons passes bill to dismiss Coyne
July 13	Senate rejects bill to fire Coyne, who then resigns
July 31	Founding convention of the NDP opens in Ottawa
August 3	Tommy Douglas elected NDP leader

1962

March 2	Bill sponsored by Nielsen gives the vote to all citizens in the Northwest Territories for the first time

April 19   Parliament dissolved, election called; polls:

	PC	Lib.	CCF	Other
March 1958*	54	34	9	3
March 1960	47	37	10	6
November 1960	39	44	11	6
January 1961	38	44	11	7
June 1961	40	42	10	8
November 1961	37	43	12	8

*election

June 18   Tories re-elected, but with minority government
                            (standings: PC 116, Lib. 100, NDP 19, Socred 30—
                            of which 26 are in Quebec)
September 27   Twenty-Fifth Parliament opened by Georges Vanier
September 29   Allister Grossart, national director of the
                            Conservative party, is named to Senate, succeeded as
                            director by Dalton Camp
October 22   President Kennedy speaks on Cuban missile crisis

1963
January 11   Pearson's Scarborough speech reverses Liberal anti-
                            nuclear stand
January 17   Conservative annual meeting opens in Ottawa;
                            Diefenbaker wins vote of confidence
April 8   Liberals win federal election (standings: Lib. 129,
                            PC 95, NDP 17, Socred 24)
April 22   Lester Pearson sworn in as prime minister
June 13   Walter Gordon's first budget
July 8   Gordon tables revised budget
July 15   Norris Report on Great Lakes violence released
July 22   Royal Commission on Bilingualism and Biculturalism
                            established
September 2   Socreds split; Ralliement des Créditistes formed with
                            thirteen seats under Réal Caouette, Socreds have
                            eleven under Robert Thompson
October 9   Canada-U.S. deal on nuclear warheads announced
October 23   Legislation proclaimed to place Seafarers'
                            International Union in trusteeship
November 22   President Kennedy assassinated
December 19   Hal Banks ordered to stand trial
December 27   Azellus Denis resigns, goes to Senate; Lionel
                            Chevrier resigns
December 31   Nuclear warheads reach North Bay, Ontario

1964

January 20	Pearson shuffles cabinet
February 1–5	Conservative annual convention in Ottawa; proposal for secret ballot on vote of confidence in leader is defeated; Dalton Camp replaces Egan Chambers as Conservative party president
February 18	Parliament opens
March 16	Second Gordon budget
March 18	Hal Banks deposed as SIU president
May 5	Hal Banks sentenced to five years in jail, released on bail; he promptly disappears
May 17	Pearson unveils new flag in Winnipeg
June 15	Flag debate begins
July 22	Conservative caucus adopts filibuster technique on flag
October 1	Hal Banks found by Robert Reguly of the *Toronto Star* on a yacht in New York
November 23	Nielsen breaks Rivard scandal in House
November 24	Guy Favreau announces Dorion Inquiry; Guy Rouleau resigns as parliamentary secretary to prime minister, remains Liberal caucus chairman
November 27	Government agrees to widen Dorion Inquiry
November 30	Flag debate resumes; Pearson sends letter on morality to cabinet
December 5	Conservative executive council meets in Ottawa
December 11	Closure announced on flag debate
December 15	Commons approves new flag at 2:13 a.m.; Dorion Inquiry opens
December 18	Parliament adjourns
December 21	Léon Balcer hints that he will leave Conservatives

1965

January 14	Ten Tory MPs from Quebec demand leadership convention
January 16	Auto Pact signed at LBJ ranch in Texas
January 22	Yvon Dupuis forced to resign over racetrack scandal
February 6	Conservative national executive meets; Léon Balcer calls for leadership convention but is defeated
February 14	Guy Rouleau resigns as chairman of Liberal caucus
February 18	Remi Paul leaves Conservatives to protest Diefenbaker's leadership
February 25	Bilingualism and Biculturalism Commission reports
March 1	Nielsen writes One Canada memo to Diefenbaker

March 2	Lucien Rivard escapes from Bordeaux jail
March 25	John Diefenbaker celebrates twenty-five years in politics
March 29	Canada Pension Plan approved
June 28	Dorion Report submitted to government
June 29	Guy Favreau resigns as minister of justice
July 7	Pearson shuffles cabinet
July 16	Rivard arrested in Montreal
July 22	Rivard extradited to United States
September 7	Pearson calls election for November 8
September 10	Jean Marchand, Gérard Pelletier, and Pierre Elliott Trudeau (Les Trois Colombes) join Liberals
November 8	Federal election, Liberals returned with minority government, 131 seats (standings: Lib. 131, PC 97, NDP 21, Socred 5, RC 9, other 2)
November 11	Walter Gordon resigns, citing bad advice in election call
November 16	Maurice Lamontagne and René Tremblay resign over furniture scandals
November 17	Major cabinet shuffle; Marchand and Robert Winters enter cabinet

1966

February 23	George Victor Spencer case breaks; Pearson says no inquiry will be held
March 4	Pearson announces Spencer Inquiry
March 10	Lucien Cardin raises ''Monseigneur'' case
March 11	Gerda Munsinger found in Munich
March 14	Pearson establishes Spence Inquiry into Munsinger affair, under Mr. Justice George Wishart Spence
March 29	Mitchell Sharp's first budget
April 18	Spence Inquiry opens in Ottawa
April 19	National Conservative director James Johnston fires Flora MacDonald from Conservative national headquarters
September 20	Dalton Camp, Conservative president, in Toronto speech calls for reappraisal of party leadership
September 23	Spence Report on Munsinger case released
October 27	Arthur Maloney announces he will run against Camp for presidency of Conservative party
November 13	Conservative national convention opens in Ottawa; Camp wins leadership reassessment motion, narrowly defeats Maloney

1967 (*Centennial Year*)

January 4	Walter Gordon returns to cabinet
January 12	Favreau resigns as Quebec Liberal party leader
January 18	Marchand named Quebec Liberal party leader
January 12	Conservative leadership convention called for September in Toronto
February 14	Fulton enters leadership race
February 16	George Hees enters leadership race
February 20	Mike Starr enters race, Erik Nielsen to run his campaign
February 9	Robert Thompson resigns as Socred leader; Trudeau and Chrétien named to federal cabinet; Lucien Cardin resigns as minister of justice
May 11	Wallace McCutcheon enters Conservative leadership race
May 26	Alvin Hamilton enters Conservative leadership race
June 7	Donald Fleming enters Conservative leadership race
July 1	Queen Elizabeth addresses Parliament in Centennial celebration
July 7	John Diefenbaker's last day as Conservative leader in House
July 11	Guy Favreau dies
July 19	Robert Stanfield enters Conservative leadership race
July 24	De Gaulle shouts "Vive le Québec libre" in Montreal
July 26	Pearson rebukes De Gaulle, who departs for France
August 3	Duff Roblin joins Conservative leadership race
August 7-10	Conservative policy conference at Montmorency, Quebec, approves "deux nations" resolution
September 5	Conservative convention opens in Toronto
September 9	Robert Stanfield elected Conservative leader
October 14	René Lévesque forced out of Liberal party in Quebec
November 3	Hal Banks ordered extradited to Canada; he appeals
November 30	Sharp "mini-budget" imposes 5 per cent surcharge on income tax
December 14	Pearson announces resignation as Liberal leader
December 21	Capital punishment abolished for five years on trial basis

1968

January 9	Liberal leadership contestants announced, beginning with Eric Kierans, Paul Hellyer (Jan. 11), Allan MacEachen (Jan. 12), John Turner (Jan. 13), Paul Martin, Mitchell Sharp, Joe Greene (Jan. 19)
February 1	Armed forces unification in effect

February 5–7	Constitutional conference in Ottawa; Justice Minister Pierre Trudeau shines in attack on Daniel Johnston
February 16	Trudeau enters leadership race
February 19	Liberals defeated on major tax bill while Pearson is out of the country; Stanfield agrees to 24-hour adjournment
February 27	Special Conservative caucus decides to allow motion to come to a vote without prolonged debate; Gordon Churchill resigns to sit as an independent Conservative
February 28	Liberals win motion 140–119
March 1	Robert Winters enters Liberal race
April 3	Mitchell Sharp drops out, supports Trudeau for Liberal leader
April 4	Martin Luther King assassinated in Memphis
April 6	Trudeau elected Liberal leader
April 20	Trudeau sworn in as prime minister
April 23	Election called for June 25
June 25	Liberals win election (standings: Lib. 154, PC 72, NDP 23, Socred 14, other 1); Gallup 1968:

	Lib.	*PC*	*NDP*	*Other*
October 1967	34	43	17	6
March 1968	42	34	16	8
June 19, 1968	47	29	18	6
Election day	45	31	17	6

1969

January 3–15	Trudeau at Commonwealth Conference in London; Parliament reconvenes
February 10–12	Federal-provincial constitutional conference
April 19	P.J. dies
April 24	Paul Hellyer resigns from cabinet when report on housing fails to get cabinet approval
May 5	Cabinet shuffle
June 3	Federal budget
July 7	Official Languages Act receives final approval
July 25	Government applies closure to end thirteen-day filibuster over new time allocation measures
October 9–13	Conservative convention in Niagara Falls
November 7	Benson White Paper on tax reform tabled
December 8–10	Federal-provincial constitutional conference

1970

| February 9–10 | National conference on price stability held in Ottawa as inflation worries grow |

March 12	Federal budget
September 24	Federal cabinet shuffle
October 5	James Cross kidnapped in Montreal by FLQ
October 8	Parliament reconvenes
October 10	Pierre Laporte, Quebec labour minister, kidnapped by FLQ
October 15	Army troops move into Montreal and Quebec City at request of Premier Bourassa
October 16	War Measures Act proclaimed, 439 arrested
October 17	Pierre Laporte's body found in trunk of a car at St. Hubert airport
November 6	Bernard Lortie arrested in Montreal for Laporte kidnapping
December 1	Commons approves temporary Public Order Bill to replace War Measures Act, 174–31
December 3	Federal budget; James Cross released unharmed
December 28	Paul and Jacques Rose and Francis Simard arrested in farm house near St. Luc, Quebec for Cross kidnapping

1971

February 8–9	Federal-provincial constitutional conference
April 24	David Lewis replaces Tommy Douglas as NDP leader
April 29	Eric Kierans resigns as communications minister
April 30	Government allows Public Order Act to elapse
June 14–16	Constitutional conference in Victoria produces Victoria Charter on patriation of constitution
June 18	Federal budget
June 23	Quebec rejects Victoria Charter
August 15	Nixon announces 10 per cent surcharge on imports to improve U.S. balance of payments
December 2	Government imposes closure to limit debate on tax reform bill
December 17	Tax reform bill passes House of Commons

1972

January 28	Federal cabinet shuffle
February 17	Parliament reconvenes
April 13–15	Nixon visits Ottawa, signs Great Lakes Water Quality Agreement
May 2	Gray Report on Foreign Investment tabled
September 1	Trudeau dissolves Parliament, calls election for October 30

October 30	Liberals win minority victory (standings: Lib. 109, PC 107, NDP 31, Socred 15, Ind. 2; popular vote: Lib. 38 per cent, PC 35 per cent, NDP 31 per cent, Socred 8 per cent, Ind. 1 per cent)
November 2	Trudeau announces that he will meet Parliament and stay in office
December 27	Lester Pearson dies in Ottawa; Gallup polls:

	Lib.	*PC*	*NDP*	*Other*
June 25, 1968★	46	32	16	6
February 1972	40	30	22	8
August 1972	42	32	16	6
October 1972	39	33	21	7
October 30★	38	35	18	8

★election

1973

| January 4 | Parliament opens |
| February 19 | Turner budget cuts taxes, wins NDP support for minority government |

1974

January 3	Parliament reconvenes
May 6	Federal budget
May 8	NDP switch defeats government on budget, 137–123
May 9	Trudeau dissolves Parliament, calls election for July 8
July 8	Trudeau wins majority, in "Zap, you're frozen" campaign (standings: Lib. 141, PC 95, NDP 16, Socred 11, Ind. 2; popular vote: Lib. 42 per cent, PC 35 per cent, NDP 15 per cent, Socred 5 per cent, Ind. 1 per cent)
August 8	Cabinet shuffle
August 14	Stanfield announces that he will step down before next election

1975

January 22	Parliament reconvenes
February 3	Robert Andras tables Green Paper on immigration
February 23	Federal budget
July 7	Ed Broadbent elected NDP leader at Winnipeg convention marked by battle over the Waffle
September 11	John Turner resigns from cabinet, reportedly over differences with Trudeau on the economy
September 26	Cabinet shuffle puts Donald Macdonald in finance ministry

October 13	Trudeau, in nation-wide television address, announces hiring freeze and wage and price controls
October 16	Wage and price controls motion introduced

1976

January 23	Consumer Affairs Minister André Ouellet held in contempt for remarks made about a judge in the sugar price-fixing case
February 12	Turner resigns Commons seat, goes into private practice with McMillan Binch
February 22	Joe Clark elected Conservative leader
March 12	Bud Drury tenders resignation over "dial-a-judge" affair; Trudeau refuses to accept his resignation
March 16	André Ouellet resigns over revelation that he had called a judge
April 20	Louis Giguere and Clarence Campbell are among five charged in Sky Shops Affair (they are later acquitted)
April 29–30	Western premiers' conference in Medicine Hat reveals increased bitterness towards Ottawa
May 25	Donald Macdonald's first budget
July 14	Parliament votes for permanent abolition of the death penalty
September 14	Cabinet shuffle
November 13	Another cabinet shuffle
November 15	PQ under René Lévesque wins upset in Quebec

1977

January 24	Parliament reconvenes
February 15	New Canadian Citizenship Act removes special status of British subjects
March 31	Federal budget
April 20	Jack Horner crosses floor, joins Liberals
April 28	Jean-Luc Pepin resigns from Anti-Inflation Board
May 24	Conservatives lose all six by-elections in Quebec and PEI
May 27	Trudeau announces separation from wife Margaret
July 6	Government orders Royal Commission to investigate wrong-doing in RCMP
September 3	Donald Macdonald resigns as federal finance minister
November 3–6	Conservative convention in Quebec City

1978

January 30	Francis Fox resigns as solicitor general after scandal over forged signature
March 10	Chrétien budget reduces sales tax for six months
March 20	Bill to patriate constitution tabled in House
March 27	James Richardson resigns from Liberal party
September 8	John Munro resigns from cabinet over phone call to a judge on behalf of a convicted constituent
October 13	Bank of Canada rate a record 10.25 per cent, dollar at $0.838 U.S.
October 30	Three-day federal-provincial constitution conference opens
November 16	Federal budget

1979

January 17	Joe Clark ends six-week world tour dubbed mostly disastrous by the media
January 25	Release of the report of the Task Force on Canadian Unity
February 5–6	First ministers' conference in Ottawa
February 21	Final report of the Task Force on Canadian Unity
May 22	Conservatives win federal election with 136 seats, a minority in a 282-seat House (standings: PC 136, Lib. 114, NDP 26, other 6; popular vote: PC 42 per cent, Lib. 35 per cent, NDP 18 per cent, other 6 per cent)
June 4	Joe Clark sworn in as prime minister; Nielsen becomes minister of public works
June 21	Lévesque announces that a referendum will be held on sovereignty-association issue in spring of 1980
August 16	John Diefenbaker dies
November 21	Trudeau resigns as Liberal leader
December 10	John Turner announces he will run to replace Trudeau
December 14	Conservative government defeated in the House, election will follow on February 18
December 18	Trudeau "unresigns," announces he will lead Liberals into next election

1980

February 18	Liberals win majority in federal election (standings: Lib. 146, PC 103, NDP 32, other 1; popular vote: Lib. 44 per cent, PC 32 per cent, NDP 20 per cent, other 3 per cent)

March 3	Trudeau sworn in as prime minister again
April 1	Canadian dollar reaches new low of $0.834 U.S.
April 14	Parliament meets
April 20	Federals win referendum in Quebec with 59.5 per cent of vote
April 21	MacEachen "mini budget"
April 27	Bill making "O Canada" the official anthem passed in House
October 6	Debate on the constitution opens in Commons
October 14	Five provinces announce that they will take Ottawa to court over constitutional proposals
December 2	Government agrees to extend deadline of Senate-Commons constitutional committee to February 6

1981

February 3	Manitoba Court of Appeal rules that the federal government doesn't need provincial assent to patriate the constitution
February 31	Newfoundland Court of Appeal rules in favour of the province on constitutional issue
April 13	Parti Québecois wins landslide victory in Quebec
July 9	StatsCan reports June unemployment rate of 7.3 per cent
July 30	Bank of Canada interest rate hits record 20.54 per cent
July 14	Provincial premiers meet in Victoria
July 28	Supreme Court rules that Ottawa has the right to patriate constitution without consent of provinces
August	Nielsen appointed opposition house leader
November 5	Ottawa and provinces agree to patriate constitution with an amending formula and Charter of Rights; Quebec opposed
November 12	First MacEachen budget
December 2	Constitution Bill passes Commons, 246-24; 17 PCs, 5 Liberals, 2 NDP oppose; Senate approves Constitution Act; constitution sent to Britain
December 22	Canada Bill tabled in London

1982

January 17	Canada Bill passes second reading in British Parliament
March 2	The bells incident begins
March 8	Canada Bill passed in Britain

March 17	Bells incident and Conservative boycott of Parliament end
March 29	Royal Assent to Canada Act
April 7	Quebec Court of Appeal rejects claim of Quebec to constitutional veto
April 17	Queen proclaims Constitution in Ottawa
June 28	Federal budget
August 4	Six-and-five restraint program passed by Commons limits prices and wages for next two years
August 26	Dominion Day becomes Canada Day
December 6	Supreme Court of Canada rejects Quebec claim of constitutional veto
December 10	Canada signs Law of the Sea Treaty

1983

January 28	Joe Clark calls leadership convention
February 2	Joe Clark resigns as Conservative leader; Nielsen appointed leader of the opposition
February 4	StatsCan reports record unemployment rate
April 4	Nielsen marries Shelley Coxford in Bermuda
April 19	Federal budget
June 11	Brian Mulroney elected Conservative leader
June 12	Nielsen gives Mulroney policy blueprint
August 12	Cabinet shuffle
August 29	Mulroney wins by-election in Central Nova
September 6	Nielsen steps down as leader of the opposition; is appointed opposition house leader, deputy leader of the opposition, and deputy national leader of the Progressive Conservative Party of Canada
September 30	Parliament ends longest session in history
December 7	Second Session of Thirty-Second Parliament opens

1984

February 15	Federal budget
February 29	Trudeau announces he will resign again
March 16	John Turner enters Liberal leadership race
April 5	Nielsen resigns as house leader, remains deputy leader of the opposition; heads up government planning
May 9	Federal deficit for year ended March 31 a new record: $29.38 billion
June 16	John Turner defeats Jean Chrétien to become Liberal leader, becoming prime minister automatically
June 30	Turner sworn in as prime minister

July 9	Turner announces an election for September 4; patronage appointments
July 24–25	French and English television debates, Mulroney a clear winner in English debate on patronage issue
August 4	Keith Davey replaces Bill Lee as Liberal campaign chairman
September 4	Conservatives win largest majority in history (standings: PC 211, Lib. 40, NDP 30, other 1; popular vote: PC 50 per cent, Lib. 28 per cent, NDP 18 per cent, other 3 per cent)
September 10	New federal deficit record: $32.354 billion
September 17	Mulroney sworn in as prime minister with forty-member cabinet: Nielsen appointed deputy prime minister and president of the Privy Council
September 18	Program Review established
September 25	Washington Summit
October 4	John Bosley named Speaker
November 5	Thirty-Third Parliament opens
November 24	Defence Minister Robert Coates visits Lahr

1985

February 12	Robert Coates resigns as defence minister
February 17	Nielsen named defence minister
March 17	Shamrock Summit in Quebec City
May 23	First Michael Wilson budget ends pension indexing
June 12	Parliament strikes down 114-year-old law that took Indian status away from Indians who married whites
June 27	Government backs down on pension de-indexing
August 17	StatsCan reports inflation down to 3.8 per cent
August 20	Minor cabinet shuffle
September 17	"fifth estate" breaks tuna scandal
September 23	John Fraser resigns as fisheries minister; Nielsen appointed acting minister of fisheries
September 25	Marcel Masse resigns as communications minister
November 8	Simon Reisman named chief negotiator of a free trade deal with the United States
November 30	Marcel Masse cleared, re-enters cabinet
December 2	De Havilland sold to Boeing for $155 million

1986

January 30	Eavesdropping story resurrected by *Toronto Star*
February 26	Second Wilson budget raises taxes, lowers deficit
March 11	Task Force on Program Review reports
April 29	*Globe and Mail* story about Sinclair Stevens

April 30	Mulroney leaves country
May 9	Mulroney speaks to Nielsen by phone about Stevens
May 11	Nielsen summons Stevens to Ottawa
May 12	Sinclair Stevens resigns
May 15	Parker Commission into Sinc Stevens Affair named
June 30	Cabinet shuffle; Nielsen dropped at own request
June 25	Dalton Camp becomes special adviser to Prime Minister Mulroney
September 5	John Bosley resigns as Speaker
September 30	John Fraser elected Speaker
November 13	Gallup has Liberals ahead of Conservatives, 39–31 per cent, with NDP at 29 per cent
November 30	Liberal party convention confirms John Turner as leader

1987

January 19	Nielsen resigns from Commons
January 22	Nielsen appointed Chairman of Canadian Transport Commission, later the National Transportation Agency

Personal Assessments of Members of the 1984 Shadow Cabinet

Harvie Andre, critic for National Defence

	Unsatisfactory	Not fully satisfactory	Fully satisfactory	Superior	Exceptional
Knowledge			X		
ABILITIES to create/innovate				X	
to analyse/evaluate				X	
to plan				X	
to organize				X	
to control				X	
to direct				X	
to communicate in writing				X	
to articulate			X		
EFFECTIVENESS quality of work				X	
industriousness					X
initiative				X	
decisiveness				X	
dependability					X
discretion			X		
judgment				X	
political judgment		X			
maturity				X	
performance under pressure					X
adaptability/flexibility				X	
LEADERSHIP tactfulness			X		
working relations with superiors and colleagues			X		
working relations with subordinates			X		
in representational capacity			X		
LOYALTY to party				X	
to leader				X	
to colleagues				X	

Andre is an obvious candidate for possible appointment at a senior level.

Perrin Beatty, critic for National Revenue

		Unsatisfactory	Not fully satisfactory	Fully satisfactory	Superior	Exceptional
	Knowledge					X
ABILITIES	to create/innovate				X	
	to analyse/evaluate					X
	to plan				X	
	to organize				X	
	to control				X	
	to direct				X	
	to communicate in writing					X
	to articulate					X
EFFECTIVENESS	quality of work				X	
	industriousness				X	
	initiative				X	
	decisiveness				X	
	dependability				X	
	discretion				X	
	judgment				X	
	political judgment				X	
	maturity				X	
	performance under pressure				X	
	adaptability/flexibility				X	
LEADERSHIP	tactfulness				X	
	working relations with superiors and colleagues				X	
	working relations with subordinates				X	
	in representational capacity				X	
LOYALTY	to party				X	
	to leader				X	
	to colleagues				X	

This assessment speaks for itself. He is obvious cabinet material at the middle or senior level.

John Bosley, critic for External Affairs

	Unsatisfactory	Not fully satisfactory	Fully satisfactory	Superior	Exceptional
Knowledge	X				
ABILITIES — to create/innovate	X				
to analyse/evaluate		X			
to plan	X				
to organize	X				
to control	X				
to direct	X				
to communicate in writing	X				
to articulate			X		
EFFECTIVENESS — quality of work	X				
industriousness	X				
initiative	X				
decisiveness			X		
dependability		X			
discretion			X		
judgment		X			
political judgment			X		
maturity		X			
performance under pressure		X			
adaptability/flexibility			X		
LEADERSHIP — tactfulness			X		
working relations with superiors and colleagues			X		
working relations with subordinates			X		
in representational capacity			X		
LOYALTY — to party			X		
to leader			X		
to colleagues			X		

John's strength is his willingness to state his political point of view even when the tide of discussion is going another way. However, his lack of industriousness contributes to his failure to establish priorities and thereby seriously impairs his reliability, his political judgment, and his potential contribution. John is not functioning on all cylinders. His latent talents are not being utilized to the extent to which he is capable.

Pat Carney, critic for Energy, Mines and Resources

		Unsatisfactory	Not fully satisfactory	Fully satisfactory	Superior	Exceptional
	Knowledge			X		
ABILITIES	to create/innovate				X	
ABILITIES	to analyse/evaluate				X	
ABILITIES	to plan			X		
ABILITIES	to organize	X				
ABILITIES	to control	X				
ABILITIES	to direct	X				
ABILITIES	to communicate in writing				X	
ABILITIES	to articulate				X	
EFFECTIVENESS	quality of work			X		
EFFECTIVENESS	industriousness	X				
EFFECTIVENESS	initiative			X		
EFFECTIVENESS	decisiveness				X	
EFFECTIVENESS	dependability	X				
EFFECTIVENESS	discretion	X				
EFFECTIVENESS	judgment	X				
EFFECTIVENESS	political judgment	X				
EFFECTIVENESS	maturity	X				
EFFECTIVENESS	performance under pressure	X				
EFFECTIVENESS	adaptability/flexibility	X				
LEADERSHIP	tactfulness		X			
LEADERSHIP	working relations with superiors and colleagues		X			
LEADERSHIP	working relations with subordinates		X			
LEADERSHIP	in representational capacity			X		
LOYALTY	to party			X		
LOYALTY	to leader			X		
LOYALTY	to colleagues		X			

Pat is a person of overwhelming self-esteem which, while enhancing the quality of decisiveness, at the same time erodes discretion, dependability, and judgment. While there is some suspicion that she has serious health and personal problems, even if they were to be solved, it would not resolve the imperfection noted above. She would pose serious political problems in any future cabinet.

John Crosbie, critic for Finance	Unsatisfactory	Not fully satisfactory	Fully satisfactory	Superior	Exceptional
Knowledge			X		
ABILITIES to create/innovate			X		
to analyse/evaluate				X	
to plan				X	
to organize				X	
to control				X	
to direct					X
to communicate in writing			X		
to articulate			X		
EFFECTIVENESS quality of work				X	
industriousness			X		
initiative			X		
decisiveness				X	
dependability		X			
discretion		X			
judgment			X		
political judgment		X			
maturity		X			
performance under pressure		X			
adaptability/flexibility		X			
LEADERSHIP tactfulness		X			
working relations with superiors and colleagues		X			
working relations with subordinates			X		
in representational capacity			X		
LOYALTY to party		X			
to leader		X			
to colleagues		X			

John has exceptional qualities, which are exercised to the fullest extent when they serve the perceived interest of John himself. There can be no doubt about his value in any future cabinet. There is, however, the ever-present potential of a determined insistence on his personal point of view notwithstanding any consensus among cabinet colleagues.

John Fraser, critic for Environment

		Unsatisfactory	Not fully satisfactory	Fully satisfactory	Superior	Exceptional
	Knowledge			X		
ABILITIES	to create/innovate	X				
	to analyse/evaluate	X				
	to plan	X				
	to organize	X				
	to control	X				
	to direct	X				
	to communicate in writing			X		
	to articulate				X	
EFFECTIVENESS	quality of work	X				
	industriousness	X				
	initiative	X				
	decisiveness			X		
	dependability	X				
	discretion			X		
	judgment			X		
	political judgment			X		
	maturity			X		
	performance under pressure	X				
	adaptability/flexibility				X	
LEADERSHIP	tactfulness			X		
	working relations with superiors and colleagues			X		
	working relations with subordinates	X				
	in representational capacity			X		
LOYALTY	to party				X	
	to leader				X	
	to colleagues				X	

John's lack of industry and initiative has so narrowed his focus over the years to limit it to one aspect of environmental matters. His sole purpose for being is re-election and a cabinet post. His total inability to organize or direct makes him a prime candidate for bureaucratic cannibalization. This critic is a one-man show.

Otto Jelinek, critic for Small Business and Tourism

		Unsatisfactory	Not fully satisfactory	Fully satisfactory	Superior	Exceptional
	Knowledge			X		
ABILITIES	to create/innovate			X		
	to analyse/evaluate			X		
	to plan			X		
	to organize			X		
	to control			X		
	to direct			X		
	to communicate in writing			X		
	to articulate			X		
EFFECTIVENESS	quality of work			X		
	industriousness				X	
	initiative				X	
	decisiveness				X	
	dependability			X		
	discretion		X*			
	judgment			X		
	political judgment			X		
	maturity			X		
	performance under pressure			X		
	adaptability/flexibility			X		
LEADERSHIP	tactfulness		X*			
	working relations with superiors and colleagues			X		
	working relations with subordinates			X		
	in representational capacity			X		
LOYALTY	to party			X		
	to leader			X		
	to colleagues			X		

*He is honest and outspoken to a fault.

Otto has the ability and discipline to be an obvious candidate for consideration for appointment at the middle to junior range in cabinet with potential for growth.

Roch LaSalle, critic for Public Works

	Unsatisfactory	Not fully satisfactory	Fully satisfactory	Superior	Exceptional
Knowledge		X			
ABILITIES to create/innovate		X			
to analyse/evaluate		X			
to plan		X			
to organize		X			
to control		X			
to direct		X			
to communicate in writing		X			
to articulate		X			
EFFECTIVENESS quality of work		X			
industriousness		X			
initiative		X			
decisiveness			X		
dependability		X			
discretion		X			
judgment		X			
political judgment		X			
maturity		X			
performance under pressure			X		
adaptability/flexibility			X		
LEADERSHIP tactfulness			X		
working relations with superiors and colleagues			X		
working relations with subordinates		X			
in representational capacity		X			
LOYALTY to party		X			
to leader			X		
to colleagues			X		

The above assessment is based primarily on a knowledge of the member gained when he functioned as minister of the Department of Supply and Services in the Clark government. DSS and Public Works perforce must function closely together. This member's view of politics is almost exclusively one of patronage, and this is viewed narrowly in Quebec terms.

Flora MacDonald, critic for Social Development

		Unsatisfactory	Not fully satisfactory	Fully satisfactory	Superior	Exceptional
	Knowledge				X	
ABILITIES	to create/innovate				X	
	to analyse/evaluate			X		
	to plan	X				
	to organize	X				
	to control	X				
	to direct	X				
	to communicate in writing			X		
	to articulate				X	
EFFECTIVENESS	quality of work		X			
	industriousness					X
	initiative				X	
	decisiveness			X		
	dependability		X			
	discretion	X				
	judgment			X		
	political judgment				X	
	maturity	X				
	performance under pressure			X		
	adaptability/flexibility	X				
LEADERSHIP	tactfulness	X				
	working relations with superiors and colleagues	X				
	working relations with subordinates	X				
	in representational capacity				X	
LOYALTY	to party				X	
	to leader		X			
	to colleagues	X				

Flora has boundless energy, intelligence, and knowledge of party politics. Regrettably she has lost any ability to act collegially and build consensus with colleagues. She would be a persistent source of disharmony in any cabinet.

Don Mazankowski, critic for Transport

		Unsatisfactory	Not fully satisfactory	Fully satisfactory	Superior	Exceptional
	Knowledge					X
ABILITIES	to create/innovate					X
	to analyse/evaluate					X
	to plan					X
	to organize					X
	to control					X
	to direct					X
	to communicate in writing				X	
	to articulate				X	
EFFECTIVENESS	quality of work					X
	industriousness					X
	initiative					X
	decisiveness					X
	dependability					X
	discretion					X
	judgment					X
	political judgment					X
	maturity					X
	performance under pressure					X
	adaptability/flexibility					X
LEADERSHIP	tactfulness					X
	working relations with superiors and colleagues					X
	working relations with subordinates					X
	in representational capacity					X
LOYALTY	to party					X
	to leader					X
	to colleagues					X

Don has the ability to take hold and direct in any responsibility you might choose to ask of him.

Sinclair Stevens, critic for External Affairs	Unsatisfactory	Not fully satisfactory	Fully satisfactory	Superior	Exceptional
Knowledge		X			
ABILITIES to create/innovate			X		
to analyse/evaluate			X		
to plan			X		
to organize			X		
to control			X		
to direct		X			
to communicate in writing			X		
to articulate			X		
EFFECTIVENESS quality of work		X			
industriousness			X		
initiative		X			
decisiveness		X			
dependability			X		
discretion			X		
judgment		X			
political judgment		X			
maturity			X		
performance under pressure			X		
adaptability/flexibility		X			
LEADERSHIP tactfulness			X		
working relations with superiors and colleagues			X		
working relations with subordinates			X		
in representational capacity		X			
LOYALTY to party			X		
to leader				X	
to colleagues			X		

While his words and actions are no doubt viewed by himself as being in the party's best interest, his weakness in exercising sound political judgment in the evaluation of his statements is, on occasion, not so. Given time and continued absolute loyalty, he will acquire the necessary judgment now lacking and hone his latent skills for effective administration. He will remain loyal as long as he perceives it to be in his personal political interest.

Michael Wilson, critic for ITC and Regional Economic Expansion

		Unsatisfactory	Not fully satisfactory	Fully satisfactory	Superior	Exceptional
	Knowledge			X		
ABILITIES	to create/innovate		X			
ABILITIES	to analyse/evaluate		X			
ABILITIES	to plan	X				
ABILITIES	to organize		X			
ABILITIES	to control		X			
ABILITIES	to direct		X			
ABILITIES	to communicate in writing			X		
ABILITIES	to articulate			X		
EFFECTIVENESS	quality of work	X				
EFFECTIVENESS	industriousness				X	
EFFECTIVENESS	initiative			X		
EFFECTIVENESS	decisiveness		X			
EFFECTIVENESS	dependability		X			
EFFECTIVENESS	discretion		X			
EFFECTIVENESS	judgment			X		
EFFECTIVENESS	political judgment		X			
EFFECTIVENESS	maturity			X		
EFFECTIVENESS	performance under pressure		X			
EFFECTIVENESS	adaptability/flexibility			X		
LEADERSHIP	tactfulness				X	
LEADERSHIP	working relations with superiors and colleagues			X		
LEADERSHIP	working relations with subordinates			X		
LEADERSHIP	in representational capacity				X	
LOYALTY	to party				X	
LOYALTY	to leader				X	
LOYALTY	to colleagues				X	

Mike's knowledge and management skills are seriously impaired by the lack of an orderly approach to the solution of problems. His weakness in the skills of analysis and evaluation impairs his ability to organize, control, and direct. His capacity for work and industriousness are valuable assets. Doubtful cabinet material.

Note: There are obvious flaws in this assessment. Wilson's natural preoccupation with the pursuit of leadership at the time was the probable cause of my failure to recognize some of his finer talents. He has been a pillar of strength in the Mulroney cabinet. (February 1989)

*I have summarized the charts for the following members and quoted in
full the comments I made at the time.*

Don Blenkarn, critic for the Ministry of State (Finance)

RATING: Don received a superior rating for knowledge, the ability
to create and innovate, industriousness, and dependability. His
ability to plan, organize, control, direct, and articulate, as well as
his discretion, tactfulness, and working relations with superiors and
colleagues were not fully satisfactory, and I noted that "he assumes
authority which he knows or should know that he ought not to
assume." In all other areas he was fully satisfactory.

COMMENTS: Don has the ability and work discipline to be considered
for appointment at a junior level. He has growth potential if he is
able to contain his sometimes misdirected enthusiasm.

David Crombie, critic for Communications

RATING: David's ability to articulate and his leadership in a representational capacity were rated exceptional. However, his ability to
organize, control, and direct, and the quality of his work in terms
of industriousness, initiative, decisiveness and performance under
pressure were considered not fully satisfactory. In all other aspects
he was fully satisfactory or superior.

COMMENTS: David has outstanding abilities for promoting causes in
which he believes, which may not always be coincidental with party
interests. He is of cabinet calibre in the middle range. His weakness
is a constant desire to be recognized at a level of importance which
he conceives should be his due.

Lloyd Crouse, critic for Fisheries and Oceans

RATING: I gave Lloyd a fully satisfactory rating for knowledge, the
ability to communicate in writing and to articulate, and for decisiveness, political judgment, maturity, leadership in a representational capacity, and loyalty. However, he was not fully satisfactory
in other aspects.

COMMENTS: The burning ambition of this member is an appointment to the Senate. Not cabinet material.

Paul Dick, Deputy House Leader (committees)

RATING: I found Paul was not fully satisfactory in terms of his ability to control, direct, and articulate, his initiative, decisiveness, judgment, maturity, adaptability, and tactfulness, and his working relations with superiors, colleagues, and subordinates. In all other matters he was fully satisfactory.

COMMENTS: Paul has shown a remarkable improvement in terms of dependability in the last six months but before that he would have been rated as unsatisfactory. His qualities fall within the category for consideration for a parliamentary secretaryship.

Bill Domm, Deputy House Leader (private members)

RATING: Bill's knowledge, ability to analyse, judgment, maturity, adaptability, and leadership in a representational capacity were unsatisfactory, and his discretion, political judgment, tactfulness, working relations with superiors and colleagues, and loyalty to the party and his colleagues were not fully satisfactory. In all other areas he was fully satisfactory.

COMMENTS: Bill has planning and organization skills, but his range of interest is far too narrow to make a quality contribution.

Jake Epp, critic for Health and Welfare

RATING: Jake received an exceptional rating for his ability to plan and organize, and for his dependability and discretion. He was judged fully satisfactory in his decisiveness, ability to articulate, judgment and political judgment, performance under pressure, and adaptability. In all other areas his performance was rated superior.

COMMENTS: The above assessment speaks for itself. The member is of obvious cabinet calibre at a senior level.

Mike Forrestall, Deputy Whip

RATING: Mike was considered unsatisfactory in terms of his ability to innovate, analyse, and articulate, and of his discretion and adaptability. His ability to control and direct, and his initiative, decisiveness, judgment and political judgment, performance under pressure, tactfulness, and leadership in a representational capacity were not fully satisfactory. He was fully satisfactory in all other ways.

COMMENTS: Mike has shown a remarkable improvement since his appointment as deputy whip and would probably continue to perform that duty satisfactorily in a Progressive Conservative government.

Benno Friesen, Chairman of Caucus

RATING: Benno's ability to control and direct were considered unsatisfactory. His ability to innovate, analyse, plan, and organize, and his quality of work, industriousness, initiative, decisiveness, and adaptability were not fully satisfactory. His knowledge, ability to articulate, dependability, judgment, and political judgment were fully satisfactory. In all other areas he received a superior rating.

COMMENTS: The caucus chairman has many admirable personal qualities but he lacks the essential skills for cabinet material. There is, however, some room for growth and he would be adequate for consideration at the level of parliamentary secretary.

Ray Hnatyshyn, critic for Solicitor General

RATING: Ray was judged unsatisfactory in terms of his ability to articulate and his decisiveness. However, his loyalty in all areas and his leadership qualities in terms of his relations with superiors, colleagues, and subordinates were superior. His knowledge, industriousness, dependability, discretion, judgment, maturity, and adaptability were fully satisfactory. In other areas he was judged not fully satisfactory.

COMMENTS: In spite of his forensic training and experience, Ray displays a marked weakness in analytical, planning, and organizational skills. His lack of ability to articulate clearly and concisely is manifest. His personal qualities, however, compel consideration for cabinet in a low responsibility/high public profile department.

Ron Huntingdon, critic for Treasury Board

RATING: Ron was judged exceptional in his ability to analyse and his industriousness, and superior in other abilities, as well as his decisiveness, performance under pressure, and loyalty to the party. Although he received a not-fully-satisfactory rating in terms of dependability, discretion, political judgment, tactfulness, and leadership in a representational capacity, he was fully satisfactory in all other respects.

COMMENTS: Ron has outstanding qualities to contribute to a future cabinet or any other organization. His weaknesses, though few, contain the potential for embarrassment. His dependability is impaired by his own sense of priorities, guided by an overwhelming, though at times scattered, industriousness, and it prevents him from carrying out assigned tasks deemed a priority by his superiors. His deep ideological convictions present a potential danger, since such convictions would compel him to resign rather than depart from his conception of principle. For example, had the Clark government survived the December vote, Huntingdon might well have resigned on the question of intellectual property.

Allan Lawrence, critic for Justice and the Attorney General

RATING: Allan's industriousness, initiative, discretion, judgment, and political judgment were rated unsatisfactory. His knowledge, ability to articulate and to communicate in writing, his adaptability, his leadership qualities in all areas, and his loyalty were fully satisfactory. In other respects he was not fully satisfactory.

COMMENTS: The experience and education of this member would normally enable him to achieve much higher levels. His central weakness is a lack of industriousness and initiative, compounded by a poor sense of priorities. As a minister he would be more interested in the perceived stature and perks of the office than in seizing control of a department and making a difference.

Doug Lewis, Chairman, Public Accounts

RATING: Doug's ability to organize, as well as his industriousness, dependability, discretion, leadership in a representational capacity, and loyalty were rated superior. His knowledge, ability to communicate in writing, quality of work, political judgment, maturity, adaptability, tactfulness, and his working relations with superiors, colleagues, and subordinates were fully satisfactory. In other areas his assessment was not fully satisfactory, and his decisiveness was rated as unsatisfactory.

COMMENTS: Doug has exceptional growth potential, but is still encumbered by dangerous weaknesses. He has shown rapid parliamentary growth since his election in 1979 and is still on a learning curve. He is not quite ready for assuming full responsibility where the skills in which he is deficient are required. Due to his promising potential he is a prime candidate for consideration as a parliamentary secretary.

Charles Mayer, critic for Agriculture

RATINGS: Charles's discretion, political judgment, adaptability, leadership qualities, and loyalty were all considered fully satisfactory. His knowledge, ability to analyse and articulate, quality of work, industriousness, decisiveness, dependability, maturity, and performance under pressure were not fully satisfactory. In other areas he was unsatisfactory.

COMMENTS: Charles requires more exposure to the basic principles of management and more experience in the political arena before achieving the level of dependability of which he is capable. He would be an ideal candidate to serve as parliamentary secretary in order to develop his potential.

John McDermid, critic for Indian and Northern Affairs

RATING: John received a fully satisfactory rating in all respects, with the exception of his ability to plan, control, and direct, and his judgment. In these areas his rating was not fully satisfactory.

COMMENTS: John has displayed in a short time an industrious and zealous approach to a completely strange and difficult responsibility (the comptroller general described the department as the worst managed in all government) and has the potential of above-average performance in the middle range of any future cabinet.

James McGrath, critic for Employment and Immigration

RATING: James's ability to articulate and his political judgment were given a superior rating. His knowledge, ability to communicate in writing, decisiveness, discretion, judgment, performance under pressure, adaptability, and loyalty were fully satisfactory. In other areas he received the rating of not fully satisfactory.

COMMENTS: There is no doubt that this critic has the ability to achieve fully satisfactory levels in the areas in which he is now rated not fully satisfactory, but he is not doing so now, nor did he in the previous ministry. With respect to his dependability, discretion, and maturity, as well as his leadership qualities, there are inherent weaknesses in his personality that would require careful monitoring should he participate in any future cabinet. His standards of loyalty would change if he were not asked to be part of any future cabinet.

NOTE: I was dead wrong about my assessment of his loyalty (February 1989).

Bill McKnight, critic for International Trade

RATING: Bill received the rating of exceptional for his industriousness, dependability, and discretion. In all other areas his performance was superior, except for his knowledge, which was rated fully satisfactory.

COMMENTS: The foregoing assessment speaks for itself. Bill is cabinet material at the middle rank with considerable further growth potential.

Tom McMillan, Deputy House Leader (Question Period)

RATING: Tom's knowledge, ability to articulate and to communicate in writing, quality of work, decisiveness, discretion, tactfulness, leadership in a representational capacity, and loyalty were fully satisfactory. In other areas he was ranked not fully satisfactory.

COMMENTS: Before assuming his present responsibilities, Tom placed personal and constituency interests above all other considerations. He was seldom a team player and displayed an insensitivity to the best interests of party and unity in his parliamentary work. In the first three and a half years of this Parliament, only eight members had a worse attendance record. While he is well-meaning, his lack of skills and abilities combined with his personality weaknesses would ensure bureaucratic captivity.

Frank Oberle, critic for Ministry of State (Mines)

RATING: Frank's ability to articulate, as well as his dependability, discretion, political judgment, maturity, leadership qualities in all areas, and loyalty were rated fully satisfactory. In all other respects (with the exception of judgment and adaptability, which were rated not fully satisfactory), he received a superior rating.

COMMENTS: Frank holds very rigid views that are difficult for him to abandon, but he is willing to do so in the party's best interest. At one time he seriously considered running as an independent because he disagreed with the party leadership. Despite these serious defects, he displays the attributes and skills that qualify him for consideration for a cabinet post in the middle range or lower with good growth potential.

Tom Siddon, critic for MSERD

RATING: Tom's rating was fully satisfactory in terms of ability to articulate and communicate in writing, performance under pressure, and loyalty to the party leader. In other respects his performance was not fully satisfactory.

COMMENTS: With his academic background and experience, Tom should score on a higher level, but he does not because his intellectual focus is far too narrow when considering matters of policy and administration. Indeed, his mind might be described as functioning as a slide rule. He is predictable as long as he is sitting at the captain's table. His stubbornly polarized views on some policy issues could prove to be volatile, as could his unpredictability.

John Wise, critic for Supply and Services

RATING: John was rated superior on his discretion and leadership qualities, and fully satisfactory on his political judgment, maturity, loyalty, and ability to articulate. His knowledge, ability to innovate, analyse, and communicate in writing, as well as his dependability, judgment, performance under pressure, and adaptability were not fully satisfactory. In other areas his performance was unsatisfactory.

COMMENTS: John's lack of industriousness, initiative, and decisiveness would result in him being captured by the bureaucrats. His almost exclusive policy interest in agriculture seriously circumscribes his usefulness.

Index